Exam Ref AZ-204
Developing Solutions
for Microsoft Azure,
Third Edition

Santiago Fernández Muñoz

Exam Ref AZ-204 Developing Solutions for Microsoft Azure, Third Edition

Published with the authorization of Microsoft Corporation by:
Pearson Education, Inc.

Copyright © 2025 by Pearson Education, Inc.

Hoboken, New Jersey

ISBN-13: 9780138312138
ISBN-10: 0138312133

Library of Congress Control Number: 2024938412

1 2024

TRADEMARKS

WARNING AND DISCLAIMER

SPECIAL SALES

For information about buying this title in bulk quantities, or for special sales opportunities (which may include electronic versions; custom cover designs; and content particular to your business, training goals, marketing focus, or branding interests), please contact our corporate sales department at *corpsales@pearsoned.com* or (800) 382-3419.

For government sales inquiries, please contact *governmentsales@pearsoned.com*.

For questions about sales outside the U.S., please contact *intlcs@pearson.com*.

CREDITS

EDITOR-IN-CHIEF
Brett Bartow

EXECUTIVE EDITOR
Loretta Yates

ASSOCIATE EDITOR
Shourav Bose

DEVELOPMENT EDITOR
Songlin Qiu

MANAGING EDITOR
Sandra Schroeder

SENIOR PROJECT EDITOR
Tracey Croom

COPY EDITOR
Dan Foster

INDEXER
Timothy Wright

PROOFREADER
Barbara Mack

TECHNICAL EDITOR
Doug Holland

EDITORIAL ASSISTANT
Cindy Teeters

COVER DESIGNER
Twist Creative, Seattle

COMPOSITOR
codeMantra

GRAPHICS
codeMantra

Contents at a glance

Contents

About the Author

SANTIAGO FERNÁNDEZ MUÑOZ is a Senior Solution Architect involved in developing international projects. He started his career as a Systems Engineer and jumped into the professional development world, attracted by the possibilities and complexities of distributed computing. He runs his own company, mainly focused on providing services to the industrial environment, specializing in photovoltaic environments and industrial cybersecurity.

Introduction

Most books take a very low-level approach, teaching you how to use individual classes and accomplish fine-grained tasks. Through this book, we review the main technologies that Microsoft offers for deploying different kinds of solutions into Azure. From the most classic and conservative approaches using Azure Virtual Machines to the latest technologies implementing event-based or message-based patterns with Azure Event Grid or Azure Service Bus, this book reviews the basics for developing most types of solutions using Azure services. The book also provides code examples that illustrate how to implement most of the concepts covered. This book should be used as an introduction to implementing more complex solutions. Although the book covers some basic concepts, you should have basic programming experience using ASP.NET, .NET Framework, or .NET Core, as well as using Git.

This book covers every major topic area found on the exam, but it does not cover every exam question. Only the Microsoft exam team has access to the exam questions, and Microsoft regularly adds new questions to the exam, making it impossible to cover specific questions. You should consider this book a supplement to your relevant real-world experience and other study materials. If you encounter a topic in this book that you do not feel completely comfortable with, use the "Need more review?" links you'll find in the text to find more information and take the time to research and study the topic. Great information is available on MSDN, TechNet, and in blogs and forums.

Organization of this book

This book is organized by the "Skills measured" list published for the exam. The "Skills measured" list is available for each exam on the Microsoft Learn website: *learn.microsoft.com/ en-us/credentials/certifications/resources/study-guides/az-204*. Each chapter in this book corresponds to a major topic area in the list, and the technical tasks in each topic area determine a chapter's organization. If an exam covers six major topic areas, for example, the book will contain six chapters.

Preparing for the exam

Microsoft certification exams are a great way to build your resume and let the world know about your level of expertise. Certification exams validate your on-the-job experience and product knowledge. Although there is no substitute for on-the-job experience, preparation through study and hands-on practice can help you prepare for the exam. This book is not designed to teach you new skills.

We recommend that you augment your exam preparation plan by using a combination of available study materials and courses. For example, you might use the *Exam Ref* and another study guide for your at-home preparation and take a Microsoft Official Curriculum course for the classroom experience. Choose the combination that you think works best for you. Learn more about available classroom training, online courses, and live events at *microsoft.com/learn*.

Note that this *Exam Ref* is based on publicly available information about the exam and the author's experience. To safeguard the integrity of the exam, authors do not have access to the live exam.

Microsoft certifications

Microsoft certifications distinguish you by proving your command of a broad set of skills and experience with current Microsoft products and technologies. The exams and corresponding certifications are developed to validate your mastery of critical competencies as you design and develop, or implement and support, solutions with Microsoft products and technologies both on-premises and in the cloud. Certification brings a variety of benefits to the individual and to employers and organizations.

> **NEED MORE REVIEW?   ALL MICROSOFT CERTIFICATIONS**
>
> For information about Microsoft certifications, including a full list of available certifications, go to *www.microsoft.com/learn*.

Access the Exam Updates chapter and online references

The final chapter of this book, "AZ-204 developing solutions for Microsoft Azure exam updates," will be used to provide information about new content per new exam topics, content that has been removed from the exam objectives, and revised mapping of exam objectives to chapter content. The chapter will be made available from the link below as exam updates are released.

Throughout this book are addresses to webpages that the author has recommended you visit for more information. Some of these links can be very long and painstaking to type, so we've shortened them for you to make them easier to visit. We've also compiled them into a single list that readers of the print edition can refer to while they read.

The URLs are organized by chapter and heading. Every time you come across a URL in the book, find the hyperlink in the list to go directly to the webpage.

Download the Exam Updates chapter and the URL list at *MicrosoftPressStore.com/ERAZ2043e/downloads*.

Errata, updates & book support

We've made every effort to ensure the accuracy of this book and its companion content. You can access updates to this book—in the form of a list of submitted errata and their related corrections—at:

MicrosoftPressStore.com/ERAZ2043e/errata

If you discover an error that is not already listed, please submit it to us at the same page.

For additional book support and information, please visit *MicrosoftPressStore.com/Support*.

Please note that product support for Microsoft software and hardware is not offered through the previous addresses. For help with Microsoft software or hardware, go to *support.microsoft.com*.

Stay in touch

Let's keep the conversation going! We're on Twitter: *twitter.com/MicrosoftPress*.

CHAPTER 1

Develop an Azure Infrastructure as a Service solution

Today, cloud computing is an established consolidating solution that any company or professional should consider when developing or maintaining new or existing products. When planning to develop or deploy an application, you can choose between two main models of cloud services: Infrastructure as a Service (IaaS) or Platform as a Service (PaaS). Each model has its pros and cons. If you choose the IaaS model, you will have more granular control over the infrastructure that supports your application.

However, once the deployment is complete in the production environment, you must maintain it. You must budget for the maintenance of the infrastructure, and you must have staff trained to conduct the maintenance.

Thanks to cloud technologies, you can drastically reduce these infrastructure planning and deployment requirements by deploying your software on a managed service known as Platform as a Service (PaaS). Doing so means you only need to worry about your code and how it interacts with other services in Microsoft Azure. PaaS products such as Azure App Service or Azure Functions relieve you from worrying about highly available or fault-tolerant configurations because the service provided by Azure already manages these things.

This chapter reviews how to work with the options that Azure provides for developing your solutions based on the IaaS model. The chapter also covers the PaaS solutions that Azure provides, which allow you to focus on your code and forget about the underlying infrastructure.

Skills covered in this chapter:

- Skill 1.1: Implement containerized solutions
- Skill 1.2: Implement Azure App Service web apps
- Skill 1.3: Implement Azure Functions

Skill 1.1: Implement containerized solutions

One of the main characteristics of the IaaS model is its higher level of control when deploying the infrastructure needed for your application. Typically, you need to work with this model because you need more control over the different elements of your application. Using IaaS, you can use different virtualization models, the traditional approach of virtual machines (VMs), or a lightweight virtualization like containers.

In the same way that IaaS and PaaS models have pros and cons, virtual machines and containers have their own pros and cons. Virtual machines allow you to run a full operating system inside a virtual server. In this model, you can run different operating systems with different versions in the same hardware as long as they run the same CPU architecture and you have enough physical resources to accommodate them. This way, your code will run as if it were deployed on a physical server.

On the other hand, using containers, your code runs in a virtualized environment but shares all the libraries, the kernel, and the resources with the host operating system. This chapter provides further details so you will become familiar with the container technology and how Azure eases the adoption of this technology in your solutions.

> **This skill covers how to**
> - Create and manage container images for solutions
> - Publish an image to the Azure Container Registry
> - Run containers by using an Azure Container Instance
> - Create solutions by using Azure Container Apps

Create and manage container images for solutions

A *container* is a piece of software that packages your code and all its dependencies in a single package that can be run directly by the computer environment. When a container is executed, it uses a read-only copy of the shared libraries of the operating system that your code needs to run. This reduces the required resources a container needs to run your code compared to running the same code on a virtual machine. Container technology was initially born on Linux environments but has also been ported to the Microsoft Windows environment. There are several implementations of container technology in the Linux ecosystem, but Docker containers are the most widely used.

When you move the container technology to an enterprise environment, scaling dynamically and automatically becomes a problem, just as with virtual machines. Several solutions are available in the market, such as Docker Swarm, DC/OS, or Kubernetes. All these solutions are orchestration solutions that automatically scale and deploy your containers in the available resources.

Azure provides several services that allow you to deploy your application in a container. It doesn't matter if you decide to use Azure Kubernetes Services, Azure Red Hat OpenShift, Azure Container Apps, Service Fabric, Azure Web Apps for Containers, Azure Container Registry, or Azure Container Instances; all these services use the same Docker container technology implementation.

Before you can deploy your application to any of these services, you must put your application into a container by creating an image of your container. A *container image* is a package that contains everything you need to run your application: code, libraries, environment variables, and configuration files. Once you have your container image, you can create instances of the image for running the code, each of which is a container. If you need to make modifications to one of your containers, you will need to modify the image definition and redeploy the container. In general, any change that you make to a container does not persist across reboots. If you need to ensure that some information in your container is not deleted when a container reboots, you must use external mount points, known as volumes.

When you create your container image, you must define your application's requirements, which are placed in a file called Dockerfile. This Dockerfile contains the definition and requirements needed for creating your container image. Use the following high-level procedure for creating an image:

1. **Create a directory for the new image.** This directory contains your Dockerfile, your code, and any other dependency that you need to include in the image that is not available in a separate image.

2. **Create the Dockerfile.** This file contains the definition of your image. Listing 1-1 shows an example of a functional Dockerfile.

LISTING 1-1 Dockerfile example

```
FROM  mcr.microsoft.com/dotnet/sdk:7.0 AS installer-env

COPY ./ /src
WORKDIR /src
RUN mkdir /myAPI_Release
RUN dotnet publish myAPI.csproj -c Release -r linux-x64 --self-contained true
--output /myAPI_Release

FROM mcr.microsoft.com/dotnet/runtime:7.0

COPY --from=installer-env ["/myAPI_Release", "/myAPI"]
WORKDIR /myAPI

ENV ASPNETCORE_URLS=http://+:8080
EXPOSE 8080

CMD [ "myAPI.dll" ]
ENTRYPOINT [ "dotnet" ]
```

3. **Open a command line.** You use this command line to run the Docker commands.

4. **Create the container image.** Use the command `docker build` to create the image. When you create an image, you should add a tag to identify the image and the version. Keep in mind that the image name must be lowercase. If you don't set a version number, Docker automatically assigns the default value *latest*. You need to provide the path of the folder that contains the Dockerfile. This command has the following structure:

```
docker build --tag=<tag_name>[:<version>] <dockerfile_dir>
```

5. **List the newly created image.** Once Docker finishes downloading all the dependencies for your image, you can ensure that your image has been created by executing this command:

```
docker image ls
```

To review the preceding high-level procedure, you can create your first image in your computer. For this example, you will need:

- Docker Desktop
- ASP.NET SDK
- Visual Studio or Visual Studio Code

Remember that Docker is a commercial solution with different subscription levels and terms of use. For this example, you can use the personal subscription level, which is free for personal use. As you will see in the following sections, Docker Desktop is not required to work with Azure containers, since you can build and deploy images directly on the cloud. Use the following procedure for building your first image on your computer:

1. Download Docker Desktop from https://www.docker.com/products/docker-desktop/.

2. Install Docker Desktop following the instructions for your environment.

3. If you don't have an ASP.NET SDK installed, install the latest version.

4. Create a new empty ASP.NET Core Web API application using your favorite IDE. From the command line, you can use the command `dotnet new webapi -n myAPI` to create a new API.

5. Open your favorite IDE and open the file Program.cs

6. Comment or remove the line with the code `app.UseHttpsRedirection();`

7. Compile and run your new API to ensure that everything runs correctly before creating the container image. You can use the command `dotnet run` from the command line. Remember to set myAPI folder as your working directory before running the `dotnet run` command.

8. If everything goes well, you should get an output showing the URL where your code awaits requests.

9. Open your browser and navigate to http://localhost:5144/WeatherForecast. Please notice that the TCP port might be different on your computer.

10. Using your favorite IDE, create a file named **Dockerfile** in the base folder of your code, in the same location as the Program.cs file.

11. Copy the content of Listing 1-1 to the Dockerfile.

12. Execute the command `docker build --tag=myapi .` in the same folder where the Dockerfile is. Notice the dot character at the end of the command.

13. Once you have created your image, you can create a container from that image. Use the following command to create a container: `docker run -d -P myapi`

14. Run the command `docker container ls` to find the port where your container is listening. You will find the correct port under the PORTS `column` with the format `0.0.0.0:32777->8080/tcp`. In this case, the container is listening on port 8080 and is forwarded to port 32774 on the local computer. You must use the local computer port to connect to the container.

15. Open your browser and navigate to http://localhost:32777/WeatherForecast. You should get the same output as you did in step 9. This time, however, your code is being executed inside the new container. You should get an output similar to Figure 1-1.

```
1    // 20230924221629
2    // http://localhost:32777/WeatherForecast
3
4  ▼ [
5  ▼   {
6          "date": "2023-09-25",
7          "temperatureC": 35,
8          "temperatureF": 94,
9          "summary": "Balmy"
10       },
11 ▼   {
12         "date": "2023-09-26",
13         "temperatureC": -6,
14         "temperatureF": 22,
15         "summary": "Cool"
16       },
17 ▼   {
18         "date": "2023-09-27",
19         "temperatureC": 38,
20         "temperatureF": 100,
21         "summary": "Balmy"
22       },
23 ▼   {
24         "date": "2023-09-28",
25         "temperatureC": 17,
26         "temperatureF": 62,
27         "summary": "Cool"
28       },
29 ▼   {
30         "date": "2023-09-29",
31         "temperatureC": 33,
32         "temperatureF": 91,
33         "summary": "Balmy"
34       }
35   ]
```

FIGURE 1-1 Web API output

Once you have an overview of what a Dockerfile looks like, let's dig into the file structure, as there are some key concepts you need to manage to deploy a container in Azure successfully.

The first element in any valid Dockerfile must be a *FROM* instruction. This instruction sets the base image for all the following instructions until the end of the Dockerfile or the next *FROM* instruction. A Dockerfile can be a compound of several build stages. Each build stage has an independent state from other stages. The *FROM* instruction sets the start of each build stage and clears the state created by previous stages. This is useful when you want to compile your code while building your image but don't want your source code to be copied to the final image. The only required argument to the *FROM* instruction is the image's name. This image can be a local image stored in your computer or a remote image stored in a container registry, such as an Azure Container Registry. In the example shown in Listing 1-1, we use two differ-ent base images because we have two separate stages. The first base image is `mcr.microsoft.com/dotnet/sdk:7.0`. We assigned the alias installer-env by using the AS keyword. We can use that alias to refer to this stage in later stages. The second base image that we are using in the example in Listing 1-1 is `mcr.microsoft.com/dotnet/runtime:7.0`.

The next instruction that we find in Listing 1-1 is *COPY*. This instruction copies the source code to the container filesystem. This instruction has two arguments: the source path and the destination path. The source path argument represents a path in your local computer. You can use wildcards in the source path. The destination path is inside the container where you want to copy the files. You can use an absolute path or a relative one. Using a relative path will be relative to the working directory set with the WORKDIR instruction. We can copy files from pre-vious stages using the `--from=<stage_name>` modifier, as shown in Listing 1-1.

After copying the needed files to the container filesystem, we set the working directory using the *WORKDIR* instruction. This instruction sets the working directory for the subsequent commands, such as *RUN, CMD, ENTRYPOINT, COPY,* or *ADD.* The argument of this instruction is the path of the working directory. If you use a relative path, this will be relative to the path of the previous *WORKDIR* instruction in the Dockerfile. If there is no previous *WORKDIR* instruc-tion, the default working directory is /. In our example, the working directory is set to /app.

The *RUN* instruction executes a command inside the container. In our example from Listing 1-1, we have two different commands: one for creating the directory `myAPI_Release` in the con-tainer filesystem and another one for publishing our code in the directory that we created with the previous command. When working with containers, remember that you need to provide all the needed libraries, packages, files, or resources that your code needs to run. Think of the image-building process as deploying your code on a new computer.

The *ENV* instruction sets an environment variable inside the container. The format of the argument of this instruction is `<key>=<value>` where `<key>` is the name of the environment variable, and `<value>` is the value of the variable. If the value has spaces, you must put the value between double quotes. The environment variables defined using the ENV instruction will be present in the final image. If you need to set environment variables only during the building phase, you can use them directly on the instruction using the same `<key>=<value>` format.

The *EXPOSE* instruction is one of the sources of issues when you start working with containers. This instruction tells the container engine that the container listens on the specified network port set as the instruction's parameter. You can think of the *EXPOSE* instruction as documentation of the ports that should be opened in the firewall of the container. You need to use the -P flag with the `docker run` command to open all ports set in the *EXPOSE* instructions. If you use the -P flag, Docker will map the exposed ports to random ports in your computer. If you want to map to specific ports, you must use the -p flag (in lowercase).

The last two instructions, *CMD* and *ENTRYPOINT*, set the command to execute when the container runs. In our example in Listing 1-1, we use the *CMD* instruction to set the command parameters to execute when the container runs, `myAPI.dll`. The *ENTRYPOINT* instruction sets the actual command to run. Notice that we didn't use the full path for telling the `dotnet` command where to find the `myAPI.dll` file. This works because we set `/myAPI` as the working directory using the *WORKDIR* instruction. Another option would be to use only the *CMD* or *ENTRYPOINT* instructions alone.

This example is not appropriate for production environments because it exposes the web application using a non-secure channel. For production environments, you should set up the HTTPS options in the code, or you could publish your web application using an inverse proxy. In that case, the inverse proxy could be another container that accepts the HTTPS requests and forwards them to your application through an HTTP call.

For scenarios in which you need to define and run multiple containers, you can use Docker Compose. You can think of Docker Compose as the definition of your images for a production environment. If your application comprises several images, you can define the relationship between those images and how they are exposed to the external world. Using Docker Compose, you can also set the limits of the resources assigned to each container when it executes and define what happens if one container associated with a service fails.

A service in the Docker world is each of the pieces that are part of your application. A service has a one-to-one relationship with an image. Remember that a service can have multiple instances of the same image, which means you can have various containers. The docker-composer.yaml file contains the definitions of the relationships and requirements needed for running your application.

Now that you have a better understanding of how to create an image and a container, let's review some useful commands that will help you manage them. All the actions that you will see here can also be performed using the Docker Desktop application. The following list includes the most common commands that you might need for managing images and containers:

- **docker image ls** List all the images currently available on your computer. The IMAGE ID field identifies the image. Notice that you may have several entries for the same IMAGE ID and different REPOSITORY.

- **`docker image rm <image_id>`** Removes the image identified by `image_id`. If you use a tag name instead of an image ID, you remove the tag from that image. If an image is tagged multiple times, you must use the -f modifier to force the removal of the image.

- **`docker pull <image_name>`** Downloads the `image_name` from the container registry that you have configured in your computer. The default container registry is Docker Hub, but you can add more container registries.

- **`docker push <image_name>`** Uploads the `image_name` from your computer to the container registry set in the `image_name`. We will review this command in depth in the next section.

- **`docker container ls`** Lists all the containers on your computer. By default, this command only shows the running containers. If you want to list all containers on your computer, use the -a modifier.

- **`docker run <image_name>`** Creates a new container based on the image you provide with the `image_name` parameter. By default, this command attaches the container's output with the standard output of the console. If you want to run the container in the background, use the -d flag between the run command and the `image_name`. By default, this command does not map any port between your computer and the container. If you want to do the mapping, use the modifier -P or -p.

- **`docker exec -it <container> <command>`** Executes a command in interactive mode inside your container. You can use this command to troubleshoot the container or test any configuration changes. Remember that file changes inside the container do not persist unless you change a mapped volume.

> ***NEED MORE REVIEW?*** **FULLY FUNCTIONAL EXAMPLE**
>
> You can run a fully functional example in your local environment by reviewing the instructions published by Microsoft at *https://docs.microsoft.com/en-us/azure/aks/ tutorial-kubernetes- prepare-app.*

EXAM TIP

The modifications you make to a container while it is running do not persist if you reboot the container. If you need to make changes to the content of a container, you must modify the image container and then redeploy it. You must use volumes if you need your container to save information that needs to be persisted across reboots.

Publish an image to the Azure Container Registry

The main purpose of creating an image is to make your code highly portable and independent from the server that executes it. To achieve this objective, your image must be accessible by all the servers that can execute your image. Therefore, you need to store your image in a centralized storage service.

Azure Container Registry (ACR) is Microsoft's implementation of a Docker registry service based on the Docker Registry 2.0 definition. Using this managed Docker registry service, you can privately store your images for later distribution to container services, such as Azure Managed Kubernetes Service or Azure Container Apps. You can also use ACR to build your images on the fly and automate the building of the image based on the commits of your source code.

Azure offers three different pricing tiers: Basic, Standard, and Premium. All three tiers provide the same programmatic capabilities. The main difference between the tiers is their performance and scale:

- **Basic tier** More suitable for lower usage scenarios, where you have low throughput requirements.

- **Standard tier** Offers the same capabilities as the Basic tier but with higher throughput and storage capacity. This tier is appropriate for most production scenarios.

- **Premium tier** Adds more storage capacity and throughput and adds additional capabilities, such as geo-replication, private links with private endpoints for accessing the registry, or content trust for image tag signing.

> **NEED MORE REVIEW? CONTAINER REGISTRY TIERS AND LIMITS**
>
> You can learn more about the container registry tries and their limits by reviewing the following Microsoft article: *https://learn.microsoft.com/en-us/azure/container-registry/container-registry-skus*

Before you can upload an image to your private container registry, you must tag the image. To do this, you need to include the name of your private container registry in the tag. You will use the name structure <acr_name>.azurecr.io/[repository_name][:version]. The following list breaks down each part of the tag:

- **acr_name** This is the name that you gave to your registry.

- **repository_name** This is an optional name for a repository in your registry. ACR allows you to create multilevel repositories inside the registry. If you want to use a custom repository, just put its name in the tag.

- **version** This is the version that you use for the image.

Use the following procedure to push your image to your ACR registry. These steps assume you have already created an Azure Container Registry and installed the latest Azure CLI. You should also have already performed the procedure on how to create a container image, shown in the previous section:

1. Log in to your Azure subscription.

   ```
   az login
   ```

2. Log in to your registry using this command. Change the parameter az204demo according to your needs:

   ```
   az acr login --name az204demo
   ```

3. Tag the image that you want to upload to the registry using this command. Change the parameters `myapi` and `az204demo.azurecr.io/chapter1/myapi` according to your needs:

```
docker tag myapi az204demo.azurecr.io/chapter1/myapi
```

4. Push the image to the registry using this command:

```
docker push az204demo.azurecr.io/chapter1/myapi
```

When Docker finishes pushing your image to the registry, you can browse the repositories, as shown in Figure 1-2, to verify that it has been successfully uploaded.

FIGURE 1-2 Browse container repositories

Another advantage of using Azure Container Registry is building your images in the cloud without installing Docker Desktop on your computer. All you need is your Azure Container Registry instance and the latest version of Azure CLI.

The following procedure shows how to create the same container image that you created in the previous section but using Azure Container Registry Tasks:

1. Log in to your Azure subscription.

```
az login
```

2. Log in to your registry using this command. The most important part of this command is the --expose-token flag. Using this flag, the `az acr` login command won't search for the

docker command in your system. You can also use the output of this command to log in to your registry from your local Docker Desktop installation. Change the parameter az204demo according to your needs:

```
az acr login --name az204demo --expose-token
```

3. Change to your source code folder.

4. Push the image to the registry using this command. Notice the period character at the end of the command. That parameter sets the current folder as the context for uploading the code to the Azure Container Registry service. You can also use remote code repositories such as GitHub or Azure DevOps. Change the parameters az204demo and chapter1/myapi according to your needs:

```
az acr build --registry az204demo --image chapter1/myapi .
```

Azure Container Registry Tasks not only allow you to build your image in the cloud but also automate the building and updating of your images based on different triggers, such as source code update, base image update, and scheduling. You can also create complex workflows using multi-step tasks.

NEED MORE REVIEW? **AZURE CONTAINER REGISTRY TASKS**

You can explore the capabilities of Azure Container Registry Tasks and review some tutorials by exploring the following Microsoft article: *https://learn.microsoft.com/en-us/azure/ container-registry/container-registry-tasks-overview*

NOTE **CONNECTED REGISTRIES**

The Premium tier enables a feature called *connected registries*. This feature lets you connect an on-premises or remote replica that synchronizes with your registry. You can expand your knowledge about connected registries by reviewing the following Microsoft article: *https://learn.microsoft.com/en-us/azure/container-registry/intro-connected-registry*

The next section reviews how to run the container from the image you have already pushed to the registry.

EXAM TIP

A container registry is useful not only for storing your container images but also for automating the deployment of containers into the Azure Container services. Use Azure Container Registry Tasks to update your images automatically based on code updates or operating system patches.

Run containers by using an Azure Container Instance

Once you have created your image and made it available to Azure services by pushing it to your container registry, it is time to run the container in any of the services Azure offers. Follow this high-level procedure:

1. Create as many images as your application needs to run correctly.

2. Upload or push your application images to a container registry.

3. Deploy the application.

When you want to create an image in the Azure Container Instance (ACI) service from your Azure Container Registry (ACR), you must authenticate before you can pull the image from your ACR. You can create a new Azure Container Instance like any other Azure resource. If you decide to use the Azure portal to create a new ACI, you must enable the admin account before proceeding. This admin account should be used only for troubleshooting purposes or for creating ACIs from the Azure portal; if you want to automate the creation of ACIs, you should consider using other authentication modes such as service principals, managed instances, or tokens.

The following procedure shows how to enable the admin account:

1. Sign in to the Azure portal (*https://portal.azure.com*).

2. In the search box at the top middle of the portal, type the name of your container registry.

3. On the result contextual page, select the name of your container registry under the Resources section.

4. On your container registry page, select Access Keys under the Settings section.

5. Ensure that the checkbox beside the Admin user label is checked. Once you check this option, you will get the admin username and two passwords to log in to this container registry. Figure 1-3 shows the admin user enabled for a container registry.

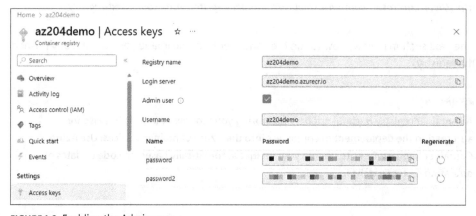

FIGURE 1-3 Enabling the Admin user

Once you have enabled the admin user, you can create a new ACI from the Azure portal. You can do this by using the Create A Resource from the main page of the Azure portal or directly from the repository on your Azure Container Registry.

The following procedure shows how to create an ACI directly from a container registry:

1. Sign in to the Azure portal (*https://portal.azure.com*).
2. In the search box at the top middle of the portal, type the name of your container registry.
3. On the result contextual page, select the name of your container registry under the Resources section.
4. On your container registry page, select Repositories under Services.
5. Select the repository you want to deploy as a new Azure Container Instance.
6. Search for the tag of the image that you want to deploy.
7. Click the three dots at the end of the line with the appropriate tag.
8. Select Run Instance on the contextual menu shown in Figure 1-4.

FIGURE 1-4 Options for a repository tag

9. On the Create Container Instance page, type a name for the container in the Container Name field.
10. Select the operating system that best matches your needs.
11. Select the Subscription where you want to create this resource.
12. Select the Resource group where you want to create the ACI. Alternatively, you can create a new resource group by clicking the Create New Link option under the Resource group dropdown menu.
13. Select the Location.
14. Select the number of cores.
15. Type the amount of Memory in GB that will be assigned to the container.

16. On the Public IP address selection, select Yes if your container needs to be accessed from outside; otherwise, keep the selection set to No.

17. Select the TCP port that your container will be listening on.

18. Click the Create button at the bottom left of the page.

The preceding procedure shows how to deploy a single container using Azure Container Instances, but this service allows you to deploy multi-container applications using container groups. Every single time that you deploy a container, the ACI service creates a container group for you. In fact, the preceding procedure deployed a container group with a single container within. The advantage of deploying multiple containers inside the same container group is that the containers can communicate between them using the internal networking associated to the container group. This way, only the container that needs to receive the requests from the outside world needs to be exposed. This is the typical usage of the sidecar pattern, where you use an inverse proxy, like nginx, for hiding your code that runs in a separate container in the same container group. To deploy a multi-container group, you must use Azure CLI and YAML, or Resource Manager, or Docker Compose.

> **NEED MORE REVIEW? SIDECAR PATTERN**
>
> You can extend your knowledge about the sidecar and other architecture patterns by review-ing the following Microsoft article: *https://learn.microsoft.com/en-us/azure/architecture/patterns/sidecar*

EXAM TIP

You can use several authentication mechanisms, such as an individual login with Azure AD, an admin account, or a service principal. Authentication with Azure AD is a good approach for your development and testing environment. Using the admin account is disabled by default and is discouraged for production environments because you must put the admin account password in your code. For production environments, the recommended way to pull images is using service principals for authentication with the ACR.

Create solutions by using Azure Container Apps

So far, we have reviewed how to deploy a container locally on your computer or by using Azure Container Instances. Those options are good for testing or situations that do not require other advanced features such as orchestration, scalability, and traffic management.

Azure Container Apps is based on Kubernetes technology so that you can run any microservice and container you might already have running on a Kubernetes cluster. The main difference with Azure Container Apps is that the Kubernetes API is not exposed, and you can-not programmatically interact with the cluster. If you need to use the API to interact with the Kubernetes cluster, you should use Azure Kubernetes Service instead.

Before starting with Azure Container Apps, you need to consider the requirements of your application to choose the most appropriate plan for your needs. Azure Container Apps is presented in two different plans:

- **Dedicated**   provides a fully managed environment where you pay for the allocated resources. In this plan, you get a single tenant where you deploy the resources you need to run your apps. You are billed for the number of seconds that vCPUs and GiBs of memory are allocated, plus a base price for the plan management. The resource assignment is done through the usage of workload profiles. You pay per instance of the workload profile, and you can run multiple apps in a single workload profile. This plan also allows you to scale-to-zero, so if you don't need resources, you can deallocate them.

- **Consumption**   provides a serverless infrastructure for running your applications. You are billed for the seconds of vCPU and GiBs your application consumes. You are also billed per application instead of workload.

Now that you have a better idea of the available plans for Azure Container Apps, let's review some concepts that we need to know before creating our first app:

- **Environment**   is a secure boundary where you can execute one or more apps or jobs. Containers in the same environment share the same virtual network, enforcing the secure boundary. Azure Container Apps runtime performs all the tasks related to operating system upgrades, scale operations, failover procedures, and resource balancing. There are two types of environments: workload profile environments and consumption-only environments. Workload profile environments support dedicated and consumption plans.

- **Container**   is the package with all the libraries, binaries, and resources needed to run your code. Azure Container Apps supports:

  - Any Linux-based x86-x64 container.

  - Containers from public and private container registries.

  - Sidecar and init containers. A sidecar container runs side by side with the main container, adding some features that are not present in the main container. An example of sidecar containers would be exposing a REST API through a reverse proxy. You can deploy your REST API in a container and deploy a sidecar container with NGINX web server as the reverse proxy. All the requests to your REST API will reach the sidecar container and then be forwarded to your REST API. An init container is run before launching the main container.

- **Revision**   is an immutable snapshot of a container version. A revision is always created the first time you deploy your container app. A new revision is automatically created when you change the container app configuration. When a new revision is created, it can automatically deactivate old revisions or keep other revisions activated. You work in single revision mode if only one revision is active. You are working in multiple revisions mode if you allow multiple revisions to work simultaneously. In single revision mode, the old revision is not deactivated until the new revision is fully operational. In multiple revision mode, you can decide when and which revisions to deactivate or decide how much traffic is routed to each revision

- **Application lifetime** comprises four different states, or phases: deployment, update, deactivation, and shutdown. It is important to mention that application lifetime only applies to container apps, not container jobs. The description of each phase is:
  - **Deployment** This is the state when the container is deployed to the environment. During this phase, the first revision is automatically created.
  - **Update** In this phase, the container is being updated with a revision scope-change. A new revision is created in this phase.
  - **Deactivate** Use this phase for revisions that are no longer needed. Once you have deactivated a revision, you can activate it again if needed.
  - **Shutdown** This happens when a container is in one of these situations: the container app scales in or is deleted or a revision is deactivated.
- **Jobs** These are tasks that need to run for a period of time and then exit. Typical uses of jobs include data processing, cache updates, or on-demand requests. You can use three types of triggers for running a job: manual, schedule, and event. If a job fails, it is not automatically restarted.

> *NOTE* **DEPLOY YOUR CODE TO AZURE CONTAINER APPS**
>
> You can deploy your code directly to Azure Container Apps from your Visual Studio or Visual Studio Code. You can review how to work with Azure Container Apps using your favorite IDE by reviewing the following Microsoft article: *https://learn.microsoft.com/en-us/azure/container-apps/deploy-visual-studio-code*

Once you understand the basic concepts that you need to work with Azure Container Apps, you can deploy an app and configure an autoscale rule. The following procedure shows how to create a Container App. This procedure assumes that you created the container image that we made in the previous sections or you have a container image that contains a web API or a web App:

1. Sign in to the Azure portal (*https://portal.azure.com*).
2. On the Azure portal, click the Create A Resource button.
3. On the Create A Resource page, select Containers under the Categories column on the left side.
4. Under the Popular Azure services, locate the Container App icon in the middle of the page and click the Create link below the icon.
5. On the Create Container App page, on the Basics tab, ensure that the correct subscription is selected on the Subscription menu.
6. On the Resource group menu, select the correct resource group. Alternatively, you can create a new resource group by clicking the Create new link below the dropdown menu.

7. On the Container App Name, type the name of your app.

8. On the Container Apps Environment section, select the deployment region on the Region dropdown menu.

9. On the Container Apps Environment, select the environment where you want to deploy your app. If you don't have any environment created, a new default environment is created for you. This default environment is a Consumption-only type. If you want to use a Dedicated plan, you need to create a Workload Profiles environment type.

10. Click the Next: Container > button on the bottom of the page.

11. On the Create Container App page, on the Container tab, type the name of your app in the Name textbox.

12. On the Image source select control, ensure that the Azure Container Registry is selected.

13. On the Registry menu, select the Azure Container Registry where your container image is stored.

14. On the Image menu, select the container image that will be used to deploy your app.

15. On the Image tag menu, select the tag to deploy. If you have doubts about which tag to use, select Latest.

16. Leave the Command Override textbox empty.

17. On the CPU and Memory menu, select the appropriate resource allocation for your app.

18. Click the Next: Ingress > button at the bottom of the page.

19. On the Create Container App page, on the Container tab, type the name of your app in the Name textbox.

20. On the Create Container App page, on the Ingress tab, check the Enabled checkbox on the Ingress control.

21. On the Ingress traffic select control, select the Accepting Traffic From Anywhere option.

22. On the Target Port textbox, type the port your container will listen to. Following the example from the previous section, type **8080**. This port is not the port where you need to connect to your application. Your application will listen in the TCP/443 port.

23. Click the Review + Create button at the bottom of the page.

24. On the Review + Create tab, click the Create button at the bottom of the page.

25. Once the resource has been created, click the Go To Resource button.

At this point, you have your app ready to run. Now, we need to create a scale rule to create the appropriate number of replicas to serve the application content. The following procedure shows how to create a new scale rule and access the app:

1. Sign in to the Azure portal (*https://portal.azure.com*).

2. In the search box on the top middle of the portal, type the name of your container app.

3. On the result contextual page, select the name of your container app under the Resources section.

4. Select the Scale and Replicas option on your container app page under the Services section.

5. Click the Edit And Deploy button, shown in Figure 1-5, on the Scale and Replicas page.

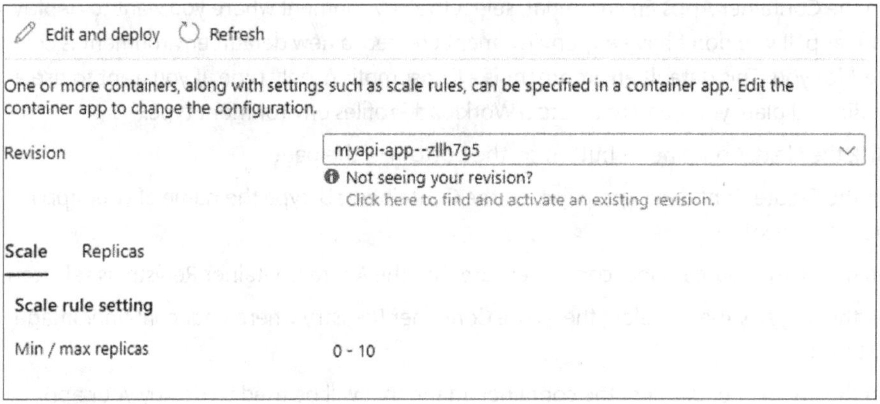

FIGURE 1-5 Configuring scale rules

6. On the Create and deploy new revision, choose the Scale tab.

7. Click the Add button below in the Scale rule section.

8. On the Add scale rule tab, type a name in the Rule name textbox.

9. On the Type menu, select HTTP scaling.

10. In the Concurrent Requests textbox, type **1**. This will create a new replica for each request. This setting makes sense only for demo purposes; in a real environment, you must find the correct value for your environment.

11. Click the Add button at the bottom left of the tab.

12. Click the Create button at the bottom left of the Create and deploy new revision page.

13. Click the refresh button on the Scale And Replicas page. You should be able to see your newly created scale rule in the Scale rule section.

Now it's time to test that everything is working properly. In the following procedure, you will test that you are able to connect to the WeatherForecast endpoint from the web API example that we created in the previous section. You will also test that the container app scales correctly when it receives multiple concurrent requests:

1. Sign in to the Azure portal (*https://portal.azure.com*).

2. In the search box on the top middle of the portal, type the name of your container app.

3. On the result contextual page, select the name of your container app under the Resources section.

4. On the Overview page of your container app, copy the Application URL located on the right side of the page.

5. Paste the application URL on a new tab in your browser. Append the string */Weather-Forecast* to the URL and press Enter. If you don't append that string, you will get a 404 error.

6. You should get a JSON document as the output of your application.

7. Switch to the Azure portal tab.

8. In your container app page, select the Scale And Replicas option in the Application section.

9. On the Scale And Replicas page, select the Replicas tab. There should be one replica running.

10. Open the URL *https://shell.azure.com* in a different tab.

11. Ensure that you have selected Bash on the top left dropdown on the Azure Shell page.

12. Execute the following command on the bash shell. Replace `application_URL` with your application URL. This command sends 50 requests to the WeatherForecast endpoint on your application API.

```
seq 1 50 | xargs -Iname -P10 curl "<application_URL>/WeatherForecast"
```

13. Switch to the Azure portal tab. Ensure that you are on the Replicas tab on the Scale And Replicas page.

14. Click the Refresh button. You should see how new replicas are created based on the scale rule you created previously in this section. Figure 1-6 shows a list of running replicas. Once all requests have been processed, all replicas should disappear automatically.

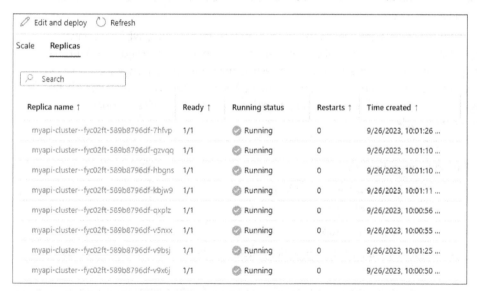

FIGURE 1-6 Running replicas of a container app

In the previous procedure, we configured an HTTP scaling trigger for the scale rule, but you can use any KEDA Scaler. This means that your container application can scale based on Azure Event Hub events, the number of messages in an Azure Queue, or the results of a query to Elasticsearch. Using Azure Container Apps gives you the power and scalability of using a Kubernetes cluster without dealing with the complexity of managing low-level details like deploying KEDA.

> **NOTE   KEDA SCALERS**
>
> KEDA stands for Kubernetes Event-Driven Autoscaling and is a Kubernetes component that you need to deploy to your Kubernetes cluster if you want your pods to scale automatically based on events different from HTTP requests. You can use KEDA scalers with your Azure Container App. You can review all the available scalers by examining the following KEDA article: *https://keda.sh/docs/2.11/scalers/*

EXAM TIP

Don't confuse the Azure Container Apps plans and the environment types. Remember that Workload profiles environments support both dedicated and consumption-only plans, whereas Consumption-only environments support only consumption-only plans.

Skill 1.2: Implement Azure App Service web apps

Azure App Service is a Platform as a Service (PaaS) solution that Microsoft offers to assist with developing your applications, mobile app back end, or REST APIs without worrying about the underlying infrastructure.

You use most of the more popular programming languages—.NET, .NET Core, Java, Ruby, Node.js, PHP, or Python—on top of your preferred platform (Linux or Windows). Azure App Service provides you with enterprise-level infrastructure capabilities, such as load balancing, security, autoscaling, and automated management. Thanks to the integration with GitHub, Docker Hub, and Azure DevOps, you can also include Azure App Service in your continuous deployment life cycle.

> **This skill covers how to**
> - Create an Azure App Service web app
> - Enable diagnostics logging
> - Deploy code to a web app
> - Configure web app settings including Secure Sockets Layer (SSL), API settings, and connection strings
> - Implement autoscaling rules, including scheduled autoscaling and scaling by operational or system metrics
> - Configure deployment slots

Create an Azure App Service web app

Azure App Service is a PaaS solution based on HTTP that allows you to deploy your web or mobile back-end applications or REST APIs to the cloud. Using Azure App Services enables you to develop your application in any of the most popular languages of the moment, such as .NET, .NET Core, Java, Ruby, Node.js, PHP, or Python. Azure App Services also offers you the flexibility of working with any of your favorite platforms: Windows, Linux, or Linux-based containers. The advantage of using Azure App Services is not limited only to the different options for developing; it also integrates quite well with different continuous integration and deployment platforms.

When you plan to create an Azure App Service, you must understand some concepts about how your application performs. Every App Service needs resources to execute your code. Virtual machines are the base of these resources. Although Azure automatically provides the low-level configuration for running these virtual machines, you still need to provide some high-level information. An App Service plan manages the group of virtual machines that host your web application.

You can think of an App Service plan like a server farm that runs in a cloud environment. This also means that you are not limited to running a single App Service in an App Service plan. You can share the same computing resources between several App Services that you deploy on the same App Service plan.

When you create a new App Service plan, you need to provide the following information:

- **Region** This is the region where you deploy the App Service plan. Any App Service in this App Service plan is placed in the same region as the App Service plan.

- **Number of instances** This is the number of VMs added to your App Service plan. Remember that the maximum number of instances you can configure for your App Service plan depends on the pricing tier you select. You can scale the number of instances manually or automatically.

- **Size of the instances** You configure the size of the VM used in the App Service plan.

- **Operating system platform** This controls whether your web application runs on Linux or Windows VMs. Depending on the operating system, you have access to different pricing tiers. Beware that once you have selected the operating system platform, you cannot change the operating system for the App Service without re-creating the App Service.

- **Pricing tier** This sets the features and capabilities available for your App Service plan and how much you pay for the plan. For Windows VMs, two basic pricing tiers use shared VMs: F1 and D1. This shared tier is not available for Linux VMs. When you use the basic pricing tiers, your code runs alongside other Azure customers' code.

When you run an App Service in an App Service plan, all instances configured in the plan execute the code corresponding to your app. This means that if you have five virtual machines, any app you deploy into the App Service runs on each of the five VMs. Other operations related to the App Service, such as additional deployment slots, diagnostic logs, backups, or WebJobs, are also executed using the resources of each virtual machine in the App Service plan.

Azure App Service also provides you with the ability to integrate the authentication and authorization of your web application, REST API, a mobile app back end, or even Azure Functions. You can use different well-known authentication providers, such as Azure, Microsoft, Google, Facebook, and Twitter, for authenticating users in your application. You can also use other authentication and authorization mechanisms on your apps. However, by using this security module, you can provide a reasonable level of security to your application with minimal or even no required code changes.

There are situations when your application may require access to resources on your on-premises infrastructure, and App Service provides you with two different approaches:

- **VNet integration** This option is available only for Standard, Premium, or PremiumV2 pricing tiers. This integration allows your web app to access resources in your virtual network. If you create a site-to-site VPN with your on-premises infrastructure, you can access your private resources from your web app.

- **Hybrid connections** This option depends on the Azure Service Bus Relay and creates a network connection between the App Service and an application endpoint. This means that hybrid connections enable the traffic between specific TCP host and port combinations.

The following procedure shows how to create an App Service plan and upload a simple web application based on .NET Core using Visual Studio 2022. Ensure that you have installed the ASP.NET and web development workload, and you have installed the latest updates.

1. Open Visual Studio 2022 on your computer.
2. In the Visual Studio 2022 Start window, in the column named Get Started, click the Continue Without Code link at the bottom of the column.
3. Select the Tools menu and choose Get Tools And Features. Verify that the ASP.NET And Web Development In The Web & Cloud section is checked.
4. In the Visual Studio 2022 window, select File > New > Project to open the New Project window.
5. In the Create a New Project window, select the C# language in the dropdown menu below the Search For Templates text box at the top right of the window.
6. In the All Project Types dropdown menu, select Web.
7. In the list of templates on the right side of the window, select ASP.NET Core Web App.
8. Click the Next button at the bottom right of the window.
9. In the Configure Your New Project window, complete the following steps:
   - Select a name for the project.
   - Enter a path for the location of the solution.

- In the Solution dropdown menu, select Create A New Solution.
- Enter a name for the solution.

10. Click the Next button in the bottom right of the Configure Your New Project window. This opens the Additional Information window.

11. In the Additional Information window, ensure that the selected framework is .NET 6.0 (Long Term Support)

12. The authentication type should be None.

13. Uncheck the option Configure For HTTPS.

14. Click the Create button in the bottom right of the Additional Information window.

At this point, you have created a simple ASP.NET Core web application. You can run this application in your local environment to ensure it is running correctly before publishing it to Azure.

Now you need to create the Resource Group and App Service plan that hosts the App Service in Azure:

1. In your Visual Studio 2022 window, ensure that you have opened the solution of the web application that you want to publish to Azure.

2. On the right side of the Visual Studio window, in the Solution Explorer window, right-click the project's name.

3. In the contextual menu, select Publish. This opens the Publish window.

4. In the Publish window, make sure that Azure is selected from the list of available Targets on the right side of the window.

5. Click the Next button on the bottom right of the window.

6. Select Azure App Service (Windows) on the list of Specific Targets.

7. Click the Next button on the bottom right of the window.

8. In the Azure App Service section, ensure that the correct Azure subscription is selected in the Subscription name dropdown menu.

9. Click the Create New button on the right side of the window, below the subscription dropdown menu. This opens the Create App Service window.

10. In the Create App Service window, add a new Azure account. This account must have enough privileges in the subscription for creating new resource groups, app services, and an App Service plan.

11. Once you have added a valid account, you can configure the settings for publishing your web application, as shown in Figure 1-7.

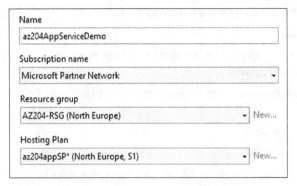

Name

az204AppServiceDemo

Subscription name

Microsoft Partner Network ▾

Resource group

AZ204-RSG (North Europe) ▾ | New...

Hosting Plan

az204appSP* (North Europe, S1) ▾ | New...

FIGURE 1-7 Creating an app service

12. In the App Name text box, enter a name for the App Service. By default, this name matches the name that you gave to your project.

13. In the Subscription dropdown menu, select the subscription in which you want to create the App Service.

14. In the Resource Group dropdown menu, select the resource group in which you want to create the App Service and the App Service plan. If you need to create a new resource group, you can do so by clicking the New link on the right side of the dropdown menu.

15. To the right of the Hosting Plan dropdown menu, click the New link to open the Configure Hosting Plan window.

16. In the Configure Hosting Plan window, type a name for the App Service plan in the App Service Plan text box.

17. Select a region from the Location dropdown menu.

18. Select a virtual machine size from the Size dropdown menu.

19. Click the OK button in the bottom right of the window. This closes the Configure Hosting Plan window.

20. At the bottom right of the Create App Service window, click the Create button. This starts the creation of the needed resources and the upload of the code to the App Service.

21. Once the Create App Service window closes automatically, ensure that the new App Service is selected on the Publish window and click the Finish button at the bottom right of the window. This will create the publish profile for the solution.

22. Click the Close button.

23. Now, the Publish tab should be open in your Visual Studio. If not, right-click your solution's name in the Solution Explorer and select Publish on the contextual menu.

24. Click the Publish button on the Publish tab.

25. Once the publishing process has finished, Visual Studio opens your default web browser with the URL of the newly deployed App Service. This URL will have the structure *https://<your_app_service_name>.azurewebsites.net*.

Depending on the pricing tier that you selected, some features are enabled, such as configuring custom domains or configuring SSL connections for your web applications. For production deployment, you should use Standard or Premium pricing tiers. As your feature needs change, you can choose different pricing tiers. You can start by using the free tier, F1, in the early stages of your deployment and then increase to an S1 or P1 tier if you need to make backups of your web application or need to use deployment slots.

Even if the premium pricing tiers do not fit your computer requirements, you can still deploy a dedicated and isolated environment, called an Isolated pricing tier. This tier provides you with dedicated VMs running on top of dedicated virtual networks where you can achieve the maximum level of scale-out capabilities. Keep in mind that you cannot use the shared tier D1 to deploy a Linux App Service plan.

EXAM TIP

Because Azure App Service does not support the same features for Linux and Windows, you cannot mix Windows and Linux apps in the same resource group in the same region. For more information about the limitations of Linux App Services, review the following article: *https://docs.microsoft.com/en-us/azure/app-service/containers/app-service-linux-intro.*

Enable diagnostics logging

Troubleshooting and diagnosing the behavior of an application is a fundamental operation in the life cycle of every application. This is especially true if you are developing your application. Azure App Service provides you with some mechanisms for enabling diagnostics logging at different levels that can affect your application:

- **Web server diagnostics** These are message logs generated from the web server itself. You can enable three different types of logs:

    - **Detailed error logging** This log contains detailed information for any request that results in an HTTP status code 400 or greater. When an error 400 happens, a new HTML file is generated, containing all the information about the error. A separate HTML file is generated for each error. These files are stored in the file system of the instance in which the web app is running. A maximum of 50 error files can be stored. When this limit is reached, the oldest 26 files are automatically deleted from the file system.

    - **Failed request tracing** This log contains detailed information about failed requests to the server. This information contains a trace of the IIS components that were involved in processing the request. It also contains the time taken by each IIS component. These logs are stored in the file system. The system creates a new folder for each new error, applying the same retention policies as for detailed error logging.

    - **Web server logging** This log registers the HTTP transaction information for the requests made to the web server. The information is stored using the W3C extended log file format. You can configure custom retention policies to these log files. By default, these diagnostic logs are never deleted, but they are restricted by the space they can use in the file system. The default space quota is 35 MB, although you can set this value from 25 to 100 MB.

- **Application diagnostics**   You can send a log message directly from your code to the log system. You use the standard logging system of the language that you use in your app for sending messages to the application diagnostics logs. This is different from Application Insights because application diagnostics are just logged information that you register from your application. If you want your application to send logs to Application Insights, you need to add the Application Insights SDK to your application.

- **Deployment diagnostics**   This log is automatically enabled for you, and it gathers all information related to the deployment of your application. Typically, you use this log for troubleshooting failures during the deployment process, especially if you are using custom deployment scripts.

You can enable the different diagnostics logs, shown in Figure 1-8, using the Azure portal. When you enable application logging, you can select the level of error log that will be registered on the files. These error levels are:

- **Disabled**   No errors are registered.
- **Error**   Critical and Error categories are registered.
- **Warning**   Registers Warning, Error, and Critical categories.
- **Information**   Registers Info, Warning, Error, and Critical log categories.
- **Verbose**   Registers all log categories (Trace, Debug, Info, Warning, Error, and Critical).

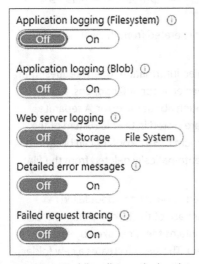

FIGURE 1-8 Enabling diagnostics logging

When you configure application logging, you can set the location for storing the log files. You can choose between saving the logs in the file system or using Blob Storage. Storing application logs in the file system is intended for debugging purposes. If you enable this option, it will be automatically disabled after 12 hours. If you need to enable the application logging for a longer period, you must save the log files in Blob Storage. When you configure application logging for storing the log files in Blob Storage, you can also provide a retention period in days. When log files become older than the value that you configured for the retention period, the files are automatically deleted. By default, there is no retention period set. You can configure the web server logging in the same way that you configure the storage for your application logging.

If you configure application or web server logging for storing the log files in the file system, the system creates the following structure for the log files:

- **/LogFiles/Application/** This folder contains the log files from the application logging.

- **/LogFiles/W3SVC#########/** This folder contains the files from the failed request traces. The folder contains an XSL file and several XML files. The XML files contain the actual tracing information, whereas the XSL file provides the formatting and filtering functionality for the content stored in the XML files.

- **/LogFiles/DetailedErrors/** This folder contains the *.htm files related to the detailed error logs.

- **/LogFiles/http/RawLogs/** This folder contains the web server logs in W3C extended log format.

- **/LogFiles/Git** This folder contains the log generated during the deployment of the application. You can also find deployment files in the folder D:\home\site\deployments.

You need this folder structure when you want to download the log files. You can use two different mechanisms for downloading the log files: FTP/S or Azure CLI. The following command shows how to download log files to the current working directory:

```
az webapp log download --resource-group <Resource group name> --name <App name>
```

The logs for the application *<App name>* are automatically compressed into a file named webapp_logs.zip. Then, this file is downloaded in the same directory where you executed the command. You can use the optional parameter `--log-file` for downloading the log files to a different path in a different zip file.

There are situations in which you may need to view the logs for your application in near real time. For these situations, App Service provides you with log streams. Using streaming, you can see the log messages as they are being saved to the log files. Any text file stored in the D:\home\LogFiles\ folder is also displayed on the log stream. You can view log streams by using the embedded viewer in the Azure portal, on the Log Stream item under the monitoring section in your App Service. You can also use the following Azure CLI command for viewing your application or web server logs in streaming:

```
az webapp log tail --resource-group <Resouce group name> --name <App name>
```

EXAM TIP

When planning to configure application logging, you should consider that not all the programming languages' codes can write the log information in Blob Storage. You can use Blob Storage only with .NET application logs. If you use Java, PHP, Node.js, or Python, you must use the application log file system option.

Deploy code to a web app

As part of the typical development life cycle of your application, there is a point where you need to deploy your code to an Azure App Service. The "Create an Azure App Service web app" section earlier in this chapter reviews how to deploy the code directly from Visual Studio 2022. This section explains how to deploy your code using other alternatives more suitable to continuous deployment or continuous integration workflows.

When developing your web application, you must test your code on both your local environment and in development or testing environments that are similar to the production environment. Starting with the Standard pricing tier, Azure App Service provides you with the deployment slots. These slots are deployments of your web application that reside in the same App Service as your web application. A deployment slot has its configuration and host name. You can use these additional deployment slots for testing your code before moving to the production slot. The main benefit of using these deployment slots is that you can swap these slots without any downtime. You can even configure an automated swap of the slots by using Auto Swap.

When planning to deploy your web application into an App Service, Azure offers several options:

- **ZIP or WAR files**   When you want to deploy your application, you can package all your files into a ZIP or WAR package. Using the Kudu service, you can deploy your code to the App Service.
- **FTP**   You can copy your application files directly to the App Service using the FTP/S endpoint configured by default in the App Service.
- **Cloud synchronization**   Powered by the Kudu deployment engine, this method allows you to have your code in a OneDrive or Dropbox folder, which then syncs with the App Service.

- **Continuous deployment** Azure can integrate with GitHub, BitBucket, or Azure Repos repositories for deploying the most recent updates of your application to the App Service. Depending on the service, you can use the Kudu build server or Azure Pipelines for implementing a continuous delivery process. You can also configure the integration manually with other cloud repositories such as GitLab.
- **Your local Git repository** You can configure your App Service as a remote repository for your local Git repository and push your code to Azure. Then the Kudu build server automatically compiles your code for you and deploys it to the App Service.
- **ARM template** You can use Visual Studio and an ARM template for deploying your code into an App Service.

> **NOTE KUDU**
>
> The Kudu platform oversees Git deployments in Azure App Service. You can find more detailed information on its GitHub site at *https://github.com/ projectkudu/kudu/wiki*.

The following example shows how to deploy your code to a web app using Azure Pipelines. For this example, you must have your code deployed in an Azure Repos repository. If you don't already have your code in an Azure Repos repository, you can use the following article for creating a new repo: *https://docs.microsoft.com/en-us/azure/devops/repos/git/creatingrepo*.

1. Open the Azure portal (*https://portal.azure.com*).
2. In the search box at the top of the Azure portal, type the name of your App Service.
3. In the result list below the search box, select your App Service.
4. On your App Service blade, on the menu on the left side of the page, under the Deployment section, select Deployment Center.
5. On the Deployment Center, shown in Figure 1-9, in the Source dropdown menu, select Azure Repos.
6. In the Azure Repos section, in the Organization dropdown menu, select your organization.
7. Select the project from the dropdown menu.
8. Select the repository in the dropdown menu.
9. Select the branch in the dropdown menu.
10. Click the Save button at the top left of the Deployment Center blade.

At this point, you have configured an Azure Pipeline in your Azure Repo that automatically deploys your code to the Azure App Service. When you make a commit to the branch that you selected in the previous example, the Azure Pipeline automatically uses the code in the last commit. Once you have configured the continuous deployment for your Azure App Service, you can review the status of the different deployments in the Deployment Center of your Azure App Service.

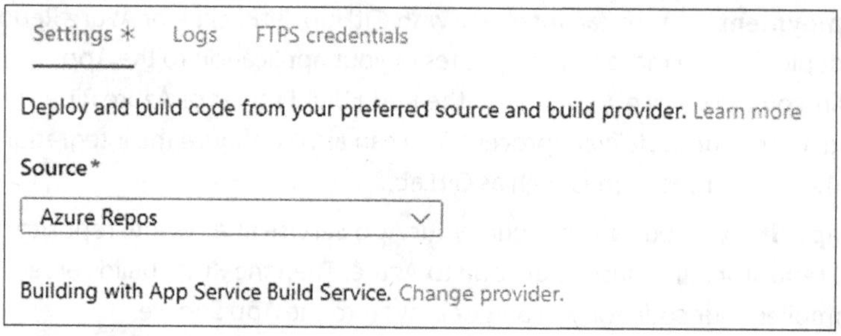

Settings ✳   Logs   FTPS credentials
_____

Deploy and build code from your preferred source and build provider. Learn more

Source *

| Azure Repos   ∨ |

Building with App Service Build Service. Change provider.

FIGURE 1-9 Configuring continuous deployment.

> **NEED MORE REVIEW?**   **APP SERVICE DEPLOYMENT EXAMPLES**
>
> You can review samples of the different types of deployments by following the cases published in the following articles:
>
> - Deploy ZIP or WAR files: *https://docs.microsoft.com/en-us/azure/app-service/deploy-zip*
> - Deploy via cloud sync: *https://docs.microsoft.com/en-us/azure/app-service/deploy-content-sync*
> - Deploy from local Git: *https://docs.microsoft.com/en-us/azure/app-service/deploy-local-git*

When you deploy your code to an Azure App Service, you can do so in different deployment slots. A deployment slot is a live app that is different from the main app. Each deployment slot has its own host name and group of settings. You usually use the various slots as a staging environment for testing purposes. You can switch between the different slots without losing requests. Deployment slots are available only to Standard, Premium, and Isolated App Services tiers.

> **NEED MORE REVIEW?**   **DEPLOYMENT SLOTS**
>
> You can learn more about how to work with deployment slots by reviewing the following article: *https://docs.microsoft.com/en-us/azure/app-service/deploy-staging-slots*.

EXAM TIP

You can use different mechanisms for deploying your code into an Azure App Service. If you decide to use continuous deployment systems for deploying your code, such as Azure Repos or GitHub, remember that you must authorize your continuous deployment system before you can perform any deployment.

_____

Configure web app settings including Secure Sockets Layer, API settings, and connection strings

After you have created your App Service application, you can manage the various parameters that might affect your application. You can access these settings in the Configuration menu on the Settings section in the App Service blade. The available parameters are grouped by the following four main categories of settings:

- **Application Settings**   You can configure the environment variables that are passed to your code. Using these settings is equivalent to setting the same variables in the <appSettings> section in the Web.config or appsettings.json files in an ASP.NET or ASP. NET Core project. If you set a variable in this section that matches a variable in Web. config or appsettings.json files, the value of the variables in the configuration files will be replaced with the value in your Azure Web App settings. These settings are always encrypted at rest—that is, when they are stored.

- **Connection Strings**   You use this section for configuring the connection strings for the database that your code needs to use. This is similar to using the <connectionString> section in the Web.config or appsettings.json files in ASP.NET or ASP.NET Core projects.

- **General Settings**   These settings are related to the environment and platform in which your app runs. You can control the following items:
  - **Stack Settings**   You configure the stack and the version used for running your application.
  - **Stack**   You can choose between .NET Core, .NET, Java, PHP, and Python.
  - **Version**   This is the version for the stack that you chose in the previous setting.
  - **Platform Settings**   This section controls the different settings related to the platform that runs your code.
  - **Platform**   This setting controls whether your application runs on a 32- or 64-bit platform.
  - **Managed Pipeline Version**   Configures the IIS pipeline mode. You should set this to *classic* if you need to run a legacy application that requires an older version of IIS.
  - **FTP State**   Configures the possibility of using FTP or FTPS to deploy your web app to the Azure App Service. By default, both FTP and FTPS protocols are enabled.
  - **HTTP Version**   This enables the HTTPS/2 protocol.
  - **Web Sockets**   If your application uses SignalR or socket.io, you need to enable web sockets.
  - **Always On**   Enabling this setting means your app is always loaded. By default, the application is unloaded if it is idle for some amount of time. You can configure this idle timeout in the host.json project file. The default value for App Service is 30 minutes.
  - **ARR Affinity**   Enabling this setting ensures that client requests are routed to the same instance for the life of the session. This setting is useful for stateful applications but can negatively affect stateless applications.

- **Debugging**   Enable remote debugging options so you can directly connect from your IDE to the Azure App Service for debugging your ASP.NET, ASP.NET Core, or Node.js apps. This option automatically turns off after 48 hours.

- **Incoming Client Certificates**   If you require mutual SSL authentication for your application, you need to enable this option.

- **Default Documents**   This setting configures which web page is displayed at the root URL of your app. You can set a list of different default documents, where the first valid match is shown at the root URL of your website.

- **Path Mappings**   The settings in this section depend on the type of operating system that you choose for your Azure App Service:

  - **Windows Apps (Uncontainerized)**   These settings are similar to the ones that you can find in IIS.

  - **Handler Mappings**   You can configure custom script processors for different file extensions.

  - **Virtual Applications And Directories**   This setting allows you to add additional virtual directories or applications to your App Service.

  - **Containerized Apps**   You can configure the mount points that are attached to the containers during the execution. You can attach up to five Azure files or blob mount points per app. Figure 1-10 shows the dialog for configuring an Azure file mount point.

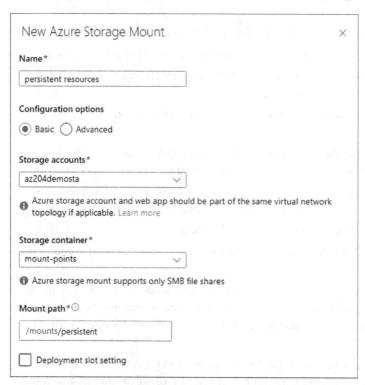

FIGURE 1-10 Configuring a new mount point

Once you have created an app setting or connection string variable, you can access these values from your code by using environment variables. The following code snippet shows how to access an app setting named `testing-var1` and connection string named `testing-connsql1` from a PHP page:

```php
<?php
    $testing_var1 = getenv('APPSETTING_testing-var1')
    $connection_string = getenv('SQLAZURECONNSTR_testing-connsql1')
?>
```

As you can see in the previous code snippet, you need to prepend the string `APPSETTING_` to your app setting variable's name. In the case of connection strings, the string that you need to prepend to your connection string's name depends on the type that you configure in the connection string in the Azure portal:

- **SQL Databases** SQLAZURECONNSTR_
- **SQL Server** SQLCONNSTR_
- **MySQL** MYSQLCONNSTR_
- **PostgreSQL** POSTGRESQLCONNSTR_
- **Custom** CUSTOMCONNSTR_

For ASP.NET applications, you can also access app settings and connection strings by using the traditional ConfigurationManager. If you decide to use the ConfigurationManager, you don't need to prepend any string to the name of your app setting or connection string. The following code snippet shows how to access your app settings or connection string from ASP.NET code:

```
System.Configuration.ConfigurationManager.AppSettings["testing-var1"]
System.Configuration.ConfigurationManager.ConnectionStrings["testing-connsql1"]
```

When configuring an Azure web app for a production environment, you usually need to secure the connections with the web app. You also need to make your Azure web app available through your own domain instead of the default *azurewebsites.net* domain. You can do so by configuring the Custom Domain and secure sockets layer (SSL) settings.

Use the following procedure for configuring SSL settings for an existing web app. Remember that SSL settings are available only for B1 or higher pricing tiers:

1. Open the Azure portal (*https://portal.azure.com*).
2. In the search box, type the name of your Azure web app.
3. In the result list, select the name of your Azure web app.
4. On your Azure web app page, on the navigation list on the left side of the page, select Custom Domain in the Settings section.
5. Click the Add Custom Domain button in the middle of the Custom Domains page.
6. On the Add Custom Domain blade on the right side of the page, in the Domain provider select control, select the All Other Domain Services option.

7. In the Domain text box, type the name of your custom domain name. Once you finish typing the domain name, the Domain Validation section appears.

8. Keep the App Service Managed Certificate option in the TLS/SSL certificate settings. This option instructs Azure to automatically create a new certificate for your custom domain and install it in your App Service at no additional cost.

9. Keep the SNI SSL option for the TLS/SSL type setting. This certificate type does not have an additional cost. The IP-based SSL certificate is available only for Standard tier or above and has additional costs.

10. Follow the instructions for validating your domain shown in the Domain Validation section.

11. Once you have validated your custom domain, click the Add button in the Add Custom Domain blade.

NEED MORE REVIEW? CONFIGURE APP SETTINGS

You can review more details about how to configure the different settings in your Azure web app by reviewing the article at *https://docs.microsoft.com/en-us/azure/app-service/configure-common*.

EXAM TIP

Remember that the settings that you configure in the Application Settings section overwrite the values that you configure in the <appSettings> or <connectionStrings> in your Web. config or appsettings.json files.

Implement autoscaling rules, including scheduled autoscaling, and scaling by operational or system metrics

One of the biggest challenges that you face when you deploy your application in a production environment is to ensure that you provide enough resources so your application has the expected performance. Determining the number of resources that you should allocate is the big question when it comes to configuring the resources for your app. If you allocate too many resources, your application will perform well during usage peaks, but you are potentially wasting resources. If you allocate too few resources, you are saving resources, but your app might not perform well during usage peaks. Another issue with the application performance is that it's challenging to anticipate when a heavy usage peak may happen. This is especially true for applications that have unpredictable usage patterns.

Fortunately, Azure provides a mechanism for addressing this issue. You can dynamically assign more resources to your application when you need them. *Autoscaling* is the action of automatically adding or removing resources to an Azure service and providing needed computing power for your application in each situation. An application can scale in two different ways:

- **Vertically**   You add more computing power by adding more memory, CPU resources, and IOPS to the application. At the end of the day, your application runs on a virtual machine. It doesn't matter if you use an IaaS virtual machine, Azure App Service, or Azure Service Fabric—you are using virtual machines under the hood. Vertically scaling an application means moving from a smaller VM to a larger VM and adding more memory, CPU, and IOPS. Vertically scaling requires stopping the system while the VM is resizing. This type of scaling is also known as "scaling up and down."

- **Horizontally**   You can also scale your application by creating or removing instances of your application. Each instance of your application is executed in a virtual machine that is part of a virtual machine scale set. The corresponding Azure service automatically manages the virtual machines in the scale set. All these instances of your application work together to provide the same service. The advantage of scaling horizontally is that the availability of your application is not affected because there is no need for rebooting all the instances of your application that provide the service. This type of scaling is also known as "scaling out and in."

When you work with autoscaling, we refer to horizontal scaling because vertical scaling requires service interruption while the Azure Resource Manager is changing the size of the virtual machine. For that reason, vertical scaling is not suitable for autoscaling.

You configure autoscaling based on some criteria that your application should meet for providing the right performance level. You configure these criteria in Azure by using autoscaling rules. A rule defines which metric should use Azure Monitor for performing the autoscaling. When that metric reaches the configured condition, Azure automatically performs the action configured for that rule. The typical action that you might think the rule should do is adding or removing a VM to the scale set, but it can also perform other actions such as sending an email or making an HTTP request to a webhook. You can configure three different types of rules when working the autoscaling rules:

- **Time-based**   The Azure Monitor executes the autoscaling rule based on a schedule. For example, if your application requires more resources during the first week of the month, you can add more instances and reduce the number of resources for the rest of the month.

- **Metric-based**   You configure the threshold for standard metrics, such as the usage of the CPU, the length of the HTTP queue, or the percentage of memory usage, as shown in Figure 1-11.

- **Custom-based**   You can create your metrics in your application, expose them using Application Insights, and use them for autoscaling rules.

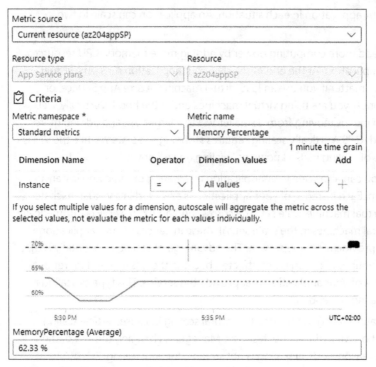

FIGURE 1-11 Configuring a metric-based autoscale rule

You can only use the built-in autoscaling mechanism with a limited group of Azure resource types:

- **Azure virtual machines** You can apply autoscaling by using virtual machine scale sets. All the VMs in a scale set are treated as a group. By using autoscaling, you can add virtual machines to the scale set or remove virtual machines from it.

- **Azure Service Fabric** When you create an Azure Service Fabric cluster, you define different node types. A different virtual machine scale set supports each node type that you define in an Azure Service Fabric cluster. You can apply the same type of autoscaling rules that you use in a standard virtual machine scale set.

- **Azure App Service** This service has built-in autoscaling capabilities that you can use for adding or removing instances to the Azure App Service. The autoscale rules apply to all apps inside the Azure App Service.

- **Azure Cloud Services** This service has built-in autoscaling capabilities that you can use for adding or removing resources to the roles in the Azure Cloud Service.

When you work with the autoscale feature in one of the supported Azure services, you define a profile condition. A profile condition defines the rule that you configure for adding or removing resources. You can also define the default, minimum, and maximum allowed instances for this profile. When you define a minimum and maximum, your service cannot decrease or grow beyond the limits you define in the profile. You can also configure the profile for scaling based on a schedule or based on the values of built-in or custom metrics. You can use the following procedure for adding a metric-based autoscale rule to an Azure App Service. This rule adds an instance to the Azure App Service plan when the average percentage of CPU usage is over 80 percent for more than 10 minutes:

1. Open the Azure portal (*https://portal.azure.com*).

2. In the search box at the top of the Azure portal, type the name of your Azure App Service.

3. Select the name of your Azure App Service in the results list.

4. On your Azure App Service blade, on the navigation menu on the left side of the blade, select the Scale-Out (App Service Plan) option in the Settings section.

5. On the Scale-Out (App Service Plan) blade, on the Scaling section, select Rules Based for the Scale-Out method setting.

6. A warning message in red appears at the bottom of the blade. Click the Manage Rules-Based Scale link inside the warning message.

7. On the Autoscale setting blade, select the Custom autoscale option.

8. On the Auto Created Default Scale Condition area, on the Scale Mode setting, select Scale Based On A Metric.

9. On the Scale-Out (App Service Plan) blade, on the Configure tab, in the Auto Created Default Scale Condition window shown in Figure 1-12, click the Add A Rule link.

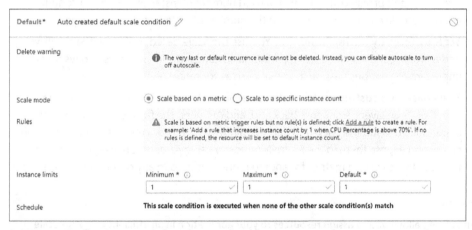

FIGURE 1-12 Configuring a metric-based autoscale rule

10. On the Scale rule panel, in the Criteria section, ensure that the CPU Percentage value is selected in the Metric Name dropdown menu.

11. Ensure that the Greater Than value is selected from the Operator dropdown menu.

12. Type the value **80** in the Metric Threshold To Trigger Scale Action text box.

13. In the Action section, ensure that the Instance count value is set to **1**.

14. Click the Add button at the bottom of the panel.

15. On the Scale-Out (App Service Plan) blade, in the Default Profile condition, set the Maximum Instance Limit to **3**.

16. Click the Save button in the top left of the blade.

> **NOTE SCALE-OUT/SCALE-IN**
>
> The previous procedure shows how to add an instance to the App Service plan (it is scaling out the App Service plan) but doesn't remove the additional instance once the CPU percentage falls below the configured threshold. You should add a Scale-In rule for removing the additional instances once they are not needed. You configure a Scale-In rule in the same way you did for the Scale-Out rule. Just set the Operation dropdown menu to the Decrease Count To value.

You can use different common autoscale patterns based on the settings that you have seen so far:

- **Scale based on CPU**   You scale your service (Azure App Service, VM Scale Set, or Cloud Service) based on CPU. You need to configure Scale-Out and Scale-In rules for adding and removing instances to the service. In this pattern, you also set a minimum and a maximum number of instances.

- **Scale differently on weekdays versus weekends**   You use this pattern when you expect to have the primary usage of your application occur on weekdays. You configure the default profile condition with a fixed number of instances. Then you configure another profile condition for reducing the number of instances during weekends.

- **Scale differently during holidays**   You use the Scale based on CPU pattern. Still, you add a profile condition for adding additional instances during holidays or days that are important to your business, such as Black Friday for retail solutions.

- **Scale based on custom metrics**   You use this pattern with a web application composed of three layers: front end, back end, and API tiers. The front end of an API tier communicates with the back-end tier. You define your custom metrics in the web application and expose them to the Azure Monitor by using Application Insights. You can then use these custom metrics for adding more resources to any of the three layers.

EXAM TIP

Autoscaling allows you to assign resources to your application in an efficient way. Autoscale rules for adding more instances to your application do not remove those instances when the rule condition is not satisfied. As a best practice, if you create a Scale-Out rule for adding instances to a service, you should create the opposite Scale-In rule for removing the instance. This ensures that the resources are assigned efficiently to your application.

Configure deployment slots

As part of your application's typical development life cycle, there is a point when you need to deploy your code to an Azure App Service. The "Create an Azure App Service web app" section earlier in this chapter reviews how to deploy the code directly from Visual Studio 2022. This section explains how to deploy your code using other alternatives more suitable to continuous deployment or continuous integration workflows.

When developing your web application, you must test your code on both your local environment and in development or testing environments similar to the production environment. Starting with the Standard pricing tier, Azure App Service provides you with the deployment slots. These slots are deployments of your web application that reside in the same App Service of your web application. A deployment slot has its configuration and host name. You can use these additional deployment slots to test your code before moving to the production slot. The main benefit of using these deployment slots is that you can swap these slots without any downtime. You can even configure an automated slot swap using Auto Swap.

To deploy your web application into an App Service, Azure offers several options:

- **ZIP or WAR files**   When you want to deploy your application, you can package all your files into a ZIP or WAR package. Using the Kudu service, you can deploy your code to the App Service.
- **FTP**   You can copy your application files directly to the App Service using the FTP/S endpoint configured by default in the App Service.
- **Cloud synchronization**   Powered by the Kudu deployment engine, this method allows you to store your code in a OneDrive or Dropbox folder and sync that folder with the App Service.
- **Continuous deployment**   Azure can integrate with GitHub, BitBucket, or Azure Repos repositories for deploying the most recent updates of your application to the App Service. Depending on the service, you can use the Kudu build server or Azure Pipelines

for implementing a continuous delivery process. You can also configure the integration manually with other cloud repositories such as GitLab.

- **Your local Git repository** You can configure your App Service as a remote repository for your local Git repository and push your code to Azure. Then the Kudu build server automatically compiles your code for you and deploys to the App Service.

- **ARM template** You can use Visual Studio and an ARM template for deploying your code into an App Service.

> *NOTE* **KUDU**
>
> The Kudu platform oversees Git deployments in Azure App Service. You can find more detailed information on its GitHub site at *https://github.com/ projectkudu/kudu/wiki*.

The following example shows how to deploy your code to a web app using Azure Pipelines. For this example, you must have your code deployed in an Azure Repos repository. If you don't already have your code in an Azure Repos repository, you can use the following article for creating a new repo: *https://docs.microsoft.com/en-us/azure/devops/repos/git/creatingrepo*.

1. Open the Azure portal (*https://portal.azure.com*).
2. In the search box at the top of the Azure portal, type the name of your App Service.
3. In the result list below the search box, select your App Service.
4. On your App Service blade, on the menu on the left side of the page, in the Settings section, select Configuration.
5. In the Platform Settings section in the Configuration blade, ensure that SCM Basic Auth Publishing Credentials is enabled by clicking the On option.
6. Click the Save button on the top of the Configuration blade and accept the warning message by clicking the Continue button.
7. On the left menu, under the Deployment section, select Deployment Center.
8. On the Deployment Center, shown in Figure 1-13, in the source dropdown, select Azure Repos.
9. In the Azure Repos section, select your Azure DevOps organization in the Organization dropdown menu.
10. Select your project in the corresponding dropdown menu.
11. Select the repository and branch from the corresponding dropdown menus.
12. Click the Save button on the top left of the Deployment Center blade.

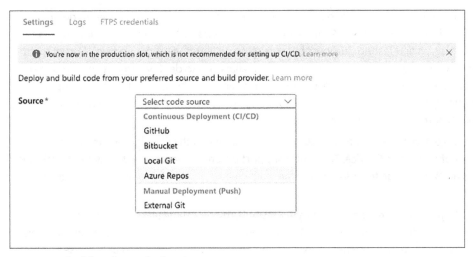

FIGURE 1-13 Enabling diagnostics logging

At this point, you have configured an Azure Pipeline in your Azure Repo that automatically deploys your code to the Azure App Service. When you make a commit to the branch that you selected in the previous example, the Azure Pipeline automatically uses the code in the last commit. Once you have configured the continuous deployment for your Azure App Service, you can review the status of the different deployments in the Deployment Center of your Azure App Service.

When you deploy your code to an Azure App Service, you can do so in different deployment slots. Deployment slots in Azure App Service are separate instances of an app that can be used for staging and testing purposes before swapping with the production slot. Deployment slots are live apps with their own host names that allow you to deploy and test your web app, web app on Linux, mobile backend, or API app in a separate environment before swapping it with the production slot. They provide a staging environment where you can validate app changes before making them available to users.

To enable deployment slots, your app must be running in the Standard, Premium, or Isolated tier of Azure App Service. These tiers support different numbers of deployment slots, and there is no extra charge for using them. The main characteristics of deployment slots are as follows:

- **Staging Environment**: Deployment slots provide a dedicated environment for testing and validating app changes before they are swapped with the production slot. This helps ensure that your app works as expected before making it available to users.

- **Zero Downtime**: When you swap a deployment slot with the production slot, all instances of the source slot are warmed up before the swap. This means all staging slot instances are running before the actual swap with the production slot. The warm-up process ensures zero downtime for your app, since the traffic redirection is seamless, and no requests are dropped during the swap operation.

- **Rollback Capability**: After a swap, the slot that previously had the production app now contains the previous version of the app. If the changes swapped into the production slot are not as expected, you can immediately perform the swap again with the previous slot, reverting the situation to the "last known good site."

- **Configuration Cloning**: When adding a new deployment slot, you have the option to clone the app configuration from another deployment slot. This includes app settings, connection strings, language framework versions, web sockets, HTTP version, and platform bitness. This eases the deployment of new slots and ensures that the new slot can run under the same circumstances as the production slot.

- **Separate Host Name**: Each deployment slot has its own host name and can be accessed independently. The URL format for a deployment slot is *http://sitename-slotname.azurewebsites.net*. Using this separate host name, you can perform all the needed checks, user acceptance tests, or integration tests before switching to the production slot.

- **Traffic Routing**: By default, all customer traffic is routed to the production slot. However, you can configure automatic or manual traffic routing to route a portion of the traffic to a nonproduction slot. This is useful for testing new updates with a subset of users or allowing users to opt in or out of a beta app.

- **Auto Swap**: The Auto Swap feature allows you to continuously deploy your app with zero cold starts and zero downtime. When enabled, any code changes pushed to a deployment slot are automatically swapped into the production slot after the app is warmed up in the source slot.

- **Rollback and Troubleshooting**:   If any errors occur during a slot swap, you can roll back the swap by swapping the same two slots immediately. Additionally, you can monitor the swap operation in the activity log and troubleshoot common swap errors using the event log and application-specific error log.

The following procedure shows how to create a new deployment slot and swap it with the production slot.

1. Open the Azure portal (*https://portal.azure.com*).

2. In the search box at the top of the Azure portal, type the name of your App Service.

3. In the result list below the search box, click your App Service.

4. On your App Service blade, on the menu on the left side of the page, in the Deployment section, click Deployment slots.

5. Click the Add Slot button on the top side of the Deployment Slots blade.

6. In the Add a Slot dialog on the right side of the window, type a name for the new slot.

7. In the Clone Settings From dropdown menu, select your production slot.

8. Click the Add button at the bottom left of the Add a Slot dialog.

9. Click the Close button.

At this point, you have your slot ready. You can select the name of your slot and configure the Continuous Integration settings following the procedure shown at the beginning of this section.

NEED MORE REVIEW?   **DEPLOYMENT SLOTS**

You can learn more about how to work with deployment slots by reviewing the following article: *https://docs.microsoft.com/en-us/azure/app-service/deploy-staging-slots*

EXAM TIP

You can use different mechanisms for deploying your code into an Azure App Service. If you decide to use continuous deployment systems for deploying your code, such as Azure Repos or GitHub, remember that you must authorize your continuous deployment system before you can perform any deployment.

Skill 1.3: Implement Azure Functions

Based on Azure App Service, Azure Functions allow you to run pieces of code that solve particular problems inside the whole application. You use these functions in the same way that you might use a class or a function inside your code. That is, your function gets some input, executes the piece of code, and provides an output.

The big difference between Azure Functions and other app services models is that with Azure Functions (using the Consumption pricing tier), you are charged per second only when your code is running. When you use the Consumption pricing tier, you are working in a serverless model.

If you use App Service, you are charged hourly when the App Service Plan is running—even if no code is executing. Because Azure Functions is based on App Service, you can also decide to run your Azure Function in your App Service Plan if you already have other app services executing. When using an App Service, you are working in a Platform as a Service (PaaS) model.

> **This skill covers how to**
> - Create and configure an Azure Function App
> - Implement input and output bindings for a function
> - Implement function triggers by using data operations, timers, and webhooks

Create and configure an Azure Function App

When developing Azure Functions, if you decide to use C# for creating your function, your natural choice for the Integrated Development Environment (IDE) would be Visual Studio. If you are not working with C# and use any other supported language, you can still use Visual Studio Code for working with Azure Functions. Independent of the language you use for your Azure function, you must create an Azure Function App to run your code. You can create Function Apps using the Azure portal, Visual Studio, or Visual Studio Code.

The following procedure shows how to create an Azure Function project and an Azure Function App in Azure using Visual Studio 2022:

1. On your local computer, open Visual Studio 2022.
2. On the Welcome page, click the Continue Without Code link at the bottom of the Get Started column.
3. Select Tools > Get Tools And Features. Check the Azure Development option in the Web & Cloud section.
4. Click the Modify button on the bottom right of the window.
5. Create a new Azure Function project. Select File > New > Project.
6. On the Create A New Project window, in the dropdown menus below the Search For Templates textbox, ensure that the following values are selected, as shown in Figure 1-14:
   a. C#
   b. All Platforms
   c. Cloud
7. In the New Project window, select Azure Functions in the template area, as shown in Figure 1-14.

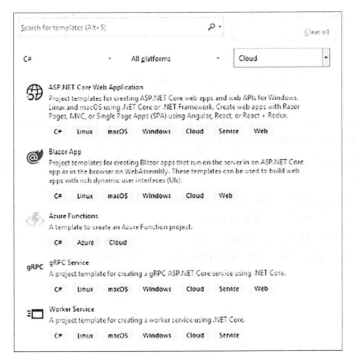

FIGURE 1-14 Cloud project templates

8. On the bottom right of the window, select Next.

9. In the Configure Your New Project window, provide a Project Name, Location, and Solution Name for your project.

10. Select Next.

11. On the Additional Information Azure Functions window, select .NET 6.0 (Long Term Support) in the Functions worker dropdown menu.

12. In the Function dropdown menu, select HTTP Trigger.

13. Ensure that the Use Azurite for runtime storage account (AzureWebJobsStorage) option is checked.

14. Ensure that the Enable Docker option is unchecked.

15. Ensure that the Authorization level is configured as Function.

16. Select Create.

17. Make the modifications that you need on the new project.

18. In Solution Explorer, right-click the Azure Function project name.

19. Select Publish, which opens the Publish tab and the Publish Profile Assistant window.

20. Ensure that the Azure option is selected in the Target list.

21. Select Next.

22. In the Specific Target list, select Azure Function App (Windows).

23. Select Next.

24. In the Functions instance area, click the Create New button on the right side of the area below the Subscription name dropdown menu.

25. On the Pick A Publish Target window, select Create Profile. This opens the App Service Create New window.

26. In the top right of the Function App Create New window, click the Add An Account Button For Connecting To Your Azure Subscription.

27. On the Function App Create New window that is connected to your Azure Subscription, type the name of your function app in the app Name field, as shown in Figure 1-15.

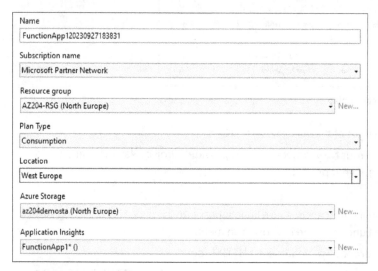

Name

FunctionApp120230927183831

Subscription name

Microsoft Partner Network

Resource group

AZ204-RSG (North Europe)   New...

Plan Type

Consumption

Location

West Europe

Azure Storage

az204demosta (North Europe)   New...

Application Insights

FunctionApp1* ()   New...

FIGURE 1-15 Creating a function app

28. On the Resource Group dropdown menu, click on the New link next to the dropdown menu.

29. Type a name for the new Resource Group and select OK.

30. On the Location dropdown menu, choose the location where you need to deploy your Azure Function.

31. Click on the New link next to the Azure Storage dropdown menu.

32. In the Azure Storage Create New window, type a name for the new Account and select OK.

33. In the bottom right of the Function App Create New window, select **Create**. This creates the needed resources in Azure. Once everything is created successfully, the Function App Create New window closes.

34. In the Publish window, ensure that the new function app is selected.

35. Click the Finish button. This will create the publish profile.

36. In the Finish area in the Publish window, click the Close button on the bottom right of the window to close the window.

37. In the Publish tab in Visual Studio, click the Publish button on the top right of the tab.

At this point, your Azure Function is ready for execution. Depending on your code, you might need to write data to some storage system, such as storage accounts or databases, or you might need to wait for external data for processing them. The connection of external data sources and triggers is done through the usage of input and output bindings. We will review them in the next section.

> **NOTE NETWORKING**
>
> In a real-world scenario, you may need to connect to other resources in Azure or even on external sites. That connection depends on the networking connectivity of your Azure Function. That connectivity is managed by virtual networks. You can find more information about Azure Functions and virtual networks by reviewing the article at *https://learn.microsoft.com/ en-us/azure/azure-functions/functions-create-vnet*.

Implement input and output bindings for a function

When writing a function in your code, that function may require data as input information for doing the job that you are writing. The function can also produce some output information as the result of the operations performed inside the function. When you work with Azure Functions, you might also need these input and output data flows.

Binding uses Azure Functions for connecting your function with the external world without hard coding the connection to the external resources. An Azure Function can have a mix of input and output bindings, or it can have no binding at all. Bindings pass data to the function as parameters.

Although triggers and bindings are closely related, you should not confuse them. Triggers are the events that cause the function to start its execution; bindings are like the connection to the data needed for the function. You can see the difference in this example:

One publisher service sends an event (to an Event Grid that reads a new image that has been uploaded to Blob Storage) to an Azure Storage account. Your function needs to read this image, process it, and place some information in a Cosmos DB document. When the image has been processed, your function also sends a notification to the user interface using SignalR.

In this example, you can find one trigger, one input binding, and two output bindings:

- **Trigger** The Event Grid should be configured as the trigger for the Azure Function.
- **Input binding** Your function needs to read the image that has been uploaded to the Blob Storage. In this case, you need to use Blob Storage as an input binding.
- **Output bindings** Your function needs to write a Cosmos DB document with the results of processing the image. You need to use the Cosmos DB output binding. Your function also needs to send a notification to the user interface using the SignalR output binding.

Depending on the language that you use for programming your Azure Function, the way you declare a binding changes:

- **C#** You declare bindings and triggers by decorating methods and parameters.
- **Other** Update the function.json configuration file.

When defining a binding for non-C# language functions, you need to define your binding using the following minimum required attributes:

- **type** This string represents the binding type. For example, you would use `eventHub` when using an output binding for Event Hub.
- **direction** The only allowed values are `in` for input bindings and `out` for output bindings. Some bindings also support the special direction `inout`.
- **name** The function uses this attribute for binding the data in the function. For example, in JavaScript, the key in a key-value list is an attribute.

Depending on the specific binding that you are configuring, there could be some additional attributes that should be defined.

NEED MORE REVIEW? **SUPPORTED BINDINGS**

For a complete list of supported bindings, please refer to the article at *https://docs.microsoft.com/en-us/azure/azure-functions/functions-triggers-bindings#supported-bindings*.

Before you can use a binding in your code, you need to register it. If you use C# for your functions, you can install the appropriate NuGet package. You need to install the package with the extension code using the `func` command-line utility for other languages. The following example installs the Service Bus extension in your local environment for non-C# projects:

```
func extensions install –package Microsoft.Azure.WebJobs.ServiceBus
```

If you are developing your Azure Function using the Azure portal, you can add the bindings in the Integrate section of your function. When you add a binding that is not installed in your environment, you will see a warning message indicating that you need to install it manually. You need to install the extensions at the Function App level. You can install the extension by using the following procedure:

1. Open the Azure portal (*https://portal.azure.com*).
2. In the search box at the top of the Azure portal, type the name of your Function App.
3. Select the name of your Function App in the results list.

4. On your Function App blade, on the navigation menu on the left side of the blade, select the Advanced Tools option in the Development Tools section.

5. Click the Go link.

6. Select the Debug console dropdown menu on the top of the window, and select CMD.

7. In the folder explorer, select site.

8. In the folder explorer, select wwwroot.

9. Click the pencil icon on the left side of the host.json file.

10. Add the following code after the logging section. Don't forget to add a comma after the closing curly braces associated with the logging object:

```
"extensionBundle": {
        "id": "Microsoft.Azure.Functions.ExtensionBundle",
        "version": "[3.3.0, 4.0.0)"
    }
```

11. Click the Save button on the top left of the editor.

12. Close the Diagnostic Console tab and switch back to your Function App.

13. Select the Overview option.

14. On the Functions section in the Overview blade, click the Create button.

15. On the Create function panel, you should be able to see the complete list of binding extensions, as shown in Figure 1-16.

Template	Description
HTTP trigger	A function that will be run whenever it receives an HTTP request, responding based on data in the body or query string
Timer trigger	A function that will be run on a specified schedule
Azure Queue Storage trigger	A function that will be run whenever a message is added to a specified Azure Storage queue
Azure Service Bus Queue trigger	A function that will be run whenever a message is added to a specified Service Bus queue
Azure Service Bus Topic trigger	A function that will be run whenever a message is added to the specified Service Bus topic
Azure Blob Storage trigger	A function that will be run whenever a blob is added to a specified container
Azure Event Hub trigger	A function that will be run whenever an event hub receives a new event

FIGURE 1-16 Binding extensions

NOTE **MANUALLY INSTALL BINDING EXTENSIONS FROM THE AZURE PORTAL**

When you develop your Azure Function using the Azure portal, you can use the standard editor or the advanced editor. When you use the advanced editor, you can directly edit the function.json configuration file. If you add new bindings using the advanced editor, you must manually install any new binding extensions that you added to the function.json. You can review the following article for manually installing binding extensions from the Azure portal: *https://docs.microsoft.com/en-us/azure/azure-functions/install-update-binding-extensions-manual*.

If you decide to program your Azure Function using C#, you make the configuration of the bindings by using decorators for functions and parameters. The function.json file is automatically constructed based on the information that you provide in your code. Listing 1-2 shows how to configure input and output bindings using parameter decorators.

LISTING 1-2 Configuring input and output bindings

```
// C# ASP.NET Core
using System;
using System.IO;
using Microsoft.Azure.WebJobs;
using Microsoft.Extensions.Logging;
using Microsoft.Azure.WebJobs.Extensions.SignalRService;
using Microsoft.Azure.WebJobs.Extensions.EventGrid;
using Microsoft.Azure.EventGrid.Models;
using System.Threading.Tasks;

namespace  Company.Functions
{
    public static class BlobTriggerCSharp
    {
        [FunctionName("BlobTriggerCSharp")]
        public static Task Run(
            [EventGridTrigger]EventGridEvent eventGridEvent,

[Blob("{data.url}", FileAccess.Read, Connection = "ImagesBlobStorage")] StreamimageBlob,
            [CosmosDB(
                databaseName: "GIS",
                collectionName: "Processed_images",
                ConnectionStringSetting = "CosmosDBConnection")] out dynamic document,

[SignalR(HubName = "notifications")]IAsyncCollector<SignalRMessage> signalRMessages,
            ILogger log)
        {
            document = new { Description = eventGridEvent.Topic,
id = Guid.NewGuid() };

log.LogInformation($"C# Blob trigger function Processed event\n Topic: {eventGridEvent.
Topic} \n Subject: {eventGridEvent.Subject} ");
            return signalRMessages.AddAsync(
            new SignalRMessage
                {
                    Target = "newMessage",
                    Arguments = new [] { eventGridEvent.Subject }
                });
        }
    }
}
```

Let's review the portions of Listing 1-2 that are related to the binding configuration. In this example, you configured one input binding and two output bindings. The parameter `imageBlob` is configured as an input binding. You have decorated the parameter with the attribute `Blob`, which takes the following parameters:

- **Path** The value {data.url} configures the path of the blobs that are passed to the function. In this case, you are using a binding expression that resolves to the full path of the blob in the Blob Storage.
- **Blob access mode** In this example, you access the blob in read-only mode.
- **Connection** This sets the connection string to the storage account where the blobs are stored. This parameter sets the app setting name that contains the actual connection string.

You have also configured two output bindings, though you have configured them differently. The first output binding is configured using the keyword `out` in the parameter definition. Just as you did with the input parameter, you configured the output parameter document by using a parameter attribute. In this case, you used the `CosmosDB` attribute. You use the following parameters for configuring this output binding:

- **databaseName** Sets the database in which you save the document that you create during the execution of the function.
- **collectionName** Sets the collection in which you save the generated document.
- **ConnectionStringSetting** Sets the name of the app setting variable that contains the actual connection string for the database. You should not put the actual connection string here.

Setting a value for this output binding is as simple as assigning a value to the parameter document. You can also configure output bindings by using the return statement of the function. In the example, you configure the second output binding this way.

The function parameter `signalRMessages` is your second output binding. As you can see in Listing 1-2, you didn't add the `out` keyword to this parameter because you can return multiple output values. When you need to return multiple output values, you need to use `ICollector` or `IAsyncCollector` types with the output binding parameter, as you did with `signalRMessages`. Inside the function, you add needed values to the `signalRMessages` collection and use this collection as the return value of the function. You used the SignalR parameter attribute for configuring this output binding. In this case, you only used one parameter for configuring the output binding.

- **HubName** This is the name of the SignalR hub where you send your messages.
- **ConnectionStringSetting** In this case, you didn't use this parameter, so it uses its default value `AzureSignalRConnectionString`. As you saw in the other bindings, this parameter sets the name of the app setting variable that contains the actual connection string SignalR.

When configuring bindings or triggers, there are situations when you need to map the trigger or binding to a dynamically generated path or element. In these situations, you can use binding expressions. You define a binding expression by wrapping your expression in curly braces. You can see an example of a binding expression shown previously in Listing 1-2.

The path that you configure for the input binding contains the binding expression {data.url}, which resolves to the full path of the blob in the Blob Storage. In this case, `EventGridTrigger` sends a JSON payload to the input binding that contains the data.url attribute.

> **NEED MORE REVIEW?** **BINDING EXPRESSION PATTERNS**
>
> You can learn about more binding expression patterns by reviewing this article about Azure Functions binding expression patterns in Microsoft Docs at *https://docs.microsoft.com/en-us/azure/azure-functions/functions-bindings-expressions-patterns*.

The way you configure the bindings for your code depends on the language that you used for your Azure Function. In the previous example, you reviewed how to configure input and output bindings using C# and parameter decorations. If you use any other supported languages in your Azure Function, the way you configure input and output bindings changes.

The first step when configuring bindings in non-C# languages is to modify the function.json configuration file. Listing 1-3 shows the equivalent function.json for the binding configuration made in Listing 1-2. Once you have configured your bindings, you can write your code to access the bindings that you configured. Listing 1-4 shows an example written in JavaScript for using bindings in your code.

LISTING 1-3 Configuring input and output bindings in function.json

```
{
  "disabled": false,
  "bindings": [
    {
      "name": "eventGridEvent",
      "type": "eventGridTrigger",
      "direction": "in"
    },
    {
      "name": "imageBlob",
      "type": "blob",
      "connection": "ImagesBlobStorage",
      "direction": "in",
      "path": "{data.url}"
    },
    {
      "name": "document",
      "type": "cosmosDB",
      "direction": "out",
      "databaseName": "GIS",
      "collectionName": "Processed_images",
      "connectionStringSetting": "CosmosDBConnection",
      "createIfNotExists": true
    },
    {
      "name": "signalRMessages",
      "type": "signalR",
      "direction": "out",
```

```
        "hubName": "notifications"
    }
  ]
}
```

LISTING 1-4 Using bindings in JavaScript

```
// NodeJS. Index.js
const uuid = require('uuid/v4');
module.exports = async function (context, eventGridEvent) {
    context.log('JavaScript Event Grid trigger function processed a request.');
    context.log("Subject: " + eventGridEvent.subject);
    context.log("Time: " + eventGridEvent.eventTime);
    context.log("Data: " + JSON.stringify(eventGridEvent.data));

    context.bindings.document = JSON.stringify({
        id: uuid(),
        Description: eventGridEvent.topic
    });

    context.bindings.signalRMessages = [{
        "target": "newMessage",
        "arguments": [ eventGridEvent.subject ]
    }];

    context.done();
};
```

Listings 1-3 and 1-4 represent the equivalent code in JavaScript to the code in the C# code shown in Listing 1-2. Most important is that name attributes in the binding definitions shown in Listing 1-3 correspond to the properties of the context object shown in Listing 1-4. For example, you created a Cosmos DB output binding and assigned the value document to the name attribute in the binding definition in Listing 1-3. In your JavaScript code, you access this output binding by using `context.bindings.document`.

EXAM TIP

Remember that you need to install the extensions in your local environment before you can use bindings or triggers. You can use the `func` command-line command from the Azure Function CLI tools.

Implement function triggers by using data operations, timers, and webhooks

When you create an Azure Function, that function is executed based on events that happen in the external world. Some examples include

- Executing a function periodically
- Executing a function when some other process uploads a file to Blob Storage or sends a message to a queue storage
- Executing a function when an email arrives in Outlook

Triggers programmatically manage all these events.

You can configure function triggers in the same way that you configure input or output bindings, but you need to pay attention to some additional details when dealing with triggers. You configure a trigger for listening to specific events. When an event occurs, the trigger object can send data and information to the function.

You can configure three different types of triggers:

- **data operation**   The trigger is started based on new data that is created, updated, or added to the system. Supported systems are Cosmos DB, Event Grid, Event Hub, Blob Storage, Queue Storage, and Service Bus.

- **timers**   You use this kind of trigger when you need to run your function based on a schedule.

- **webhooks**   You use HTTP or webhooks triggers when you need to run your function based on an HTTP Request.

Triggers send data to the function with information about the event that caused the trigger to start. This information depends on the type of trigger. Listing 1-5 shows how to configure a data operation trigger for Cosmos DB.

LISTING 1-5 Configuring a Cosmos DB trigger

```
// C# ASP.NET Core
using System.Collections.Generic;
using Microsoft.Azure.Documents;
using Microsoft.Azure.WebJobs;
using Microsoft.Azure.WebJobs.Host;
using Microsoft.Extensions.Logging;
namespace Company.Function
{
    public static class CosmosDBTriggerCSharp
    {
        [FunctionName("CosmosDBTriggerCSharp")]
        public static void Run([CosmosDBTrigger(
            databaseName: "databaseName",
            collectionName: "collectionName",
            ConnectionStringSetting = "AzureWebJobsStorage",
            LeaseCollectionName = "leases",

CreateLeaseCollectionIfNotExists = true)]IReadOnlyList<Document> input, ILogger log)
        {
            if (input != null && input.Count > 0)
            {
                log.LogInformation("Documents modified " + input.Count);
                log.LogInformation("First document Id " + input[0].Id);
                log.LogInformation("Modified document: " + input[0]);
            }
        }
    }
}
```

Just as with bindings, you need to install the corresponding NuGet package with the appropriate extension for working with triggers. In this case, you need to install the package Microsoft.Azure.WebJobs.Extensions.CosmosDB. You used the CosmosDBTrigger parameter attribute for configuring the trigger with the following parameters:

- **databaseName**   This is the name of the database that contains the collection this trigger should monitor.

- **collectionName**   This is the name of the collection that this trigger should monitor. This collection must exist before your function runs.

- **ConnectionStringSetting**   This is the name of the app setting variable that contains the connection string to the Cosmos DB database. If you want to debug your function in your local environment, you should configure this variable in the local.settings. json file and assign the value of the connection string to your development Cosmos DB database. This local.settings.json file is used by Azure Functions Core Tools to store app settings, connection strings, and settings locally and won't be automatically uploaded to Azure when you publish your Azure Function.

- **LeaseCollectionName**   This is the name of the collection used for storing leases over partitions. By default, this collection is stored in the same database as the collection-Name. Use the parameter leaseDatabaseName if you need to store this collection in a separate database or leaseConnectionStringSetting if you need to store the database in a separate Cosmos DB account.

- **CreateLeaseCollectionIfNotExists**   This creates the lease collection set by the LeaseCollectionName parameter if it does not exist in the database. Lease collection should be a nonpartitioned collection and must exist before your function runs.

The Cosmos DB trigger monitors for new or updated documents in the database that you configure in the parameters of the trigger. Once the trigger detects a change, it passes detected changes to the function using an IReadOnlyList<Document>. Once you have the information provided by the trigger in the input list, you can process the information inside your function. If you have enabled Application Insight integration, you should be able to see the log messages from your function, as shown in Figure 1-17.

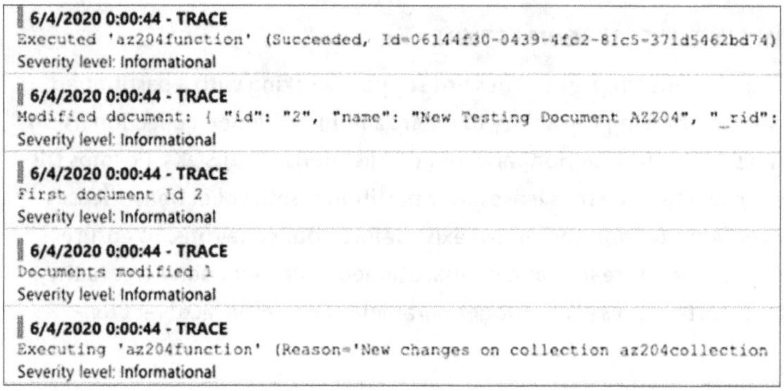

```
6/4/2020 0:00:44 - TRACE
Executed 'az204function' (Succeeded, Id=06144f30-0439-4fc2-81c5-371d5462bd74)
Severity level: Informational

6/4/2020 0:00:44 - TRACE
Modified document: { "id": "2", "name": "New Testing Document A2204", "_rid":
Severity level: Informational

6/4/2020 0:00:44 - TRACE
First document Id 2
Severity level: Informational

6/4/2020 0:00:44 - TRACE
Documents modified 1
Severity level: Informational

6/4/2020 0:00:44 - TRACE
Executing 'az204function' (Reason='New changes on collection az204collection
Severity level: Informational
```

FIGURE 1-17 View Azure function logs in Application Insight

> **NOTE VERSION 1.0 VERSUS VERSION 2.0 VERSUS VERSION 3.0**
>
> When you work with Azure Functions, you can choose between versions 1.0, 2.0, and 3.0. The main difference between version 1.0 and the other versions is that you can only develop and host Azure Functions 1.0 on Azure portal or Windows computers. Functions 2.0 and 3.0 can be developed and hosted on all platforms supported by .NET Core. The Azure Function you use affects the extension packages that you must install when configuring triggers and bindings. Review the overview of Azure Functions runtime versions at *https://docs.microsoft.com/en-us/azure/azure-functions/functions-versions*.

When you work with timer and webhooks triggers, the main difference between them and a data operations trigger is that you do not need to install the extension package that supports the trigger explicitly.

Timer triggers execute your function based on a schedule. This schedule is configured using a CRON expression that is interpreted by the NCronTab library. A CRON expression is a string compound of six different fields with this structure:

```
{second} {minute} {hour} {day} {month} {day-of-week}
```

Each field can have numeric values that are meaningful for the field:

- **second** Represents the seconds in a minute. You can assign values from 0 to 59.
- **minute** Represents the minutes in an hour. You can assign values from 0 to 59.
- **hour** Represents the hours in a day. You can assign values from 0 to 23.
- **day** Represents the days in a month. You can assign values from 1 to 31.
- **month** Represents the months in a year. You can assign values from 1 to 12. You can also use names in English, such as January, or you can use abbreviations of the name in English, such as Jan. Names are case insensitive.
- **day-of-week** Represents the days of the week. You can assign values from 0 to 6, where 0 is Sunday. You can also use names in English, such as Monday, or you can use abbreviations of the name in English, such as Mon. Names are case insensitive.

All fields must be present in a CRON expression. If you don't want to provide a value for a field, you can use the asterisk character *. This means that the expression uses all available values for that field. For example, the CRON expression * * * * * * means that the trigger is executed every second, in every minute, in every hour, in every day, and every month of the year. You can also use some operators with the allowed values in fields:

- **Range of values**   Use the dash operator (–) for representing all the values available between two limits. For example, the expression 0 10–12 * * * * means that the function is executed at hh:10:00, hh:11:00, and hh:12:00 where hh means every hour. That is, it is executed three times every hour.

- **Set of values**   Use the comma operator (,) for representing a set of values. For example, the expression 0 0 11,12,13 * * * means that the function will be executed three times a day, every day, once at 11:00:00, a second time at 12:00:00, and finally at 13:00:00.

- **Interval of values**   Use the forward slash operator (/) for representing an interval of values. The function is executed when the value of the field is divisible by the value that you put on the right side of the operator. For example, the expression */5 * * * * * will execute the function every five seconds.

Listings 1-6 and 1-7 show how to configure a timer trigger and how to use the trigger with JavaScript code.

LISTING 1-6 Configuring a timer trigger in function.json

```
{
  "disabled": false,
  "bindings": [
    {
      "name": "myTimer",
      "type": "timerTrigger",
      "direction": "in",
      "schedule": "0 */5 * * * *",
      "useMonitor": true,
      "runOnStartup": true
    }
  ]
}
```

LISTING 1-7 Using a timer trigger with JavaScript

```
//NodeJS. Index.js file
module.exports = async function (context, myTimer) {
    var timeStamp = new Date().toISOString();

    if(myTimer.isPastDue)
    {
        context.log('JavaScript is running late!');
    }
    context.log('JavaScript timer trigger Last execution: ', myTimer.ScheduleStatus.Last);
    context.log('JavaScript timer trigger Next execution: ', myTimer.ScheduleStatus.Next);
};
```

Just as you did when you configured bindings in the previous section, when you configure a trigger for non-C# languages, you must add them to the function.json configuration file. You configure your triggers in the bindings section. Listing 1-6 shows the appropriate properties for configuring a timer trigger:

- **name**   This is the name of the variable that you use on your JavaScript code for accessing the information from the trigger.

- **type**   This is the type of trigger that you are configuring. In this example, the value for the timer trigger is `timerTrigger`.

- **direction**   This is always included in a trigger.

- **schedule**   This is the CRON expression used for configuring the execution scheduling of your function. You can also use a `TimeSpan` expression.

- **useMonitor**   This property monitors the schedule even if the function app instance is restarted. The default value for this property is true for every schedule with a recurrence greater than one minute. Monitoring the schedule occurrences ensures that the schedule is maintained correctly.

- **runOnStartup**   This indicates that the function should be invoked as soon as the runtime starts. The function will be executed after the function app wakes up after going idle because of inactivity or if the function app restarts because of changes in the function. Setting this parameter to true is not recommended in production environments because it can lead to unpredictable execution times of your function.

> **NOTE**   **TROUBLESHOOTING FUNCTIONS IN YOUR LOCAL ENVIRONMENT**
>
> While developing your Azure Functions, you need to troubleshoot your code in your local environment. If you are using non-HTML triggers, you need to provide a valid value for the `AzureWebJobsStorage` attribute in the local.settings.json file.

You use `TimeSpan` expressions to specify the time interval between the invocations of the function. If the function execution takes longer than the specified interval, then the function is invoked immediately after the previous invocation finishes. `TimeSpan` expressions are strings with the format hh:mm:ss where hh represents hours, mm represents minutes, and ss represents seconds. Hours in a `TimeSpan` expression need to be less than 24. The `TimeSpan` expression 24:00:00 means the function will be executed every day. 02:00:00 means the function will be invoked every two hours. You can use `TimeSpan` expressions only on Azure Functions that are executed on App Service Plans. That is, you cannot use `TimeSpan` expressions when you are using the Consumption pricing tier.

You use HTTP triggers for running your Azure Function when an external process makes an HTTP request. This HTTP request can be a regular request using any of the available HTTP methods or a webhook. A web callback or webhook is an HTTP request made by third-party systems or external web applications, or as a result of an event generated in the external system. For example, if you are using GitHub as your code repository, GitHub can send a webhook to your Azure Function each time a new pull request is opened.

When you create an Azure Function using HTTP triggers, the runtime automatically publishes an endpoint with the following structure:

```
http://<your_function_app>.azurewebsites.net/api/<your_function_name>
```

This is the URL or endpoint that you must use when calling to your function using a regular HTTP request or when you configure an external webhook for invoking your function. You can customize the route of this endpoint by using the appropriate configuration properties. This means that you can also implement serverless APIs using HTTP triggers. You can even protect the access to your function's endpoints by requesting authorization for any request made to your API using the App Service Authentication/Authorization. Listing 1-8 shows how to configure an HTTP trigger with a custom endpoint.

LISTING 1-8 Configuring an HTTP trigger

```csharp
// C# ASP.NET Core
using System.Security.Claims;
using System;
using System.IO;
using System.Threading.Tasks;
using Microsoft.AspNetCore.Mvc;
using Microsoft.Azure.WebJobs;
using Microsoft.Azure.WebJobs.Extensions.Http;
using Microsoft.AspNetCore.Http;
using Microsoft.Extensions.Logging;
using Newtonsoft.Json;

namespace Company.Function
{
    public static class HttpTriggerCSharp
    {
        [FunctionName("HttpTriggerCSharp")]
        public static async Task<IActionResult> Run(
            [HttpTrigger(AuthorizationLevel.Anonymous, "get", "post", Route = "devices/
            {id:int?}")] HttpRequest req,
             int? id,
             ILogger log)
        {
            log.LogInformation("C# HTTP trigger function processed a request.");
            //We access the parameter in the address by adding a function parameter
            //with the same name
            log.LogInformation($"Requesting information for device {id}");

            //If you enable Authentication/Authorization at Function App level,
            //information
            //about the authenticated user is automatically provided in the
            //HttpContext
            ClaimsPrincipal identities = req.HttpContext.User;
            string username = identities.Identity?.Name;

            log.LogInformation($"Request made by user {username}");

            string name = req.Query["name"];
```

```
        string requestBody = await new StreamReader(req.Body).ReadToEndAsync();
        dynamic data = JsonConvert.DeserializeObject(requestBody);
        name = name ?? data?.name;

        //We customize the output binding
        return name != null

            ? (ActionResult)new JsonResult(new { message = $"Hello, {name}",
username = username, device = id})

            : new BadRequestObjectResult("Please pass a name on the query string or
in the request body");
        }
    }
}
```

The example in Listing 1-8 shows the following points when working with HTTP triggers:

- How to work with authentication.
- How to work with the authorization level.
- How to customize the function endpoint, using route parameters.
- How to customize the output binding.

HTTP triggers are automatically provided to you out-of-the-box with the function runtime. There is no need to install a specific NuGet package for working with this extension. You use the HTTPTrigger parameter attribute for configuring the HTTP trigger. This trigger accepts the following parameters:

- **AuthLevel** This parameter configures the authorization key that you should use for accessing the function. Allowed values are
  - **anonymous** No key is required.
  - **function** This is the default value. You need to provide a function-specific key.
  - **admin** You need to provide the master key.
- **Methods** You can configure the HTTP methods that your function accepts. By default, the function runtime accepts all HTTP methods. Listing 1-8 reduces these accepted HTTP methods to GET and POST. Don't use this parameter if you set the WebHookType parameter.
- **Route** You can customize the route of the endpoint used for the function to listen to a new request. The default route is https://<your_function_app>.azurewebsites.net/api/<your_function_name>.
- **WebHookType** This parameter is available only for version 1.x runtime functions. You should not use the Methods and WebHookType parameters together. This parameter sets the webhook type for a specific provider. Allowed values are
  - **genericJson** This parameter is used for nonspecific providers.
  - **github** This parameter is used for interacting with GitHub webhooks.
  - **slack** This parameter is used for interacting with Slack webhooks.

When you declare the variable type that your function uses as the input from the trigger, you can use `HttpRequest` or a custom type. If you use a custom type, the runtime tries to parse the request body as a JSON object to get needed information for setting your custom type properties. If you decide to use `HttpRequest` for the type of trigger input parameter, you get full access to the request object.

Every Azure Function App that you deploy automatically exposes a group of admin endpoints that you can use for programmatically accessing some aspects of your app, such as the status of the host. These endpoints look like this:

```
https://<your_function_app_name>.azurewebsites.net/admin/host/status
```

By default, these endpoints are protected by an access code or authentication key that you can manage from your Function App in the Azure portal, as shown in Figure 1-18.

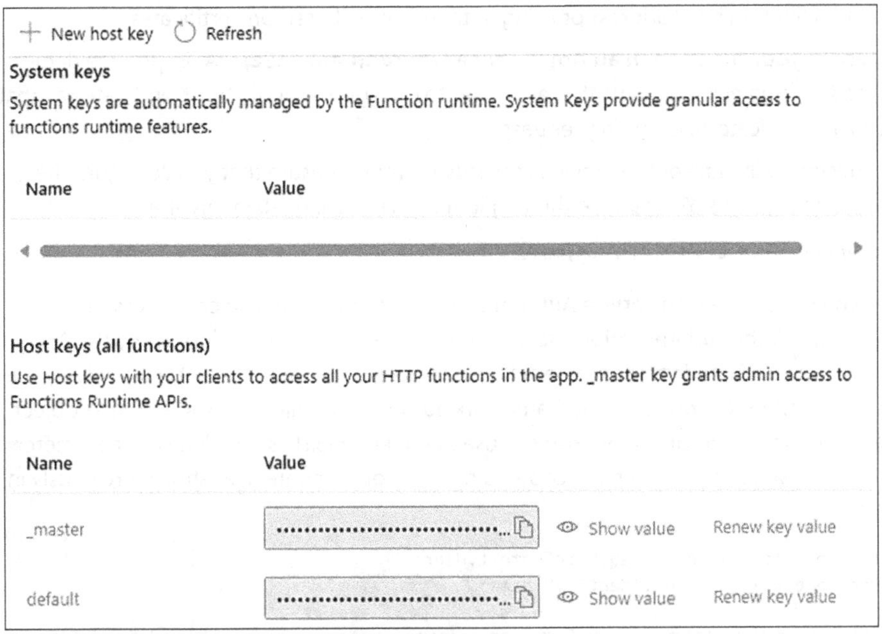

+ New host key   ↻ Refresh

System keys
System keys are automatically managed by the Function runtime. System Keys provide granular access to functions runtime features.

Name	Value
◀ ━━ ▶	

Host keys (all functions)
Use Host keys with your clients to access all your HTTP functions in the app. _master key grants admin access to Functions Runtime APIs.

Name	Value		
_master	•••••••••••••••••••••••••••••••…▢	👁 Show value	Renew key value
default	•••••••••••••••••••••••••••••••…▢	👁 Show value	Renew key value

FIGURE 1-18 Managing host keys for a Function App

When you use the HTTP trigger, any endpoint that you publish is also protected by the same mechanism, although the keys that you use for protecting those endpoints are different. You can configure two types of authorization keys:

- **host** These keys are shared by all functions deployed in the Function App. This type of key allows access to any function in the host.
- **function** These keys only protect the function where they are defined.

When you define a new key, you assign a name to the key. If you have two keys of a different type—host and function—with the same name, the function key takes precedence. There are also two default keys—one per type of key—that you can use for accessing your endpoints.

These default keys take precedence over any other key that you created. If you need access to the admin endpoints mentioned earlier, you must use a particular host key called _master. You also must use this administrative key when you set the admin value to the AuthLevel trigger configuration parameter. You can provide the appropriate key when you make a request to your API by using the code parameter or by using the x-function-key HTTP header.

Protecting your endpoints using the authorization keys is not a recommended practice for production environments. You should only use authorization keys in testing or development environments for controlling access to your API. For a production environment, you should use one of the following approaches:

- **Enable Function App Authorization/Authentication**   This integrates your API with Azure Active Directory or other third-party identity providers to authenticate clients.
- **Use Azure API Management (APIM)**   This secures the incoming request to your API, such as filtering by IP address or using authentication based on certificates.
- **Deploy your function in an App Service Environment (ASE)**   ASEs provide dedicated hosting environments that allow you to configure a single front-end gateway that can authenticate all incoming requests.

If you decide to use any of the previous security methods, ensure that you configure the AuthLevel as anonymous. You can see this configuration in Listing 1-8 in this line:

```
HttpTrigger(AuthorizationLevel.Anonymous…
```

When you enable the App Service Authentication/Authorization, you can access the information about the authentication users by reading special HTTP headers set by the App Service. These special headers cannot be set by external resources; they can be set only by the App Service. For ASP.NET projects, the framework automatically fills a ClaimsPrincipal object with the authentication information. You can use ClaimsPrincipal as an additional parameter of your function signature or from the code, using the request context, as shown previously in Listing 1-8.

```
ClaimsPrincipal identities = req.HttpContext.User;
string username = identities.Identity?.Name;
```

As described in this section, Azure Functions runtime exposes your function by default using the following URL schema:

```
https://<your_function_app_name>.azurewebsites.net/api/<your_function_name>
```

You can customize the endpoint by using the route HTTPTrigger parameter. In Listing 1-8, you set the route parameter to devices/{id:int?}. This means that your endpoint looks like this:

```
https://<your_function_app_name>.azurewebsites.net/api/devices/{id:int?}
```

When you customize the route for your function, you can also add parameters to the route, which are accessible to your code by adding them as parameters of your function's signature. You can use any Web API Route Constraint (see *https://www.asp.net/web-api/overview/web-api-routing-and-actions/attribute-routing-in-web-api-2#constraints*) that you may use when defining a route using Web API 2.

By default, when you make a request to a function that uses an HTTP trigger, the response is an empty body with these status codes:

```
HTTP 200 OK in case of Function 1.x runtime
HTTP 204 No Content in case of Function 2.x runtime
```

If you need to customize the response of your function, you need to configure an output binding. You can use any of the two types of output bindings, using the return statement or a function parameter. Listing 1-8 shows how to configure the output binding for returning a JSON object with some information.

It is important to remember the limits associated with the function when you plan to deploy your function in a production environment. These limits are

- **Maximum request length**   The HTTP request should not be larger than 100 MB.
- **Maximum URL length**   Your custom URL is limited to 4096 bytes.
- **Execution timeout**   Your function should return a value in less than 230 seconds. Your function can take more time to execute, but if it doesn't return anything before that time, the gateway will time out with an HTTP 502 error. If your function needs to take more time to execute, you should use an async pattern and return a ping endpoint to allow the caller to ask for the status of the execution of your function.

> **NEED MORE REVIEW?   HOST PROPERTIES**
>
> You can also make some adjustments to the host where your function is running by using the host.json file. Visit the following article to review all the properties available in the host.json file: *https://docs.microsoft.com/en-us/azure/azure-functions/functions-bindings-http-webhook#trigger---hostjson-properties*.
>
> You can also review which are the limits associated with the different framework versions and hosting plans by reviewing the article at *https://docs.microsoft.com/en-us/azure/azure-functions/functions-scale*.

> **EXAM TIP**
>
> In earlier versions of Azure Functions, the authentication information was available only to ASP.NET projects using the `ClaimsPrincipal` class. Now you can access that information by reading the special HTTP Headers set by the App Service. For a complete list of authentication headers, refer to the article *https://docs.microsoft.com/en-us/azure/app-service/app-service-authentication-how-to#access-user-claims*.

Chapter summary

- Azure provides computing services for deploying your own virtualized infrastructure directly in the cloud. You can also deploy hybrid architectures to connect your on-premises infrastructure with your IaaS resources.

- Azure Resource Manager is the service in Azure that manages the different resources that you can deploy in the cloud. You can define the resources and their dependencies by using a JSON-based file called an ARM template.

- A container image is a package of software in which you store your code and any library or dependencies for running your application in a highly portable environment.

- When you create a new instance of a container image, each of these instances is named a "container."

- You can store your container images in a centralized store called a registry.

- Azure Container Registry is a managed registry based on the open-source specification of Docker Registry 2.0.

- You can run your containers in several Azure services, such as Azure Managed Kubernetes Service, Azure Container Instance, Azure Batch, Azure App Service, or Azure Container Service.

- Azure provides you with the services needed for deploying serverless solutions, allowing you to focus on the code and forget about the infrastructure.

- Azure App Services is the base of the serverless offering. On top of App Services, you can deploy web apps, mobile back-end apps, REST APIs, or Azure Functions and Azure Durable Functions.

- When you work with App Services, you are charged only by the time that your code is running.

- App Services runs on top of App Services Plans.

- An App Service Plan provides the resources and virtual machines needed for running your App Services code.

- You can run more than one App Service on top of a single App Service Plan.

- When troubleshooting your App Service application, you can use several types for diagnostics logging: webserver logging and diagnostics, detailed error, failed requests, application diagnostics, and deployment diagnostics.

- Diagnostics logging is stored locally on the VM, where the instance of your application is running.

- Horizontal scaling, or in-out scaling, is the process of adding or removing instances of an application.

- Vertical scaling, or up-down scaling, is the process of adding or removing resources to the same virtual machine that hosts your application.

- Scale In/Out doesn't have an effect on the availability of the application.

- Vertical scaling affects the availability of the application because the application must be deployed in a virtual machine with the new resources assignment.

- You can add and remove resources to your applications by using autoscale rules.

- You can apply autoscale only to some Azure Resource types.

- Autoscale depends on Azure virtual machine scale sets.

- Your application must be aware of the changes in the resources assignment.

- Azure Functions is the evolution of WebJobs.

- Azure Functions uses triggers and bindings for creating instances of Azure functions and sending or receiving data to or from external services, like Queue storage or Event Hub.

- There are three versions of Azure Functions. Version 1.0 only supports .NET Framework and Windows environments. Version 2.0 and later support .NET Core and Windows and Linux environments.

- When you work with triggers and bindings, you must install the appropriate NuGet package for function extensions that contain that trigger or binding.

- Azure Function runtime already includes extensions for Timers and HTTP triggers. You don't need to install specific packages to use these trigger bindings.

- Triggers that create function instances can be based on data operations, timers, or webhooks.

- Azure Durable Functions is the evolution of Azure Functions that allows you to create workflows where the state of the instances is preserved in case of VM restart or function host process respawn.

- Orchestration functions define the activity and the order of execution of the functions that do the job.

- Activity functions contain the code that makes the action that you need for a step in the workflow, such as sending an email, saving a document, or inserting information in a database.

- Client functions create the instance of the orchestration function using an orchestration client.

- Azure Function Apps provides the resources needed for running Azure Functions and Durable Functions.

Thought experiment

In this Thought Experiment, you can demonstrate your skills and knowledge about the topics covered in this chapter. You can find the answers to this Thought Experiment in the next section.

You are developing an application for integrating several systems. One of the systems is a legacy application that generates some reports in a specific file format. Those file reports are uploaded to an Azure Storage account. Your application reads the information from these file reports and inserts the information in different destination systems. Answer the following questions related to the described scenario:

1. Before your application can insert information in the target destination, the information must be approved. The approval workflow needs to start when a new report file is added to the Azure Storage Account. Which Azure service best fits your needs?

2. Your application is suffering from performance issues. The performance issues only happen during some days in the month. You need to ensure that your application doesn't suffer performance issues during the usage peaks. How can you achieve this?

Thought experiment answers

This section contains the solutions to the Thought Experiment.

1. Because the information needs to be approved before it can be inserted in the target systems, you should use Azure Durable Functions. By implementing a Human Interaction pattern, you can wait for the information to be validated before inserting it into the correct destination system. You can also use Azure Blob Storage triggers for starting the workflow. Because you must wait for human confirmation, you should use Azure Durable Functions instead of Azure Functions.

2. You can deploy Azure Durable Functions to Azure App Service Plans. Starting with the Standard pricing tier, you can configure autoscale rules for your Azure App Service Plan. Using autoscale rules, you can add or remove resources to the App Service Plan based on your needs. In this scenario, you can add more resources based on CPU consumption or during specific days. Because no specific pattern has been described in the scenario, you should first study the usage pattern before configuring the appropriate autoscale rules.

CHAPTER 2

Develop for Azure storage

All applications work with information or data. Applications create, transform, model, or operate with that information. Regardless of the type or volume of data that your application uses, eventually you need to save it persistently so that it can be used later.

Storing data is not a simple task, and designing storage systems for that purpose is even more complicated. Perhaps your application must deal with terabytes or even petabytes of information, or you might work with an application that needs to be accessed from different countries, and you need to minimize the time required to access it. Cost efficiency is also a requirement in any project. In general, many requirements make designing and maintaining storage systems difficult.

Microsoft Azure offers different storage solutions in the cloud to satisfy your application storage requirements. Azure offers solutions for making your storage cost-effective and for minimizing latency.

Skills covered in this chapter:

- Skill 2.1: Develop solutions that use Cosmos DB storage
- Skill 2.2: Develop solutions that use Blob Storage

Skill 2.1: Develop solutions that use Cosmos DB storage

Cosmos DB is a premium storage service that Azure provides for satisfying your need for a globally distributed, low-latency, highly responsive, and always-online database service. Cosmos DB has been designed with scalability and throughput in mind. One of the most significant differences between Cosmos DB and other storage services offered by Azure is how easily you can scale your Cosmos DB solution across the globe by merely clicking a button and adding a new region to your database.

Another essential feature that you should consider when evaluating this type of storage service is how you can access this service from your code and how hard it would be to migrate your existing code to a Cosmos DB–based storage solution. The good news is that Cosmos DB offers different APIs for accessing the service. The best API for you depends on the type of data that you want to store in your Cosmos DB database. You store your data using Key-Value, Column-Family, Documents, or Graph approaches. Each of the different

APIs that Cosmos DB offers allows you to store your data with different schemas. Currently, you can access Cosmos DB using SQL, Cassandra, Table, Gremlin, and MongoDB APIs.

This skill covers how to

- Perform operations on containers and items by using the SDK
- Set the appropriate consistency level for operations
- Implement change feed notifications

Perform operations on containers and items by using the SDK

When working with Cosmos DB, you have several layers in the hierarchy of entities managed by the Cosmos DB account. The first layer is the Azure Cosmos DB account, where you choose the API you want to use to access your data. Remember that this API has implications for how the data is stored in the databases.

The second layer in the hierarchy is the database. You can create as many databases as you need in your Cosmos DB account. Databases are a way of grouping containers; you can think of databases like namespaces. At this level, you can configure the throughput associated with the containers included in the database.

When planning how to store the information that your application needs to work, you must consider the structure you need to use for storing that information. You may find that some parts of your application need to store information using a key-value structure. In contrast, others may need a more flexible, schema-less structure in which you save the information into documents. One fundamental characteristic of your application might be that you need to store the relationship between entities and use a graph structure for storing your data.

Cosmos DB offers a variety of APIs for storing and accessing your data, depending on the requirements of your application:

- **NoSQL**   This is the core and default API for accessing your data in your Cosmos DB account. This core API allows you to query JSON objects using SQL syntax, which means you don't need to learn another query language. Under the hood, the SQL API uses the JavaScript programming model for expression evaluation, function invocations, and typing systems. You use this API when you need to use a data structure based on documents.

- **Table**   You can think of the Table API as the evolution of the Azure Table Storage service. This API benefits from the high-performance, low-latency, and high-scalability features of Cosmos DB. You can migrate from your current Azure Table Storage service with no code modification in your application. Another critical difference between Table API for Cosmos DB and Azure Table Storage is that you can define your own indexes in your tables. In the same way you do with the Table Storage service, the Table API allows you to store information in your Cosmos DB account using a data structure based on documents.

- **Cassandra** Cosmos DB implements the wire protocol for the Apache Cassandra database into the options for storing and accessing data in the Cosmos DB database. This allows you to forget about operations and performance-management tasks related to managing Cassandra databases. In most situations, you can migrate your application from your current Cassandra database to Cosmos DB using the Cassandra API by merely changing the connection string. Azure Cosmos DB Cassandra API is compatible with the CQLv4 wire protocol. Cassandra is a column-based database that stores information using a key-value approach.

- **MongoDB** You can access your Cosmos DB account by using the MongoDB API. This NoSQL database allows you to store the information for your application in a document-based structure. Cosmos DB implements the wire protocol compatible with MongoDB 3.2. This means that any MongoDB 3.2 client driver that implements and understands this protocol definition can connect seamlessly with your Cosmos DB database using the MongoDB API.

- **PostgreSQL** This service is built on top of native PostgreSQL, which means you can use your code directly with Azure Cosmos DB for PostgreSQL without any substantial modification. This is a managed service, so Microsoft takes care of all the details regarding performance, availability, geo-replication, and all the features that the Cosmos DB service offers.

- **Gremlin** Based on the Apache TinkerPop graph transversal language or Gremlin, this API allows you to store information in Cosmos DB using a graph structure. This means that instead of storing only entities, you store:

  - **Vertices** You can think of a vertex as an entity in other information structures. In a typical graph structure, a vertex could be a person, a device, or an event.

  - **Edges** These are the relationships between vertices. A person can know another person, a person might own a type of device, or a person might attend an event.

  - **Properties** These are attributes you can assign to a vertex or an edge.

Beware that you cannot mix these APIs in a single Cosmos DB account. You must define the API you want to use for accessing your Cosmos DB account when creating the account. Once you have created the account, you won't be able to change the API to access it.

Azure offers SDKs for working with the different APIs you can use to connect to Cosmos DB. Supported languages are .NET, Java, Node.js, and Python. Depending on the API you want to use for working with Cosmos DB, you can also use other languages such as Spring Data, Spark V3, or Golang.

> *NOTE* **AZURE COSMOS DB EMULATOR**
>
> You can use the Azure Cosmos DB emulator during the development stage of your application. You should keep in mind that there are some limitations when working with the emulator instead of a real Cosmos DB account. The emulator is only supported on Windows platforms or Docker for Windows. You can review all characteristics of the Cosmos DB emulator at *https://docs.microsoft.com/en-us/azure/cosmos-db/local-emulator*.

EXAM TIP

You can use different APIs for accessing your Cosmos DB database. Each API offers different features depending on the way you need to represent your data. Remember that you cannot change the API once you have created your Cosmos DB database.

A container in an Azure Cosmos DB account is the unit of scalability for throughput and storage. When you create a new container, you must set the partition key to establish how the items that will be stored in the container are distributed across the different logical and physical partitions. The concept of a container maps to different elements depending on the API you choose:

- **NoSQL API**   Database.
- **Cassandra API**   Keyspace.
- **PostgreSQL API**   Database.
- **MongoDB API**   Database.
- **Gremlin API**   Database.
- **Table API**   This concept does not apply to Table API, although under the hood, when you create your first Table, Cosmos DB creates a default database for you.

Before going further with containers, we should review how data is stored in a container and how choosing the right partition key is crucial for performance.

When you save data to your Cosmos DB account, independently of the API you choose to use for accessing your data, Azure places the data in different servers to accommodate the performance and throughput you require from a premium storage service like Cosmos DB. The storage services use partitions to distribute the data. Cosmos DB slices your data into smaller pieces called *partitions* placed on the storage server. There are two different types of partitions when working with Cosmos DB:

- **Logical**   You can divide a Cosmos DB container into smaller pieces based on your criteria. Each of these smaller pieces is a logical partition. All items stored in a logical partition share the same partition key.
- **Physical**   These partitions are a group of replicas of your data that are physically stored on the servers. Azure automatically manages this group of replicas or replica sets. A physical partition can contain one or more logical partitions.

NEED MORE REVIEW?   PHYSICAL PARTITION

Setting the partition keys is the only control you have over how the data is distributed across physical partitions. If you want to review how the logical and physical partitions are related, consult the following article: *https://docs.microsoft.com/en-us/azure/cosmos-db/partition-data#physical-partitions*.

By default, any logical partition has a limit of 20 GB for storing data. This limit cannot be configured or modified. When configuring a new collection, you must decide whether you want your collection to be stored in a single logical partition and keep it under the limit of 20 GB or allow it to grow over that limit and span across multiple logical partitions. If you need your container to split over several partitions, Cosmos DB needs some way to know how to distribute your data across the different logical partitions. This is where the partition key comes into play. Keep in mind that this partition key is immutable, which means you cannot change the property that you want to use as the partition key once you have selected it.

Another important attribute that you must consider when choosing a partition key is that a logical partition is the limit of the scope for transactions. This means that all the operations inside the scope of the logical partition are executed using transactions with snapshot isolation. You don't need to worry about creating or deleting logical partitions. The system automatically creates new logical partitions as needed and deletes any partition that becomes empty after deleting all data.

Choosing the correct partition key is critical for achieving the best performance. Choosing the proper partition key is so important because Azure creates a logical partition for each distinct value of your partition key. Listing 2-1 shows an example of a JSON document.

LISTING 2-1 Example JSON document

```
{
    "id": "1",
    "firstName": "Santiago",
    "lastName": "Fernández",
    "city": "Sevilla",
    "country": "Spain"
}
```

City or country properties would be the right choice for the partition key, depending on your data. You might find in your data that some documents have the same value for the country property, so they are stored together in the same logical partition. Using the id property as the partition key means that you end with a logical partition with a single document on each partition. This configuration can be beneficial when your application usually performs read workloads and uses parallelization techniques for getting the data.

On the other hand, if you select a partition key with just a few possible values, you can end up with "hot" partitions. A "hot" partition is a partition that receives most of the requests when working with your data. The main implication for these "hot" partitions is that they usually reach the throughput limit for the partition, which means you must provision more throughput. Another potential drawback is that you can reach the limit of 20 GB for a single logical partition. Because a logical partition is the scope for efficient multi-document transactions, selecting a partition key with a few possible values allows you to execute transactions on many documents inside the same partition.

Use the following guidelines when selecting your partition key:

- The storage limit for a single logical partition is 20 GB. Select another partition key if you foresee that your data will require more space for each partition value. If your partition reaches the size limit of 20 GB, you must re-architect your solution and choose another partition key. In that situation, you can create a support ticket to request a temporary increase in the partition size. This is a temporary solution to help you re-architect your solution.

- The requests to a single logical partition cannot exceed the throughput limit for that partition. If your requests reach that limit, they are throttled to avoid exceeding it. If you reach this limit frequently, you should select another partition key because there is a good chance that you have a "hot" partition. The minimum throughput limit is different from databases to containers. The database's minimum throughput is 100 request units per second (RU/s). The minimum throughput for containers is 400 RU/s.

- Choose partition keys with a wide range of values and access patterns that can evenly distribute requests across logical partitions. This allows you to achieve the right balance between executing cross-document transactions and scalability. Using timestamp-based partition keys is usually a lousy choice for a partition key.

- Review your workload requirements. The partition key that you choose should allow your application to perform well on reading and writing workloads.

- The parameters that you usually use on your requests and filtering queries are good candidates for a partition key.

> **NEED MORE REVIEW? PARTITIONING**
>
> You can review more information about how partitioning works in the following article:
> *https://docs.microsoft.com/en-us/azure/cosmos-db/partitioning-overview*

There could be situations for which none of the properties of your items are appropriate for the partition keys. In those situations, you can create synthetic partition keys. A synthetic partition key is a key compound of two concatenated properties. In the previous document example shown in Listing 2-1, you created a new property named partitionKey containing a string that concatenates the values of city and country. For the example document, the value of the partitionKey should be Sevilla-Spain. The same rules you consider for a regular partition key apply to synthetic partition keys.

> **EXAM TIP**
>
> Remember that your data is distributed across the different logical partitions by using the partition key. For this reason, once you have chosen a partition key, you cannot change it.

Once you have a clearer idea of how partitions work and the importance of choosing the right partition key, you can create containers. When you create a new container, you can decide whether the throughput for the container is one of the following two modes:

- **Dedicated** All the throughput is provisioned for a container. In this mode, Azure makes a reservation of resources for the container that is backed by service-level agreements (SLAs).

- **Shared** The throughput is shared between all the containers configured in the database, excluding those containers that have been configured as dedicated throughput mode. The shared throughput is configured at the database level.

You cannot switch to a different mode once you have created a container of one mode. If you need to change the mode assigned to a container, you must create a new container with the needed mode and copy all data from the old container to the new one.

Containers are schema-agnostic. This means you can store in the same container documents or entities with different properties as long as they share the same partition key. For example, you could store the information about a device in a container, and all the incidents and repair orders related to that device, also in the same container. The only limitation is that all these entities must share the same partition key.

When you create a Cosmos DB container, you can configure a set of properties. These properties affect different aspects of the container or how the items are stored or managed. The following list details the properties of a container that can be configured. Keep in mind that not all properties are available for all APIs:

- **ID** This is the name of the container.

- **IndexingPolicy** When you add an item to a container, all the item properties are automatically indexed by default. It doesn't matter whether all the items in the collection share the same schema or each item has its own schema. This property allows you to configure how to index the items in the container. You can configure different types of indexes and include or exclude some properties from the indexes.

- **TimeToLive (TTL)** You can configure your container to delete items after a period of time automatically. TimeToLive is expressed in seconds. For example, if you implement a cache system using Cosmos DB, this TTL could be the period of time the items are stored in the cache. Once the TTL is reached, the item is automatically deleted from your container. You can configure the TTL value at the container or item level. If you configure the TTL at the container level, all items in the container have the same TTL, except if you configure a TTL for a specific item. A value of -1 in the TTL means that the item does not expire. If you set a TTL value to an item where its container does not have a TTL value configured, then the TTL at item level has no effect.

- **ChangeFeedPolicy** You can read the changes made to an item in a container. The change feed provides you with the original and modified values of an item. Because the changes are persisted, you can process the changes asynchronously. You can use this feature for triggering notifications or calling APIs when a new item is inserted or an existing item is modified.

- **UniqueKeyPolicy** You can configure which item's property is used as the unique key. Using unique keys, you ensure that you cannot insert two items with the same value for the same item. Keep in mind that the uniqueness is scoped to the logical partition. For example, if your item has the properties email, firstname, lastname, and company, and you define email as the unique key and company as the partition key, you cannot insert an item with the same email and company values. You can also create compound unique keys, such as email and firstname. Once you have created a unique key, you cannot change it. You can only define the unique key during the creation process of the container.

- **AnalyticalTimeToLive** Sets the time that an item will be kept in an analytical store container. The item is deleted from the container after the time specified in this property is reached. An analytical store is a special type of column store that is schematized to optimize for analytical query performance.

Apart from the properties that you reviewed in the previous list, there is a group of properties that are automatically generated and managed by the system. You can read these system-generated properties, but you cannot modify them. These properties are: _rid, _etag, _ts, and _self.

> **NOTE CONTAINER PROPERTIES**
>
> The properties available to the containers depend on the API you configured for your Azure Cosmos DB account. For a complete list of properties available for each API, please review the article at *https://docs.microsoft.com/en-us/azure/cosmos-db/databases-containers-items#azure-cosmos-containers*.

Before starting with the examples, you must create a Cosmos DB account to store your data. The following procedure shows how to create a Cosmos DB free account with the SQL API. You can use this same procedure for creating accounts with the other APIs reviewed in this skill:

1. Sign in to the Azure portal (*http://portal.azure.com*).

2. In the top left of the Azure portal, click the menu icon represented by three horizontal bars, and then select Create A Resource.

3. On the Create A Resource panel, under the Categories column, select Databases. On the Popular Azure Services column, click the Create link under Azure Cosmos DB.

4. On the Create An Azure Cosmos DB Account blade, click the Create button in the Azure Cosmos DB For NoSQL section, as shown in Figure 2-1.

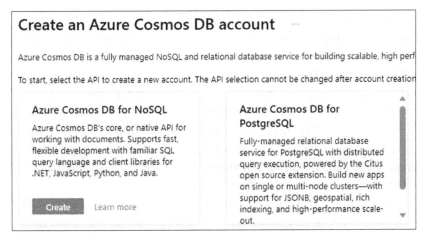

Create an Azure Cosmos DB account ···

Azure Cosmos DB is a fully managed NoSQL and relational database service for building scalable, high perf

To start, select the API to create a new account. The API selection cannot be changed after account creation

Azure Cosmos DB for NoSQL

Azure Cosmos DB's core, or native API for working with documents. Supports fast, flexible development with familiar SQL query language and client libraries for .NET, JavaScript, Python, and Java.

Create   Learn more

Azure Cosmos DB for PostgreSQL

Fully-managed relational database service for PostgreSQL with distributed query execution, powered by the Citus open source extension. Build new apps on single or multi-node clusters—with support for JSONB, geospatial, rich indexing, and high-performance scale-out.

FIGURE 2-1 Selecting a Cosmos DB API

5. On the Create Azure Cosmos DB Account blade, in the Resource Group dropdown menu, click the Create New link below the dropdown menu. Type a name for the new Resource Group in the pop-up dialog box. Alternatively, you can select an existing Resource Group from the dropdown menu.

6. In the Instance Details section, type an Account Name.

7. On the Location dropdown menu, select the region most appropriate for you. If you are using App Services or virtual machines, select the region in which you deployed those services.

8. In the Capacity mode selection control, keep Provisioned throughput selected.

9. Ensure that the Apply Free Tier Discount switch is set to Apply.

10. Click the Next: Global Distribution button at the bottom of the blade.

11. Leave Geo-Redundancy, Multi-Region Write, and Availability Zones disabled.

12. Leave all other options in the other tabs with their default values.

13. In the bottom left of the Create An Azure Cosmos DB Account blade, click the Review + Create button.

14. In the bottom left of the Review + Create tab, click the Create button to start deploying your Cosmos DB account.

Once you have created an Azure Cosmos DB account, you can use the following procedure to create a new collection in your Cosmos DB account. This procedure might be slightly different depending on the API you choose for your Cosmos DB account. In this procedure, you use a Cosmos DB account configured with the NoSQL API:

1. Sign in to the Azure portal (*http://portal.azure.com*).

2. In the search box at the top of the Azure portal, type the name of your Cosmos DB account and then select your account name.

3. On your Cosmos DB account blade, select Data Explorer.

4. On the Data Explorer blade, click the New Container icon in the top left of the blade.

5. On the New Container panel, shown in Figure 2-2, provide a name for the new database. If you want to add a container to an existing database, you can select the database by clicking the Use Existing radio button.

6. Ensure that the Share Throughput Across Containers checkbox is selected. You are configuring this container as a shared throughput container using this option. If you want to create a dedicated throughput container, uncheck this option.

7. Leave the Database Throughput (Autoscale) value set to Autoscale. This is the value for the database throughput if the previous option is checked. Otherwise, this value represents the dedicated throughput reserved for the container.

8. Leave the Database Max RU/s value set to 1000. This is the maximum value of Request Units per second configured for your container. The capacity is scaled between the minimum 10 percent of the configured value and the maximum value. This option appears only if you select the Autoscale option for the Database Throughput setting.

9. In the Container ID text box, type a name for the container.

10. Keep the Indexing setting as Automatic.

11. Type a partition key in the Partition Key text box. The partition key must start with the slash character.

12. If you want to create a unique key for this container, click the Add Unique Key button.

13. Click the OK button at the bottom of the panel.

Estimated monthly cost (USD). This cost is an estimate and may vary based on the regions where your account is deployed and potential discounts applied to your account: $8.76 - $87.60 (1 region, 100 - 1000 RU/s, $0.00012/RU)" The Container ID setting shows a blank text box into which you can type a new Container ID. The Indexing option offers the options Automatic and Off. The Automatic option is selected. The last setting, Partition Key, does not show any options. An Add Unique Key button appears at the bottom of the dialog box.

> **NEED MORE REVIEW?** **TIME TO LIVE, INDEXES, AND CHANGES FEED**
>
> You can review the details of how to configure the Time To Live, Index Policies, and Changes Feed by reading the following articles:
>
> - **Configure Time to Live in Azure Cosmos DB** *https://docs.microsoft.com/en-us/azure/cosmos-db/how-to-time-to-live*
>
> - **Unique Key Constraints in Azure Cosmos DB** *https://docs.microsoft.com/en-us/azure/cosmos-db/unique-keys*
>
> - **Change Feed Design Patterns in Azure Cosmos DB** *https://docs.microsoft.com/en-us/azure/cosmos-db/change-feed-design-patterns*

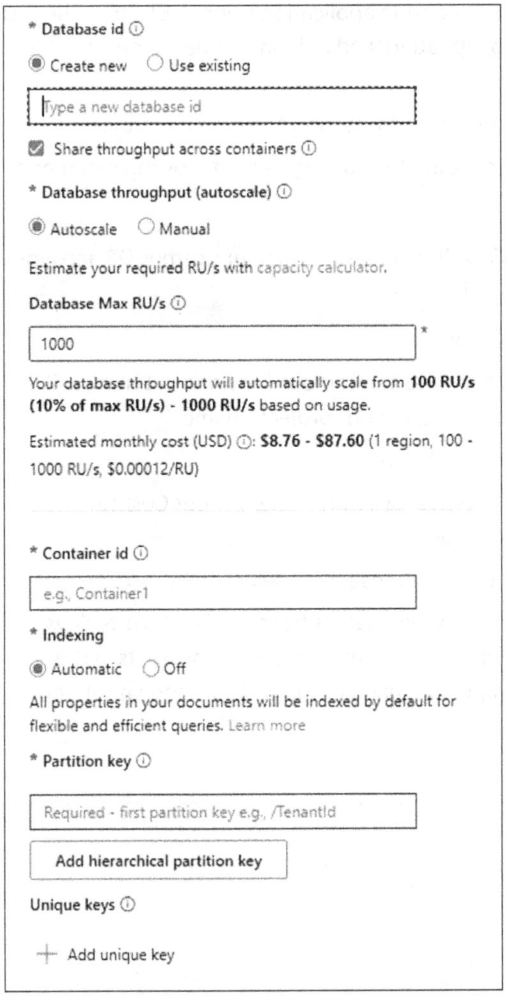

* Database id ⓘ

◉ Create new   ○ Use existing

[Type a new database id]

☑ Share throughput across containers ⓘ

* Database throughput (autoscale) ⓘ

◉ Autoscale   ○ Manual

Estimate your required RU/s with capacity calculator.

Database Max RU/s ⓘ

[1000]   *

Your database throughput will automatically scale from **100 RU/s (10% of max RU/s) - 1000 RU/s** based on usage.

Estimated monthly cost (USD) ⓘ: **$8.76 - $87.60** (1 region, 100 - 1000 RU/s, $0.00012/RU)

* Container id ⓘ

[e.g., Container1]

* Indexing

◉ Automatic   ○ Off

All properties in your documents will be indexed by default for flexible and efficient queries. Learn more

* Partition key ⓘ

[Required - first partition key e.g., /TenantId]

[Add hierarchical partition key]

Unique keys ⓘ

+ Add unique key

FIGURE 2-2 Creating a new collection

EXAM TIP

You must plan carefully how to create a new container in Azure Cosmos DB. You can configure some of the properties only during creation. Once you have created the container, if you need to modify those properties, you must create a new container with the needed values and migrate the data to the new container.

Once you have configured your container, you can create items on it. As mentioned in this section, you can use different languages, such as .NET, Node.js, Java, Python, or Go.

The following example shows how to create a console application using .NET Core. The first example uses Cosmos DB SQL API for creating, updating, and deleting some elements in the Cosmos DB account:

1. Open Visual Studio Code and create a directory for storing the example project.

2. Open the Terminal, switch to the project's directory, and type the following command:

   ```
   dotnet new console
   ```

3. Install the NuGet package using the SQL API to interact with your Cosmos DB account. Type the following command in the Terminal:

   ```
   dotnet add package Microsoft.Azure.Cosmos
   ```

4. Change the content of the Program.cs file using the content provided in Listing 2-2. You need to change the namespace according to your project's name.

5. Sign in to the Azure portal (*http://portal.azure.com*).

6. In the search box at the top of the Azure portal, type the name of your Cosmos DB account and then click the name of the account.

7. On your Cosmos DB Account blade, in the Settings section, select Keys.

8. On the Keys panel, copy the URI and Primary Keys values from the Read-Write Keys tab. You need to provide these values to the EndpointUri and Key Constants in the code shown in Listing 2-2. (The most important parts of the code are shown with bold format.)

LISTING 2-2 Cosmos DB NoSQL API example

```csharp
//C# .NET 6.0 LTS. Program.cs
using System.Collections.Immutable;
using System.Xml.Linq;
using System.Diagnostics;
using System.Runtime.CompilerServices;
using System;

using System.Linq;
using Microsoft.Azure.Cosmos;
using System.Threading.Tasks;
using ch2_1_1_NoSQL.Model;
using System.Net;

namespace ch2_1_1_NoSQL
{
    class Program
    {
        private const string EndpointUri = "<PUT YOUR ENDPOINT URL HERE>";
        private const string Key = "<PUT YOUR COSMOS DB KEY HERE>";
        private CosmosClient client;
        private Database database;
        private Container container;

        static void Main(string[] args)
        {
```

```
        try
        {
            Program demo = new Program();
            demo.StartDemo().Wait();
        }
        catch (CosmosException ce)
        {
            Exception baseException = ce.GetBaseException();
            System.Console.WriteLine($"{ce.StatusCode} error ocurred:
            {ce.Message}, Message: {baseException.Message}");
        }
        catch (Exception ex)
        {
            Exception baseException = ex.GetBaseException();
            System.Console.WriteLine($"Error ocurred: {ex.Message},
Message: {baseException.Message}");
        }

    }

    private async Task StartDemo()
    {
        Console.WriteLine("Starting Cosmos DB NoSQL API Demo!");

        //Create a new demo database

        string databaseName = "demoDB_" + Guid.NewGuid().ToString().
Substring(0, 5);

        this.SendMessageToConsoleAndWait($"Creating database {databaseName}...");

        this.client = new CosmosClient(EndpointUri, Key);
        this.database = await this.client.CreateDatabaseIfNotExistsAsync
(databaseName);

        //Create a new demo collection inside the demo database.
        //This creates a collection with a reserved throughput. You can customize
        //the options using a ContainerProperties object
        //This operation has pricing implications.
        string containerName = "collection_" + Guid.NewGuid().ToString().
Substring(0, 5);


        this.SendMessageToConsoleAndWait($"Creating collection demo
{containerName}...");

        this.container = await this.database.CreateContainerIfNotExistsAsync
(containerName, "/LastName");

        //Create some documents in the collection
        Person person1 = new Person
        {
            Id = "Person.1",
            FirstName = "Santiago",
            LastName = "Fernandez",
```

```
            Devices = new Device[]
            {

                new Device { OperatingSystem = "iOS", CameraMegaPixels = 7,
                Ram = 16, Usage = "Personal"},
                new Device { OperatingSystem = "Android", CameraMegaPixels = 12,
                Ram = 64, Usage = "Work"}
            },
            Gender = "Male",
            Address = new Address
            {
                City = "Seville",
                Country = "Spain",
                PostalCode = "28973",
                Street = "Diagonal",
                State = "Andalucia"
            },
            IsRegistered = true
        };


        await this.CreateDocumentIfNotExistsAsync(databaseName, containerName,
    person1);

        Person person2 = new Person
        {
            Id = "Person.2",
            FirstName = "Agatha",
            LastName = "Smith",
            Devices = new Device[]
            {

                new Device { OperatingSystem = "iOS", CameraMegaPixels = 12,
                Ram = 32, Usage = "Work"},
                new Device { OperatingSystem = "Windows", CameraMegaPixels = 12,
                Ram = 64, Usage = "Personal"}
            },
            Gender = "Female",
            Address = new Address
            {
                City = "Laguna Beach",
                Country = "United States",
                PostalCode = "12345",
              Street = "Main",
                State = "CA"
            },
            IsRegistered = true
        };


        await this.CreateDocumentIfNotExistsAsync(databaseName, containerName,
    person2);
```

```
        //Make some queries to the collection
        this.SendMessageToConsoleAndWait($"Getting documents from the collection
{containerName}...");

        //Find documents using LINQ

        IQueryable<Person> queryablePeople = this.container.GetItemLinqQueryable
<Person>(true)
            .Where(p => p.Gender == "Male");

        System.Console.WriteLine("Running LINQ query for finding men...");
        foreach (Person foundPerson in  queryablePeople)
        {
            System.Console.WriteLine($"\tPerson: {foundPerson}");
        }

        //Find documents using SQL

        var sqlQuery = "SELECT * FROM Person WHERE Person.Gender = 'Female'";

        QueryDefinition queryDefinition = new QueryDefinition(sqlQuery);
        FeedIterator<Person> peopleResultSetIterator = this.container.GetItemQuery
Iterator<Person>(queryDefinition);

        System.Console.WriteLine("Running SQL query for finding women...");
        while (peopleResultSetIterator.HasMoreResults)
        {
            FeedResponse<Person> currentResultSet = await peopleResultSetIterator.
ReadNextAsync();
            foreach (Person foundPerson in currentResultSet)
            {
                System.Console.WriteLine($"\tPerson: {foundPerson}");
            }
        }

        Console.WriteLine("Press any key to continue...");
        Console.ReadKey();

        //Update documents in a collection
        this.SendMessageToConsoleAndWait($"Updating documents in the collection
{containerName}...");
        person2.FirstName = "Mathew";
        person2.Gender = "Male";

        await this.container.UpsertItemAsync(person2);
        this.SendMessageToConsoleAndWait($"Document modified {person2}");

        //Delete a single document from the collection
        this.SendMessageToConsoleAndWait($"Deleting documents from the collection
{containerName}...");

        PartitionKey partitionKey = new PartitionKey(person1.LastName);
        await this.container.DeleteItemAsync<Person>(person1.Id, partitionKey);
        this.SendMessageToConsoleAndWait($"Document deleted {person1}");
```

```
        //Delete created demo database and all its children elements
        this.SendMessageToConsoleAndWait("Cleaning-up your Cosmos DB account...");
        await this.database.DeleteAsync();
    }
    private void SendMessageToConsoleAndWait(string message)
    {
        Console.WriteLine(message);
        Console.WriteLine("Press any key to continue...");
        Console.ReadKey();
    }

    private async Task CreateDocumentIfNotExistsAsync(string database,
string collection, Person person)
    {
        try
        {
            await this?.container.ReadItemAsync<Person>(person.Id,
new PartitionKey(person.LastName));

            this.SendMessageToConsoleAndWait($"Document {person.Id} already exists
in collection {collection}");
        }
        catch (CosmosException dce)
        {
            if (dce.StatusCode == HttpStatusCode.NotFound)
            {

                await this?.container.CreateItemAsync<Person>(person,
new PartitionKey(person.LastName));

                this.SendMessageToConsoleAndWait($"Created new document
{person.Id} in collection {collection}");
            }
        }
    }
}
```

> **_NOTE_ AUTHENTICATE THE COSMOS DB CLIENT**
>
> As you may notice in the Listing 2-2 example, we are authenticating the Cosmos DB Client using the Cosmos DB account key. This is a bad idea in a real-life scenario, as that key is like a password for accessing your data stored in the Cosmos DB account. You should consider using passwordless authentication, using the Azure Identity client library for .NET. The following article explains how to use passwordless authentication: *https://learn.microsoft.com/en-us/ azure/cosmos-db/nosql/quickstart-dotnet?tabs=azure-portal%2Cwindows%2Cpasswordless%2 Csign-in-azure-cli#authenticate-the-client*

When you work with the SQL API, the Azure Cosmos DB SDK provides you with the appropriate classes for working with the different elements of the account. In the Listing 2-2 example, you must create a CosmosClient object before accessing your Azure Cosmos DB account.

The Azure Cosmos DB SDK also provides the classes Database and Container for working with these elements. When you need to create a Database or a Container, you can use `Create-DatabaseIfNotExistsAsync` or `CreateContainerIfNotExistsAsync`. These `IfNotExists` methods automatically check to determine whether the Container or Database exists in your Cosmos DB account; if they don't exist, the method automatically creates the Container or the Database. When you create a new container in your database, notice that in this example, you have provided the PartitionKey using the appropriate constructor overload.

However, when you need to create a new document in the database, you don't have this type of `IfNotExists` method available. In this situation, you have two options:

1. Use the method `UpsertItemAsync`, which creates a new document if the document doesn't exist or updates an existing document.

2. Implement your own version of the `IfNotExists` method, so you need to check whether the document already exists in the container. If the document doesn't exist, then you create the actual document, as shown in the following fragment from Listing 2-2. (The code in bold shows the methods that you need to use for creating a document.)

```
try
{

    await this?.container.ReadItemAsync<Person> (person.Id, new PartitionKey
(person.LastName));

    this.SendMessageToConsoleAndWait($"Document {person.Id} already exists in
collection {collection}");
}
catch (CosmosException dce)
{
    if (dce.StatusCode == HttpStatusCode.NotFound)
    {

    await this?.container.CreateItemAsync<Person>(person,
new PartitionKey(person.LastName));

    this.SendMessageToConsoleAndWait($"Created new document {person.Id}
in collection {collection}");
    }
}
```

When you create the document using the `CreateItemAsync` method, notice that you can provide the value for the partition key by using the following code snippet `new PartitionKey(person.LastName)`. If you don't provide the value for the partition key, the correct value is inferred from the document that you are trying to insert into the database.

You need to do this verification because you get a CosmosException with StatusCode 409 (Conflict) if you try to create a document with the same Id as an already existing document in the collection. Similarly, you get a CosmosException with StatusCode 404 (Not Found) if you try to delete a document that doesn't exist in the container using the `DeleteItemAsync` method or if you try to replace a document that doesn't exist in the container using the `Replace-ItemAsync` method. Notice that these two methods also accept a partition key parameter.

When you create a document, you need to provide an Id property of type string to your document. This property needs to identify your document inside the collection uniquely. If you don't provide this property, Cosmos DB automatically adds it to the document for you, using a GUID string.

As you can see in the example code in Listing 2-2, you can query your documents using LINQ or SQL sentences. In this example, I have used a simple SQL query for getting documents that represent a person with the male gender. However, you can construct more complex sentences such as a query that returns all people who live in a specific country, using the WHERE Address.Country = 'Spain' expression, or people that have an Android device by using the WHERE ARRAY_CONTAINS(Person.Devices, { 'OperatingSystem': 'Android'}, true) expression.

> **NEED MORE REVIEW?** **SQL QUERIES WITH COSMOS DB**
>
> You can review all the capabilities and features of the SQL language that Cosmos DB implements by reviewing this article:
>
> - **Queries in Azure Cosmos DB for NoSQL** *https://learn.microsoft.com/en-us/azure/cosmos-db/nosql/query/*

Once you have modified the Program.cs file, you need to create some additional classes that you use in the main program for managing documents. You can find these new classes in Listings 2-3 to 2-5.

1. In the Visual Studio Code window, create a new folder named **Model** in the project folder.

2. Create a new C# class file in the Model folder and name it **Person.cs**.

3. Replace the content of the Person.cs file with the content of Listing 2-3. Change the namespace as needed for your project.

4. Create a new C# class file in the Model folder and name it **Device.cs**.

5. Replace the content of the Device.cs file with the content of Listing 2-4. Change the namespace as needed for your project.

6. Create a new C# class file in the Model folder and name it **Address.cs**.

7. Replace the content of the Address.cs file with the content of Listing 2-5. Change the namespace as needed for your project.

8. At this point, you can run the project by pressing F5 in the Visual Studio Code window. Check to see how your code is creating and modifying the different databases, document collections, and documents in your Cosmos DB account. You can review the changes in your Cosmos DB account using the Data Explorer tool in your Cosmos DB account in the Azure portal.

LISTING 2-3 Cosmos DB NoSQL API example: Person.cs

```csharp
//C# .NET 6.0 LTS.
using Newtonsoft.Json;

namespace ch2_1_1_NoSQL.Model
{
    public class Person
    {
        [JsonProperty(PropertyName="id")]
        public string Id { get; set; }
        public string FirstName { get; set; }
        public string LastName { get; set; }
        public Device[] Devices { get; set; }
        public Address Address { get; set; }
        public string Gender { get; set; }
        public bool IsRegistered { get; set; }
        public override string ToString()
        {
            return JsonConvert.SerializeObject(this);
        }
    }
}
```

LISTING 2-4 Cosmos DB NoSQL API example: Device.cs

```csharp
//C# .NET 6.0 LTS.
namespace ch2_1_1_NoSQL.Model
{
    public class Device
    {
        public int Ram { get; set; }
        public string OperatingSystem { get; set; }
        public int CameraMegaPixels { get; set; }
        public string Usage { get; set; }
    }
}
```

LISTING 2-5 Cosmos DB NoSQL API example: Address.cs

```csharp
//C# .NET 6.0 LTS.
namespace ch2_1_1_NoSQL.Model
{
    public class Address
    {
        public string City { get; set; }
        public string State { get; set; }
        public string PostalCode { get; set; }
        public string Country { get; set; }
        public string Street { get; set; }
    }
}
```

At this point, you can press F5 in your Visual Studio Code window to execute the code. The code stops on each step for you to view the operation's result directly on the Azure portal. Use the following steps to view the modifications in your Cosmos DB account:

1. Sign in to the Azure portal (*http://portal.azure.com*).

2. In the search box at the top of the Azure portal, type the name of your Cosmos DB account and then click the account name.

3. On your Cosmos DB Account blade, select Data Explorer.

4. On the Data Explorer blade, on the left side of the panel, under the label SQL API, you should be able to see the list of databases created in your Cosmos DB account.

NOTE **MONGODB, POSTGRESQL, GREMLIN, AND CASSANDRA EXAMPLES**

As you can see in the previous examples, integrating your existing code with Cosmos DB doesn't require much effort or many changes to your code. For the sake of brevity, we omitted the examples of connecting your PostgreSQL, Cassandra, or Gremlin applications with Cosmos DB. You can learn how to do these integrations by reviewing the following articles:

- **Quickstart: Azure Cosmos DB for MongoDB for .NET with the MongoDB driver** *https://learn.microsoft.com/en-us/azure/cosmos-db/mongodb/quickstart-dotnet*

- **Quickstart: Use C# to connect and run SQL commands on Azure Cosmos DB for PostgreSQL** *https://learn.microsoft.com/en-us/azure/cosmos-db/postgresql/quickstart-app-stacks-csharp*

- **Quickstart: Build a .NET Framework or Core application using the Azure Cosmos DB Gremlin API account** *https://docs.microsoft.com/en-us/azure/cosmos-db/create-graph-dotnet*

- **Quickstart: Build a Cassandra App with .NET SDK and Azure Cosmos DB** *https://docs.microsoft.com/en-us/azure/cosmos-db/create-cassandra-dotnet*

Set the appropriate consistency level for operations

One of the main benefits that Cosmos DB offers is the ability to have your data distributed globally with low latency when accessing the data. This means that you can configure Cosmos DB for replicating your data between any of the available Azure regions while achieving minimal latency when your application accesses the data from the nearest region. If you need to replicate your data to an additional region, you only need to add to the list of regions where your data should be available.

This replication across the different regions has a drawback: the consistency of your data. To avoid corruption, your data must be consistent among all copies of your database. Fortunately, the Cosmos DB protocol offers five levels of consistency replication. Going from consistency to performance, you can select how the replication protocol behaves when copying your data between all the replicas that are configured across the globe. These consistency levels are region agnostic, which means the region that started the read or write operation or the number of regions associated with your Cosmos DB account doesn't matter, even if you configured a single region for your account. You configure this consistency level at the Cosmos DB level, and it applies to all databases, collections, and documents stored inside the same account. You can choose from the consistency levels shown in Figure 2-3. Use the following procedure to select the consistency level:

1. Sign in to the Azure portal (*http://portal.azure.com*).

2. In the search box at the top of the Azure portal, type the name of your Cosmos DB account and then click the account name.

3. Select Default Consistency in the Settings section on your Cosmos DB account blade.

4. On the Default Consistency blade, select the desired consistency level. Your choices are Strong, Bounded Staleness, Session, Consistent Prefix, and Eventual.

5. Click the Save icon at the top left of the Default Consistency blade.

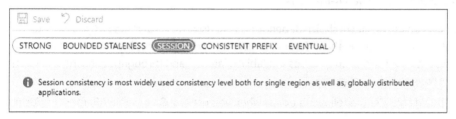

FIGURE 2-3 Selecting the consistency level

When configuring the consistency level, you must choose one of the following five options:

- **Strong**   The read operations are guaranteed to return the most recently committed version of an element; that is, the user always reads the latest committed write. This consistency level is the only one that offers a linearizability guarantee. This guarantee comes at a price. It has higher latency because of the time needed to write operation confirmations, and the availability can be affected during failures.

- **Bounded Staleness**   The reads are guaranteed to be consistent within a precon- figured lag. This lag can consist of a number of the most recent (K) versions or a time interval (T). This means that if you make write operations, the read of those operations happens in the same order but with a maximum delay of K versions of the written data or T seconds since you wrote the data in the database. For reading operations that hap- pen within a region that accepts writes, the consistency level is identical to the Strong consistency level. This level is also known as "time-delayed linearizability guarantee."

- **Session**   Scoped to a client session, this consistency level offers the best balance between a strong consistency level and the performance provided by the eventual consistency level. It best fits applications in which write operations occur in the context of a user session.

- **Consistent Prefix** This level guarantees that you always read data in the same order that you wrote the data, but there's no guarantee that you can read all the data. This means that if you write "A, B, C" you can read "A", "A, B", or "A, B, C" but never "A, C" or "B, A, C."

- **Eventual** There is no guarantee for the order in which you read the data. In the absence of a write operation, the replicas eventually converge. This consistency level offers better performance at the cost of the complexity of the programming. Use this consistency level if the order of the data is not essential for your application.

> **NOTE** **CONSISTENCY, AVAILABILITY, AND PERFORMANCE TRADE-OFFS**
>
> Every consistency level shown in this section has implications regarding data consistency, data availability, and application performance. You can review the implications of choosing each consistency level by reviewing the following article: *https://docs.microsoft.com/en-us/azure/cosmos-db/consistency-levels-tradeoffs.*

The best consistency level choice depends on your application and the API you want to store data. As you can see in the different consistency levels, your application's requirements regarding data read consistency versus availability, latency, and throughput are critical factors you must consider when selecting.

You should consider the following points when you use NoSQL or Table API for your Cosmos DB account:

- The recommended option for most applications is the level of session consistency.

- If you are considering the strong consistency level, we recommend that you use the bonded staleness consistency level because it provides a linearizability guarantee with a configurable delay.

- If you are considering the eventual consistency level, we recommend that you use the consistent prefix consistency level because it provides comparable levels of availability and latency with the advantage of guaranteed read orders.

- Carefully evaluate the strong and eventual consistency levels because they are the most extreme options. In most situations, other consistency levels can provide a better balance between performance, latency, and data consistency.

> **NEED MORE REVIEW?** **CONSISTENCY LEVELS TRADE-OFF**
>
> Each consistency level comes at a price. You can review the implications of choosing each consistency level by reading the article "Consistency, Availability, and Performance Tradeoffs" at *https://docs.microsoft.com/en-us/azure/cosmos-db/consistency-levels-tradeoffs.*

When you use Cassandra or MongoDB APIs, Cosmos DB maps the consistency levels offered by Cassandra and MongoDB to the consistency level offered by Cosmos DB. The reason for doing this is because when you use these APIs, neither Cassandra nor MongoDB offers a well-defined consistency level. Instead, Cassandra provides write or read consistency levels that map to the Cosmos DB consistency level in the following ways:

- **Cassandra write consistency level**   This level maps to the default Cosmos DB account consistency level.

- **Cassandra read consistency level**   Cosmos DB dynamically maps the consistency level specified by the Cassandra driver client to one of the Cosmos DB consistency levels.

On the other hand, MongoDB allows you to configure the following consistency levels: Write Concern, Read Concern, and Master Region. Similar to the mapping of Cassandra consistency levels, Cosmos DB consistency levels map to MongoDB consistency levels in the following ways:

- **MongoDB write concern consistency level**   This level maps to the default Cosmos DB account consistency level.

- **MongoDB read concern consistency level**   Cosmos DB dynamically maps the consistency level specified by the MongoDB driver client to one of the Cosmos DB consistency levels.

- **Configuring a master region**   You can configure a region as the MongoDB "master" by configuring the region as the first writable region.

> **NEED MORE REVIEW?   CASSANDRA AND MONGODB CONSISTENCY LEVEL MAPPINGS**
>
> You can review how the different consistency levels map between Cassandra and MongoDB and Cosmos DB consistency levels in the article "Consistency Levels and Azure Cosmos DB APIs" at *https://docs.microsoft.com/en-us/azure/cosmos-db/consistency-levels-across-apis*.

EXAM TIP

The consistency level impacts the latency and availability of the data. In general terms, you should avoid the most extreme levels as they significantly impact your program and should be carefully evaluated. If you are unsure which level of consistency you should use, you should use the session level, as this is the best-balanced level.

Implement change feed notifications

Working with data means you need to perform operations on that data. Maybe you need to do some actions just when the data arrives, or when the data is modified or even deleted. In other systems, you can implement this using triggers or events raised when a new create, update, or delete operation happens. Azure Cosmos DB provides change feed notifications, a built-in mechanism for performing actions when a new operation occurs.

Change feed notifications persist the changes on the items in your collection as soon as they happen, keeping the order in which they occurred. The engine listens for the changes in your container, creates a list of changed documents, and persists the list in a change feed.

The changes are added to the list in the same order as they happen. You can connect one or more consumers to the change feed to process those changes. The changes can be processed synchronously or asynchronously.

When working with change feed, we must distinguish between reading the change feed and the change feed mode. The change feed mode is which and how changes are published to the change feed.

You have two modes when reading information from the change feed: push and pull. In push mode, the change feed processor sends the changes to a client with the business logic to process the change. The advantage of the push mode is that the client doesn't need to keep track of the state of the last processed work. The change feed processor does this tracking for you and stores this information in a lease container.

With pull mode, the client asks the change feed for the latest change. In this mode, the client is responsible for providing the business logic for processing the change, the mechanism for storing and tracking the state, and distributing the load between the workers with the business logic for processing the changes. We will go deeper into this topic later in this section.

Regarding the change feed modes, or which changes are saved to the change feed, you can find two different modes:

- **Latest version change feed mode**   This mode saves a record of each creation and update operation performed over the items in a container to the change feed. Only the last version of the item is saved. This means that if you create a new item in a container and later make a modification to the same item before reading the change feed, you will only get the latest modification. This mode does not record the delete operations on an item, and once you delete an item, the change feed for that item is no longer available. This is the default mode for all containers. The lifetime of the record associated with each item is the same as the item. This means that the record exists in the feed as long as the item exists in the container.

- **All versions and deletes change feed mode**   In this mode, the record in the change feed associated with an item stores all the versions, modifications, and deletes that happen to that item. This means that if you create an item in a container, modify it, and later delete the item, you will find those three operations stored in the record associated with the item. This mode requires configuring the continuous backup feature at the Cosmos DB account level. The lifetime of each record matches the retention period configured in the continuous backup.

When deciding which change feed mode to use, keep in mind that you can use both modes in the same container with different applications.

> ### NEED MORE REVIEW?   MORE ON THE CHANGE FEED MODES.
>
> Although change feed is enabled by default in all containers, not all APIs support all modes. You can learn more about which Cosmos DB API supports change feed and the appropriate use cases for each mode by reviewing the following Microsoft article: *https://learn.microsoft.com/en-us/azure/cosmos-db/nosql/change-feed-modes*.

Now that we have reviewed the different modes of changes and the types of changes that are published to the change feed, we must review how to read that information from the change feed. As reviewed previously in this section, there are two modes for reading data from the change feed: pull and push. Independent of the reading mode, we need to decide which type of consumer we will use to read those changes. Depending on the reading mode, you have different options:

- **pull** You can use two different consumer types:

  - **Azure Functions** This is the simplest option and is recommended for most use cases. You create a trigger associated to an Azure Cosmos DB container. As soon as a change happens on the container, the Azure Function is executed.

  - **Change feed processor library** Starting with Azure Cosmos DB .NET V3 and JAVA V4 SDK, this library abstracts you from the complexities of managing the changes in the change feed. The library allows you to easily distribute the event processing between multiple consumers. You should use this library if you need more control over the event processing or you need to implement a fault-tolerant solution.

- **push** You use the FeedIterator class from the Azure Cosmos DB SDK for reading the information from the change feed. Remember that in push mode, you are responsible for keeping track of the processing point on the change feed, and the behavior when there are no new changes on the change feed.

Now that you have an overview of how change feed works and its different options, let's review how to implement a change feed consumer. The following procedure shows how to create and register an Azure Function as a change feed consumer. This procedure assumes you already have an Azure Cosmos DB account with a container created. If not, please review the previous sections in this chapter to learn how to create one:

1. Open Visual Studio Code.

2. Ensure that the Azure Functions extension is installed.

3. Click on the Azure icon on the left side of the Visual Studio Code window.

4. Sign in to your Azure Subscription by selecting the Sign In To Azure option in the Resources section.

5. Click the Azure Functions icon on the Workspace area. The icon should be located next to the Workspace area title.

6. Select the Create New Project option in the contextual menu.

7. Select the folder for your new project. Remember that the folder's name will also be your project's name.

8. Select C# as the language for your project.

9. Select .NET 6.0 LTS as the runtime for your project.

10. Select CosmosDBTrigger as the template for the first function in your project.

11. Provide a name for the Azure Function.

12. Provide a namespace for your code.

13. Provide a name for the setting that will store the connection string for your Cosmos DB container.

14. Enter the name of the database that you want to monitor.

15. Enter the name of the collection to monitor.

16. Press Enter to open the new project in the current Visual Studio Code window.

17. Open your function's .cs file.

18. Add the following code to the `CosmosDBTrigger` constructor's parameters:

```
CreateLeaseCollectionIfNotExists = true
```

At this point, you should have code similar to that shown in Listing 2-6. The most important things you need to understand from this code are the `LeaseCollectionName` and `CreateLease-CollectionIfNotExists` settings. These settings control the name of the container that will be used for storing the lease information to track the change feed pointer status, and the trigger extension should automatically create the lease collection if it does not exist. Keep in mind that if this collection does not exist, your code won't run.

LISTING 2-6 Cosmos DB Azure function trigger

```csharp
//C# .NET 6.0 LTS
public static class CosmosDBTriggerCSharp1
    {
        [FunctionName("CosmosDBTriggerCSharp1")]
        public static void Run([CosmosDBTrigger(
            databaseName: "demoDB_328a8",
            collectionName: "collection_02ddc",
            ConnectionStringSetting = "CosmosDBConnection",
            LeaseCollectionName = "leases",
            CreateLeaseCollectionIfNotExists = true)]IReadOnlyList<Document> input,
            ILogger log)
        {
            if (input != null && input.Count > 0)
            {
                log.LogInformation("Documents modified " + input.Count);
                log.LogInformation("First document Id " + input[0].Id);
            }
        }
    }
```

You must configure your code with your CosmosDB account's connection string. The following procedure shows how to make this configuration in your development environment:

1. Sign in to the Azure portal (*http://portal.azure.com*).

2. In the search box at the top of the Azure portal, type the name of your Cosmos DB account and then click the account name.

3. Select the Keys option in the Settings section.

4. On the Keys blade, click the eye icon to the right of the Primary Connection String text box.

5. When the Primary Connection String appears, copy it.

6. Switch back to your Visual Studio Code window.

7. Open the local.settings.json

8. In the Values object, add a new property for the connection string. The name of this property should be the same as you set in step 13 of the previous procedure. For this example, the property name is `CosmosDBConnection`.

9. Paste the connection string you copied in step 5 as the property value.

10. Save the file.

11. Press F5 to run your code.

At this point, any modification or creation of new items in your collection should trigger your Azure Function, and you should see a message in your console showing the number of modified documents, the reason for the trigger, and the document ID of the first document in the change feed.

NEED MORE REVIEW?   **MORE ON THE CHANGE FEED CONSUMERS**

Using Azure Functions trigger for Cosmos DB is the easiest and recommended way to implement change feed consumers. If you need to use push consumers or need fault-tolerance features, you should review the following Microsoft articles that explain how to implement the other types of consumers mentioned in this section:

- **Change feed processor in Azure Cosmos DB**   *https://learn.microsoft.com/en-us/azure/cosmos-db/nosql/change-feed-processor?tabs=dotnet*

- **Change feed pull model in Azure Cosmos DB**   *https://learn.microsoft.com/en-us/azure/cosmos-db/nosql/change-feed-pull-model?tabs=dotnet*

Skill 2.2: Develop solutions that use Blob Storage

Storing information in SQL or NoSQL databases is a great way to save that information when you need to save schema-less documents or when you need to guarantee the integrity of the data. The drawback of these services is that they are relatively expensive for storing data that doesn't have such requirements.

Azure Blob Storage allows you to store information that doesn't fit the characteristics of SQL and NoSQL storage in the cloud. This information can be images, videos, office documents, or more. The Azure Blob Storage still provides high-availability features that make it an ideal service for storing a large amount of data but at a lower price compared to the other data storage solutions covered earlier in this chapter.

> **This skill covers how to**
> - Set and retrieve properties and metadata
> - Interact with data using the appropriate SDK
> - Implement storage policies and data life cycle management
> - Implement static site hosting

Set and retrieve properties and metadata

When you work with Azure Storage services, you can work with some additional information assigned to your blobs. This additional information is stored in the form of system properties and user-defined metadata:

- **System properties** This is information that the Storage services automatically add to each storage resource. You can modify some of these system properties, while others are read-only. Some of these system properties correspond with some HTTP headers. You don't need to worry about maintaining these system properties because the Azure Storage client libraries automatically make any needed modifications for you.

- **User-defined metadata** You can assign key-value pairs to an Azure Storage resource. This metadata is for your own purposes and doesn't affect the behavior of the Azure Storage service. You need to take care of updating the value of the metadata according to your needs.

When working with blob metadata, you can use the appropriate SDK from your preferred language or the command az storage blob metadata from the Azure CLI. The following example shows how to work with properties and metadata using the .NET SDK. You need to create an Azure Storage Account and have Azure CLI installed to run this example:

1. Open Visual Studio Code and create a folder for your project.

2. In the Visual Studio Code window, open a new terminal.

3. Use the following command to create a new console project:

   ```
   dotnet new console
   ```

4. Use the following command to install NuGet packages:

   ```
   dotnet add package <NuGet_package_name>
   ```

5. Install the following NuGet packages:

   - Azure.Storage.Blob
   - Azure.Storage.Common
   - Azure.Identity
   - Microsoft.Extensions.Configuration

- Microsoft.Extensions.Configuration.Binder

- Microsoft.Extensions.Configuration.Json

6. Create a new JSON file in the project folder and name it **AppSettings.json**. Copy the content from Listing 2-7 to the JSON file and replace the value of the variables with the values of your storage accounts.

7. Create a C# class file and name it **AppSettings.cs**.

8. Replace the contents of the AppSettings.cs file with the contents of Listing 2-8. Change the name of the namespace to match your project's name.

9. Create a C# class file and name it **Common.cs**.

10. Replace the contents of the Common.cs file with the contents of Listing 2-9.

11. Change the name of the namespace to match your project's name.

12. Replace the contents of the Program.cs file with the contents of Listing 2-10. Change the name of the namespace to match your project's name.

13. Edit your .csproj project file and add the following code inside the ItemGroup section:

```
<None Update="AppSettings.json">
    <CopyToOutputDirectory>PreserveNewest</CopyToOutputDirectory>
</None>
```

14. At this point, you can set some breakpoints in the Program.cs file to see, step by step, how the code moves the blob items between the different containers and Storage Accounts.

15. In the Visual Studio window, press F5 to build and run your code.

LISTING 2-7 AppSettings.json configuration file

```
{
    "AccountName": "<name_of_your_storage_account>",
    "ContainerName": "<source_container_name>"
}
```

LISTING 2-8 AppSettings.cs C# class

```
//C# .NET 6.0 LTS

using Microsoft.Extensions.Configuration;

namespace ch2_2_1
{
    public class AppSettings
    {
        public string AccountName { get; set; }
        public string ContainerName { get; set; }

        public static AppSettings LoadAppSettings()
        {
            IConfigurationRoot configRoot = new ConfigurationBuilder()
                .AddJsonFile("AppSettings.json",false)
```

```
                .Build();
            AppSettings appSettings = configRoot.Get<AppSettings>();
            return appSettings;
        }
    }
}
```

LISTING 2-9 Common.cs C# class

```
//C# .NET 6.0 LTS

using System;
using Azure.Storage;
using Azure.Storage.Auth;
using Azure.Storage.Blob;

namespace ch2_2_1
{
    public class Common
    {

        public static BlobContainerClient CreateBlobContainerClientFromDefaultAzureCrede
ntial(string accountName, string containerName)
        {
            BlobContainerClient blobContainerClient;
            try
            {
                var storageCredentials = new DefaultAzureCredential();
                blobContainerClient = new BlobContainerClient(new Uri($"https://
{accountName}.blob.core.windows.net/{containerName}"), storageCredentials, null);
            }
            catch (System.Exception)
            {
                throw;
            }

            return blobContainerClient;

        }
    }
}
```

Listing 2-10 shows how to create a new container and get a list of some system properties assigned automatically to the container when you create it.

LISTING 2-10 Program.cs C# class

```
//C# .NET 6.0 LTS
// Getting system properties from a storage resource
using Azure.Storage.Blobs;
using ch2_2_1;

Console.WriteLine("Getting System properties Demo!");

AppSettings appSettings = AppSettings.LoadAppSettings();
```

```
//Create a BlobContainerClient for working with the container in the storage account
BlobContainerClient container =
Common.CreateBlobContainerClientFromDefaultAzureCredential(appSettings.AccountName,
appSettings.ContainerName);

//Create the container if it does not already exist
container.CreateIfNotExists();

//Fetch the container properties before getting their values
var containerProperties = container.GetProperties();
Console.WriteLine($"Properties for container {appSettings.ContainerName}");
System.Console.WriteLine($"ETag: {containerProperties.Value.ETag}");
System.Console.WriteLine($"LastModifiedUTC: {containerProperties.Value.LastModified.
ToString()}");
System.Console.WriteLine($"Lease status: {containerProperties.Value.LeaseStatus.
ToString()}");
System.Console.WriteLine();
```

As you can see in the previous code in Listing 2-10, you need to use the GetProperties() or GetPropertiesAsync() method before you can read the properties from the container, stored in the Properties property of the BlobContainerClient or BlobClient objects. If you get null values for system properties, ensure that you called the GetProperties() method before accessing the system property.

> **NOTE   MICROSOFT IDENTITY**
>
> The previous example uses the DefaultAzureCredential object from the Microsoft Identity Library instead of shared access signature (SAS) authentication. This approach is recommended for authenticating resources as it does not require storing passwords or connection strings on the code. If you get an access error when running the previous example, run the az login command from your terminal and ensure that your user has enough privileges to access the storage account. You can learn more about DefaultAzureCredentials by reviewing the Microsoft article *https://learn.microsoft.com/en-us/dotnet/api/azure.identity.defaultazurecredential*

Working with user-defined metadata is quite similar to working with system properties. The main difference is that you can add your custom key pairs to the storage resource. This user-defined metadata is stored in the Metadata property of the storage resource. Listing 2-11 extends the example in Listing 2-10 and shows how to set and read user-defined metadata in the container that you created in Listing 2-10. Copy the content from Listing 2-11 and insert the code in the Program.cs file after the last System.Console.WriteLine().

LISTING 2-11 Setting user-defined metadata

```
//C# .NET 6.0 LTS
//Add some metadata to the container that you created previously
container.SetMetadata(new Dictionary<string, string>
{
    {"department", "Technical Support"},
    {"category", "Knowledge Base"},
    {"author", "John Doe"},
```

```
        {"editor", "Jane Doe"},
        {"publishDate", "2023-01-01"},
        {"reviewDate", "2023-12-31"},
});

//List newly added metadata. We need to fetch all attributes before being
//able to read; otherwise, we could get nulls or weird values
containerProperties = container.GetProperties();

System.Console.WriteLine($"User-defined metadata for container
{appSettings.ContainerName}");
foreach (var metadata in containerProperties.Value.Metadata)
{
    System.Console.WriteLine($"{metadata.Key}: {metadata.Value}");
}
```

> **NEED MORE REVIEW?   SYSTEM PROPERTIES**
>
> You can find a complete list of system properties in the Azure.Storage.Blob .NET client reference at *https://learn.microsoft.com/es-es/dotnet/api/ azure.storage.blobs.models.blobcontainerproperties*

The `BlobContainerProperties` and `BlobProperties` classes are responsible for storing the system properties for the storage resources in a Blob Storage account.

You can also view and edit system properties and user-defined metadata by using the Azure portal, using the Properties and Metadata sections in the Settings section of your container, or clicking on the ellipsis next to the blob item and selecting the Blob Properties option in the contextual menu, as shown in Figure 2-4

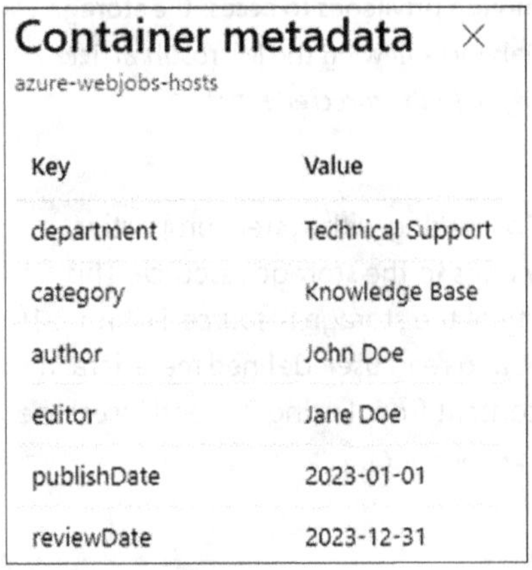

Container metadata ✕
azure-webjobs-hosts

Key	Value
department	Technical Support
category	Knowledge Base
author	John Doe
editor	Jane Doe
publishDate	2023-01-01
reviewDate	2023-12-31

FIGURE 2-4 Container metadata

Interact with data using the appropriate SDK

Microsoft provides several SDKs for working with data in your Storage Accounts. You can find SDKs for the main programming languages supported by Microsoft, such as .NET, Java, Python, JavaScript (Node.js or browser), Go, PHP, or Ruby.

The following example written in .NET shows how to move a blob item between two containers in the same Storage Account and how to move a blob item between two containers in different Storage Accounts. Before you can run this example, you must create two Storage Accounts with two blob containers. For the sake of simplicity, you should create two containers with the same name in the two different Storage Accounts. Also, you need to upload two control files as blob items to one of the containers in one Storage Account:

1. Open Visual Studio Code and create a folder for your project.

2. In the Visual Studio Code window, open a new terminal.

3. Use the following command to create a new console project:

   ```
   dotnet new console
   ```

4. Use the following command to install NuGet packages:

   ```
   dotnet add package <NuGet_package_name>
   ```

5. Install the following NuGet packages:

   - Azure.Storage.Blobs
   - Azure.Storage.Common
   - Microsoft.Extensions.Configuration
   - Microsoft.Extensions.Configuration.Binder
   - Microsoft.Extensions.Configuration.Json

6. Create a new JSON file in the project folder and name it **AppSettings.json**. Copy the content from Listing 2-12 to the JSON file.

7. Create a C# class file and name it **AppSettings.cs**.

8. Replace the contents of the AppSettings.cs file with the contents of Listing 2-13. Change the name of the namespace to match your project's name.

9. Create a C# class file and name it **Common.cs**.

10. Replace the contents of the Common.cs file with the contents of Listing 2-14.

11. Change the name of the namespace to match your project's name.

12. Replace the contents of the Program.cs file with the contents of Listing 2-15. Change the name of the namespace to match your project's name.

13. Edit your .csproj project file and add the following code inside the ItemGroup section:

    ```
    <None Update="AppSettings.json">
      <CopyToOutputDirectory>PreserveNewest</CopyToOutputDirectory>
    </None>
    ```

14. At this point, you can set some breakpoints in the Program.cs file to see, step by step, how the code moves the blob items between the different containers and Storage Accounts.

15. In the Visual Studio window, press F5 to build and run your code. You can use the Azure portal or the Microsoft Azure Storage Explorer desktop application to review how your blob items change their locations.

LISTING 2-12 AppSettings.json configuration file

```
{
    "SourceSASConnectionString": "<SASConnectionString_from_your_first_storage_account>",
    "SourceAccountName": "<name_of_your_first_storage_account>",
    "SourceContainerName": "<source_container_name>",
    "DestinationSASConnectionString": "<SASConnectionString_from_your_second_storage_
account>",
    "DestinationAccountName": "<name_of_your_second_storage_account>",
    "DestinationContainerName": "<destination_container_name>"
}
```

LISTING 2-13 AppSettings.cs C# class

```csharp
//C# .NET 6.0 LTS
using Microsoft.Extensions.Configuration;

namespace ch2_2_2
{
    public class AppSettings
    {
        public string SourceSASConnectionString { get; set; }
        public string SourceAccountName { get; set; }
        public string SourceContainerName { get; set; }
        public string DestinationSASConnectionString { get; set; }
        public string DestinationAccountName { get; set; }
        public string DestinationContainerName { get; set; }

        public static AppSettings LoadAppSettings()
        {
            IConfigurationRoot configRoot = new ConfigurationBuilder()
                .AddJsonFile("AppSettings.json",false)
                .Build();
            AppSettings appSettings = configRoot.Get<AppSettings>();
            return appSettings;
        }
    }
}
```

LISTING 2-14 Common.cs C# class

```csharp
//C# .NET 6.0 LTS
using Azure.Storage.Blobs;

namespace ch2_2_2
{
    public class Common
    {
```

```
        public static BlobServiceClient CreateBlobClientStorageFromSAS
(string SASConnectionString)
        {
            BlobServiceClient blobClient;
            try
            {
                blobClient = new BlobServiceClient(SASConnectionString);
            }
            catch (System.Exception)
            {
                throw;
            }

            return blobClient;

        }
    }
}
```

In Listing 2-15, portions of the code significant to working with the Azure Blob Storage service are shown in bold.

LISTING 2-15 Program.cs C# class

```
//C# .NET 6.0 LTS
using System.Threading.Tasks;
using System;
using Azure.Storage.Blobs;
using Azure.Storage.Blobs.Models;

namespace ch2_2_2
{
    class Program
    {
        static void Main(string[] args)
        {
            Console.WriteLine("Copy items between Containers Demo!");
            Task.Run(async () => await StartContainersDemo()).Wait();
            Console.WriteLine("Move items between Storage Accounts Demo!");
            Task.Run(async () => await StartAccountDemo()).Wait();
        }

        public static async Task StartContainersDemo()
        {
            string sourceBlobFileName = "Testing.zip";
            AppSettings appSettings = AppSettings.LoadAppSettings();

            //Get a cloud client for the source Storage Account
            BlobServiceClient sourceClient = Common.CreateBlobClientStorageFromSAS
(appSettings.SourceSASConnectionString);

            //Get a reference for each container
            var sourceContainerReference = sourceClient.GetBlobContainerClient
(appSettings.SourceContainerName);
            var destinationContainerReference = sourceClient.GetBlobContainer
Client(appSettings.DestinationContainerName);
```

```
        //Get a reference for the source blob
        var sourceBlobReference = sourceContainerReference.GetBlobClient
(sourceBlobFileName);
        var destinationBlobReference = destinationContainerReference. GetBlobClient
(sourceBlobFileName);

        //Copy the blob from the source container to the destination container
        await destinationBlobReference.StartCopyFromUriAsync(sourceBlob Reference.Uri);

    }

    public static async Task StartAccountDemo()
    {
        string sourceBlobFileName = "Testing.zip";
        AppSettings appSettings = AppSettings.LoadAppSettings();

        //Get a cloud client for the source Storage Account
        BlobServiceClient sourceClient = Common.CreateBlobClientStorageFromSAS
(appSettings.SourceSASConnectionString);
        //Get a cloud client for the destination Storage Account
        BlobServiceClient destinationClient = Common.CreateBlobClientStorage
FromSAS(appSettings.DestinationSASConnectionString);

        //Get a reference for each container
        var sourceContainerReference = sourceClient.GetBlobContainerClient
(appSettings.SourceContainerName);
        var destinationContainerReference = destinationClient.GetBlobContainer
Client(appSettings.DestinationContainerName);

        //Get a reference for the source blob
        var sourceBlobReference = sourceContainerReference.GetBlobClient
(sourceBlobFileName);
        var destinationBlobReference = destinationContainerReference. GetBlobClient
(sourceBlobFileName);

        //Move the blob from the source container to the destination container
        await destinationBlobReference.StartCopyFromUriAsync(sourceBlob Reference.Uri);
        await sourceBlobReference.DeleteAsync();
    }
  }
}
```

> ***NOTE*** **MICROSOFT ENTRA ID AUTHENTICATION**
>
> Notice that we didn't use the `DefaultAzureCredentials` object for authenticating the `BlobSer-`
> `viceClient`. This is because Microsoft Entra ID authorization (formerly Azure AD authoriza-
> tion) is not supported for making cross-account blob copies. You can learn more about this
> by reading the Microsoft article *https://learn.microsoft.com/en-us/rest/api/storageservices/*
> *copy-blob*

In this example, you made two different operations—a copy between containers in the same Storage Account and a movement between containers in different Storage Accounts. As you can see in the code shown previously in Listing 2-15, the high-level procedure for moving blob items between containers is as follows:

1. Create a `BlobServiceClient` instance for each Storage Account that is involved in the blob item movement.

2. Create a reference for each container. If you need to move a blob item between containers in a different Storage Account, you must use the `BlobServiceClient` object that represents each Storage Account.

3. Create a reference for each blob item. You need a reference to the source blob item because this is the item you will move. You use the destination blob item reference for performing the actual copy operation.

4. Once you finish the copy, you can delete the source blob item using the `DeleteAsync()` method.

Although this code is quite straightforward, it has a critical problem that you can solve in the following sections. If someone else modifies the source blob item while the write operation is pending, the copy operation fails with an HTTP status code 412. We will fix this later in this section.

NEED MORE REVIEW? **CROSS-ACCOUNT BLOB COPY**

You can review the details of how the asynchronous copy between Storage Accounts works by reading the MSDN article, "Introducing Asynchronous Cross-Account Copy Blob" at *https://blogs.msdn.microsoft.com/windowsazurestorage/2012/06/12/ introducing-asynchronous- cross-account-copy-blob/.*

EXAM TIP

When you need to move a blob to any destination, container, or Storage Account, remember that you first need to perform a copy operation and then delete the source blob. There is no such move method in the `CloudBlockBlob` class.

When working with the Blob Storage service—in which several users or processes can simultaneously access the same Storage Account—you can face a problem when two users or processes are trying to access the same blob. Azure provides a leasing mechanism for solving this kind of situation. A lease is a short block that the blob service sets on a blob or container item to grant exclusive access to that item. When you acquire a lease to a blob, you get exclusive write and delete access to that blob. If you acquire a lease in a container, you get exclusive delete access to the container.

When you acquire a lease for a storage item, you must include the active lease ID on each write operation that you want to perform on the blob with the lease. You can choose the duration of the lease time when you request it. This duration can last from 15 to 60 seconds or forever. Each lease can be in one of the following five states:

- **Available** The lease is unlocked, and you can acquire a new lease.

- **Leased** There is a lease granted to the resource, and the lease is locked. You can acquire a new lease if you use the same ID that you got when you created the lease. You can also release, change, renew, or break the lease when it is in this status.

- **Expired** The duration configured for the lease has expired. When you have a lease in this status, you can acquire, renew, release, or break the lease.

- **Breaking** You have broken the lease, but it's still locked until the break period expires. In this status, you can release or break the lease.

- **Broken** The break period has expired, and the lease has been broken. In this status, you can acquire, release, and break a lease. You need to break a lease when the process that acquired the lease finishes suddenly, such as when network connectivity issues or any other condition results in the lease not being released correctly. In these situations, you may end up with an orphaned lease, and you cannot write or delete the blob with the orphaned lease. In this situation, the only solution is to break the lease. You may also want to break a lease when you need to force the release of the lease manually.

You use the Azure portal for managing the lease status of a container or blob item, or you use it programmatically with the Azure Blob Storage client SDK. In the example shown in Listings 2-12 to 2-15, in which we reviewed how to copy and move items between containers or Storage Accounts, we saw that if some other process or user modifies the blob while our process is copying the data, we get an error. You can avoid that situation by acquiring a lease for the blob that you want to move. Listing 2-16 shows in bold the modification that you need to add to the code in Listing 2-15 so that you can acquire a lease for the blob item.

LISTING 2-16 Program.cs modification

```
//C# .NET 6.0 LTS
//Add lines in bold to the StartContainersDemo method in Listing 2-15
//Add the following using statement to the beginning of the file:
//using Azure.Storage.Blobs.Specialized;
public static async Task StartContainersDemo()
        {
            string sourceBlobFileName = "Testing.zip";
            AppSettings appSettings = AppSettings.LoadAppSettings();

            //Get a cloud client for the source Storage Account
            BlobServiceClient sourceClient = Common.CreateBlobClientStorageFromSAS
(appSettings.SourceSASConnectionString);

            //Get a reference for each container
            var sourceContainerReference = sourceClient.GetBlobContainerClient
(appSettings.SourceContainerName);
            var destinationContainerReference = sourceClient.GetBlobContainerClient
(appSettings.DestinationContainerName);
```

```
            //Get a reference for the source blob
            var sourceBlobReference = sourceContainerReference.GetBlobClient
(sourceBlobFileName);
            var destinationBlobReference = destinationContainerReference.GetBlobClient(
sourceBlobFileName);

            //Get the lease status of the source blob
            BlobProperties sourceBlobProperties = await sourceBlobReference.
GetPropertiesAsync();
            System.Console.WriteLine($"Lease status: {sourceBlobProperties.LeaseStatus}" +
                    $"\tstate: {sourceBlobProperties.LeaseState}" +
                    $"\tduration: {sourceBlobProperties.LeaseDuration}");

            //Acquire an infinite lease. If you want to set a duration for the lease
            //use
            //TimeSpan.FromSeconds(seconds). Remember that seconds should be a value
            //between 15 and 60.
            //We need to save the lease ID automatically generated by Azure to release
            //the lease later.
            string leaseID = Guid.NewGuid().ToString();
            BlobLeaseClient sourceLease = sourceBlobReference.GetBlobLeaseClient(leaseID);

            sourceLease.Acquire(new TimeSpan(-1));

            sourceBlobProperties = await sourceBlobReference.GetPropertiesAsync();
            System.Console.WriteLine($"Lease status: {sourceBlobProperties.LeaseStatus}" +
                    $"\tstate: {sourceBlobProperties.LeaseState}" +
                    $"\tduration: {sourceBlobProperties.LeaseDuration}");

            //Copy the blob from the source container to the destination container
            await destinationBlobReference.StartCopyFromUriAsync (sourceBlobReference.Uri);

            //Release the lease acquired previously
            sourceLease.Release();

    }
```

As you can see in the previous example, you need to get a reference to a `BlobLeaseClient`. This object allows you to acquire new leases by invoking the method `Acquire()`. In this example, we created an infinite lease because we used a `TimeSpan` with the value -1. Once we have copied the blob, we need to release the lease by using the `Release()` method of the `BlobLeaseClient`.

NEED MORE REVIEW? **LEASING BLOBS AND CONTAINERS**

You can review the details of how leasing works for blobs and containers by consulting the following articles:

- **Lease Blob**   *https://docs.microsoft.com/en-us/rest/api/storageservices/lease-blob*

- **Lease Container**   *https://docs.microsoft.com/en-us/rest/api/storageservices/ lease-container*

Implement storage policies and data life cycle management

When working with data, the requirements for accessing the data change during the lifetime of the data. Data that has been recently placed on your storage system is usually accessed more frequently and requires faster access than older data. If you are using the same type of storage for all your data, that means you are using storage for rarely accessed data. If your storage is based on an SSD disk or any other technology that provides proper performance levels, this means that you can potentially be wasting expensive storage for data that is rarely accessed. A solution to this situation is to move less frequently accessed data to a cheaper storage system. The drawback of this solution is that you need to implement a system for tracking the last time data has been accessed and moving it to the right storage system.

Azure Blob Storage provides you with the ability to set different levels of access to your data. These different access levels, or tiers, provide different levels of performance when accessing the data. Each different access level has a different price. The following are the available access tiers:

- **Hot** You use this tier for data that you need to access more frequently. This is the default tier that you use when you create a new Storage Account.
- **Cool** You can use this tier for data that is less frequently accessed and is stored for at least 30 days.
- **Cold** Similar to the cool tier, you use this tier for data that is infrequently accessed or modified. Data in this tier should be stored for at least 90 days.
- **Archive** You use this tier for storing data that is rarely accessed and is stored for at least 180 days. This access tier is available only at the blob level. You cannot configure a Storage Account with this access tier.

Hot, cool, and cold tiers are online, while archive is offline. An online access tier allows the user to access the data immediately so you can read or modify the data. An offline access tier means you cannot access the data. You need to extract the data from the Archive access tier, change the blob to any online access tiers, and then perform the operation you might need on the blob.

The different access tiers have the following performance and pricing implications:

- The cool tier provides slightly lower availability than the hot tier, reflected in the service-level agreement (SLA) because of lower storage costs; however, it has higher access costs.
- The cold tier provides slightly lower availability than the cool tier.

- Hot, cool, and cold tiers have similar characteristics in terms of time-to-access and throughput.

- Archive storage is offline storage. It has the lowest storage cost rates but has higher access costs.

- The lower the storage costs, the higher the access costs.

- You can use storage tiering only on General Purpose v2 (GPv2) Storage Accounts.

- If you want to use storage tiering with a General Purpose v1 (GPv1) Storage Account, you must convert to a GPv2 Storage Account.

Moving between the different access tiers is a transparent process for the user, but it has some implications in terms of pricing. In general, when moving from a warmer tier to a cooler tier—hot to cool or hot to archive—you are charged for the write operations to the destination tier. When you move from a cooler tier to a warmer tier—from the archive to cold or from cold to hot—you are charged for the read operations from the source tier. Another essential thing to remember is how the data is moved when you change your data tier from the archive to any other access tier. Because data in the archive tier is saved in offline storage, when you move data out of the access tier, the storage service needs to move the data back to online storage. This process is known as *blob rehydration* and can take up to 15 hours.

NEED MORE REVIEW? BLOB REHYDRATION FROM ARCHIVE TIER

There are additional details when considering rehydrating your data from the archive tier, such as the rehydration priority. You can review those details by reading the Microsoft article: *https://learn.microsoft.com/en-us/azure/storage/blobs/archive-rehydrate-overview*

If you don't manually configure the access tier for a blob, it inherits the access from its container or Storage Account. Although you can manually change the access tier using the Azure portal, this process creates an administrative overload that could lead to human errors. Instead of manually monitoring the different criteria for moving a blob from one tier to another, you can implement policies that make that movement based on the criteria that you define. You use these policies for defining the life cycle management of your data. You can create these life cycle management policies by using the Azure portal, Azure PowerShell, Azure CLI, or REST API.

A life cycle management policy is a JSON document in which you define several rules that you want to apply to the different containers or blob types. Each rule consists of a filter set and an action set.

- **Filter set**   The filter set limits the actions to only a group of items that match the filter criteria.

- **Action set**   You use this set to define the actions that are performed on the items that match the filter.

The following procedure is for adding a new policy using the Azure portal:

1. Sign in to the Azure portal (*http://portal.azure.com*).

2. In the search box at the top of the Azure portal, type the name of your Storage Account and then select your account.

3. In the Data Management section, select Lifecycle Management.

4. Select the Code View tab in the Lifecycle Management blade.

5. Copy the content from Listing 2-17 and paste it into the Lifecycle Management panel.

6. Click the Save button at the top left of the panel.

LISTING 2-17 Life cycle management policy definition

```
{
    "rules": [
        {
            "enabled": true,
            "name": "rule1",
            "type": "Life cycle",
            "definition": {
                "actions": {
                    "baseBlob": {
                        "tierToCool": {
                            "daysAfterModificationGreaterThan": 30
                        },
                        "tierToArchive": {
                            "daysAfterModificationGreaterThan": 90
                        },
                        "delete": {
                            "daysAfterModificationGreaterThan": 2555
                        }
                    },
                    "snapshot": {
                        "delete": {
                            "daysAfterCreationGreaterThan": 90
                        }
                    }
                },
                "filters": {
                    "blobTypes": [
                        "blockBlob"
                    ],
                    "prefixMatch": [
                        "container-a"
                    ]
                }
            }
        }
    ]
}
```

The previous policy applies to all blobs under the container named container-a, as stated by the prefixMatch in the filters section. In the actions sections, you can see the following things:

- Blobs that are not modified in 30 days or more are moved to the cool tier.
- Blobs that are not modified in 90 days or more are moved to the archive tier.
- Blobs that are not modified in 2,555 days or more are deleted from the Storage Account.

Snapshots that are older than 90 days are also deleted. The life cycle management engine processes the policies every 24 hours. This means that it is possible that you won't see your changes reflected in your Storage Account until several hours after you make changes.

> **NEED MORE REVIEW?** **STORAGE ACCESS TIERS AND LIFE CYCLE MANAGEMENT POLICIES**
>
> You can extend your knowledge about storage access tiers and life cycle management by reviewing the following articles from Microsoft Docs:
>
> - **Azure Blob Storage: Hot, Cool, and Archive Access Tiers** *https://docs.microsoft.com/en-us/azure/storage/blobs/storage-blob-storage-tiers*
> - **Manage the Azure Blob Storage Lifecycle** *https://docs.microsoft.com/en-us/azure/storage/blobs/storage-lifecycle-management-concepts*

Apart from the automatic management of the life cycle of the blobs done by the management policies, you may also want to directly change the access tier from your code. The following example shows how to switch a blob between the different access tiers:

1. Open Visual Studio Code and create a folder for your project.
2. In the Visual Studio Code window, open a new terminal.
3. Use the following command to create a new console project:

   ```
   dotnet new console
   ```

4. Use the following command to install NuGet packages:

   ```
   dotnet add package <NuGet_package_name>
   ```

5. Install the following NuGet packages:
   - Azure.Storage.Blobs
   - Azure.Storage.Common
   - Microsoft.Extensions.Configuration
   - Microsoft.Extensions.Configuration.Binder
   - Microsoft.Extensions.Configuration.Json
6. In the project folder, create a new JSON file and name it **AppSettings.json**. Copy the content from Listing 2-18 to the JSON file.
7. Create a C# class file and name it **AppSettings.cs**.

8. Replace the contents of the AppSettings.cs file with the contents of Listing 2-19. Change the name of the namespace to match your project's name.

9. Create a C# class file and name it **Common.cs**.

10. Replace the contents of the Common.cs file with the contents of Listing 2-20.

11. Change the name of the namespace to match your project's name.

12. Replace the contents of the Program.cs file with the contents of Listing 2-21. Change the name of the namespace to match your project's name.

13. Edit your .csproj project file and add the following code inside the ItemGroup section:

```
<None Update="AppSettings.json">
    <CopyToOutputDirectory>PreserveNewest</CopyToOutputDirectory>
</None>
```

14. At this point, you can set some breakpoints in the Program.cs file to see, step by step, how the code moves the blob items between the different containers and Storage Accounts.

15. In the Visual Studio Window, press F5 to build and run your code. You can use the Azure portal or the Microsoft Azure Storage Explorer desktop application to review how your blob items change their locations.

LISTING 2-18 AppSettings.json configuration file

```
{
    "SASConnectionString": "<SASConnectionString_from_your_first_storage_account>",
    "AccountName": "<name_of_your_first_storage_account>",
    "ContainerName": "<source_container_name>"
}
```

LISTING 2-19 AppSettings.cs C# class

```
//C# .NET 6.0 LTS
using Microsoft.Extensions.Configuration;

namespace ch2_2_3
{
    public class AppSettings
    {
        public string SASConnectionString { get; set; }
        public string AccountName { get; set; }
        public string ContainerName { get; set; }

        public static AppSettings LoadAppSettings()
        {
            IConfigurationRoot configRoot = new ConfigurationBuilder()
                .AddJsonFile("AppSettings.json",false)
                .Build();
            AppSettings appSettings = configRoot.Get<AppSettings>();
            return appSettings;
        }
    }
}
```

LISTING 2-20 Common.cs C# class

```
//C# .NET 6.0 LTS
using Azure.Storage.Blobs;

namespace ch2_2_3
{
    public class Common
    {

        public static BlobServiceClient CreateBlobClientStorageFromSAS
(stringSASConnectionString)
        {
            BlobServiceClient blobClient;
            try
            {
                blobClient = new BlobServiceClient(SASConnectionString);
            }
            catch (System.Exception)
            {
                throw;
            }
            return blobClient;
        }
    }
}
```

In Listing 2-21, portions of the code that are significant to the process of working with the different access tiers are shown in bold.

LISTING 2-21 Program.cs C# class

```
//C# .NET 6.0 LTS
using System.Threading.Tasks;
using System;
using Azure.Storage.Blobs;
using Azure.Storage.Blobs.Models;
using Azure.Storage.Blobs.Specialized;

namespace ch2_2_3
{
    class Program
    {
        static void Main(string[] args)
        {
            Console.WriteLine("Moving blobs between Access Tiers");
            Task.Run(async () => await StartContainersDemo()).Wait();
        }

        public static async Task StartContainersDemo()
        {
            string BlobFileName = "Testing.zip";
            AppSettings appSettings = AppSettings.LoadAppSettings();
```

```
            //Get a cloud client for the Storage Account
            BlobServiceClient blobClient = Common.CreateBlobClientStorageFromSAS
(appSettings.SASConnectionString);

            //Get a reference for each container
            var containerReference = blobClient.GetBlobContainerClient(appSettings.
ContainerName);

            //Get a reference for the blob
            var blobReference = containerReference.GetBlobClient(BlobFileName);

            //Get current Access Tier
            BlobProperties blobProperties = await blobReference.GetPropertiesAsync();
            System.Console.WriteLine($"Access Tier: {blobProperties.AccessTier}\t" +
                    $"Inferred: {blobProperties.AccessTierInferred}\t" +
                    $"Date last Access Tier change: {blobProperties.
AccessTierChangedOn}");

            //Change Access Tier to Cool
            blobReference.SetAccessTier(AccessTier.Cool);

            //Get current Access Tier
            blobProperties = await blobReference.GetPropertiesAsync();
            System.Console.WriteLine($"Access Tier: {blobProperties.AccessTier}\t" +
                    $"Inferred: {blobProperties.AccessTierInferred}\t" +
                    $"Date last Access Tier change: {blobProperties.
AccessTierChangedOn}");

            //Change Access Tier to Archive
            blobReference.SetAccessTier(AccessTier.Archive);

            //Get current Access Tier
            blobProperties = await blobReference.GetPropertiesAsync();
            System.Console.WriteLine($"Access Tier: {blobProperties.AccessTier}\t" +
                    $"Inferred: {blobProperties.AccessTierInferred}\t" +
                    $"Date last Access Tier change: {blobProperties.
AccessTierChangedOn}");

            //Change Access Tier to Hot
            blobReference.SetAccessTier(AccessTier.Hot);

            //Get current Access Tier
            blobProperties = await blobReference.GetPropertiesAsync();
            System.Console.WriteLine($"Access Tier: {blobProperties.AccessTier}\t" +
                    $"Inferred: {blobProperties.AccessTierInferred}\t" +
                    $"Date last Access Tier change: {blobProperties.
AccessTierChangedOn}\t" +
                    $"Archive Status: {blobProperties.ArchiveStatus}" );
        }
    }
}
```

As you can see, you can change to the different access tiers by using the SetAccessTier()
method from the BlobClient object representing the blob that you are working with. You
should also use the metadata property AccessTier from the blob for getting the current access

tier where the blob is stored. You should pay special attention to the `ArchiveStatus` property. If you try to change the access tier for a blob that is being rehydrated from the archive tier, you get an exception. The `AccessTierInferred` property is also essential, as it indicates whether the current access tier is inherited from the container or is configured in the blob.

EXAM TIP

You should not try to change the access tier for a blob that is stored in an Azure Storage Account Gen1. Only Azure Storage Account Gen2 allows working with access tiers. If you try to use the `SetAccessTier()` method with a blob in an Azure Storage Account Gen1, you will get an exception.

EXAM TIP

You can move between hot, cool, and cold access tiers without waiting for rehydration. The rehydration process only happens when you move a blob from the archive to any other access tier.

Implement static site hosting

Azure Blob Storage allows you to serve static web content from your storage account. You can serve HTML, CSS, JavaScript, or image files from a special container named *$web*. These static websites have some limitations that you should consider when evaluating this solution:

- **You cannot configure HTTP headers.** If you need to customize the HTTP headers for your static website, you need to use Azure Content Delivery Network (Azure CDN).
- **All access to your site is anonymous.** There is no option to use authentication or authorization, even if you configure the *$web* container as private. If you need authentication and authorization to access your static website, you should consider using Azure Static Web Apps instead.
- **You can use a custom domain with your static website.**
- **You can use HTTPS with your custom domain and static website,** but this configuration requires additional services, like Azure Front Door or Azure CDN. This is because the Azure Storage account does not natively support HTTPS with custom domains.
- **You can use redundancy.** You can configure replication with a secondary region, and your site will be available using a secondary endpoint. The replication between regions is asynchronous, so there is no guarantee that both regions are fully synced all the time.
- **Changing the access level for the web container does not impact the static website access level.** When configuring a static website in Azure Blob Storage, the website is always accessed anonymously, even if the *$web* container is configured as Private. If you decide to change the access level of the *$web* container from Private to Public, you will make accessible not only the static website but also the files in the *$web* container.
- **You can configure the index document and the 404 error page.**

The following procedure shows how to configure a static website in an Azure Storage account. This procedure assumes that you already have created an Azure Storage account:

1. Sign in to the Azure portal (*http://portal.azure.com*).

2. In the search box at the top of the Azure portal, type the name of your Storage Account and then select your account.

3. Select the Capabilities tab in the Overview section in your Azure Storage account blade.

4. Select the Static Website option.

5. Change the Static Website switch to Enabled.

6. On the Static Website blade, in the Index Document Name box, type **index.html**.

7. Click the Save button on the top left of the Static Website blade. If the *$web* container doesn't exist on your Storage account, Azure will create it for you. Once you enable the static website feature, you will get the URL for accessing your static website, as shown in Figure 2-5.

8. Copy the URL from the Primary Endpoint text box.

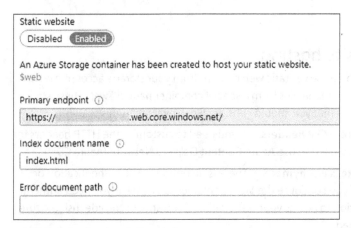

FIGURE 2-5 Configuring static websites

9. Select the storage browser in the Storage Account blade.

10. In the storage browser, navigate to the *$web* container under the Blob Containers section.

11. Create a basic index.html file on your computer and upload it to the *$web* container.

12. Open another tab in your web browser and paste the URL you copied in step 8.

13. The content should appear in your web browser. If you get a not found content error, check that the content-type tag for the index.html is text/html.

NEED MORE REVIEW? **MAPPING CUSTOM DOMAINS**

You can review how to map your custom domain to your Storage Account static website by visiting the Microsoft article *https://learn.microsoft.com/en-us/azure/storage/blobs/ storage-custom-domain-name*

EXAM TIP

Pay special attention to the limitation of using Azure Storage static websites. Even if you can access your storage account using HTTPS, you cannot directly configure HTTPS with custom domains, and you need to deploy additional Azure services, such as Front Door or CDN, to enable custom domains HTTPS.

Chapter summary

- Cosmos DB is a premium storage service that provides low-latency access to data distributed across the globe.
- The `PartitionKey` system property defines the partition where the entity is stored.
- Choosing the correct `PartitionKey` is critical for achieving the right performance level.
- You can access Cosmos DB using different APIs: NoSQL, Table, Gremlin (Graph), MongoDB, PostgreSQL, and Cassandra.
- You can create your custom indexes in Cosmos DB.
- You can choose the property that is used as the partition key.
- You should avoid selecting partition keys that create too many or too few logical partitions.
- A logical partition has a hard limit of 20 GB of storage.
- Consistency levels define how the data is replicated between the different regions in a Cosmos DB account.
- There are five consistency levels: strong, bounded staleness, session, consistent prefix, and eventual.
- The Strong consistency level provides a higher level of consistency but also has a higher latency.
- The Eventual consistency level provides lower latency and lower data consistency.
- You can move blob items between containers in the same Storage Account or containers in different Storage Accounts.
- The Azure Blob Storage service offers four access tiers with different prices for storing and accessing data.
- You can move less-frequently-accessed data to cool, cold, or archive access tiers to save money.
- You can automatically manage the movement between access tiers by implementing life cycle management policies.

Thought experiment

In this thought experiment, you can demonstrate your skills and knowledge about the topics covered in this chapter. You can find the answers to this thought experiment in the next section.

You are developing a web application that must work with information in a structure that can change during the lifetime of the development process. You need to query this information using different criteria. You need to ensure that your application returns the results of the queries as fast as possible. Your application needs to get information from an external system. The external system uploads information to an Azure Blob Storage Gen1 account.

With this information in mind, answer the following questions:

1. During the testing phases, you realize that the partition key is creating "hot spots." What should you do to solve the situation?

2. The information provided by the external system should be stored for several years due to legal reasons. Once the information is processed by your application, the information is no longer needed. What would be a secure and cost-effective solution for this scenario?

Thought experiment answers

This section contains the solutions to the thought experiment.

1. A "hot spot" appears in a Cosmos DB container when you choose a partition key that stores most of the items in the same logical partition. You can resolve the "hot spot" by changing the partition key and choosing a partition key that distributes the items evenly across the different logical partitions. Unfortunately, you cannot modify a partition key once you have created the container. In this scenario, you must create a new container with the new partition key, and then migrate all the data to the new container using the AzCopy tool.

2. Because you need to keep the data for several years, you need to use the Storage Account access tiers. Because you are using a Gen1 Storage Account, you cannot use access tiers in that Storage Account. You must upgrade your Blob Storage account to a Gen2. Once you have your Gen2 Storage Account, you can configure a life cycle management policy for automatically moving to the archive tier those files that have not been accessed for some time.

CHAPTER 3

Implement Azure security

Most applications have a standard requirement: to protect the information they manage. Regarding security, you must consider the five dimensions of information security awareness: integrity, availability, confidentiality, authorization, and non-repudiation. Each of these dimensions is useful for evaluating the different risks and countermeasures that you must implement to mitigate the associated risks.

Implementing the appropriate security mechanism on your application can be tedious and potentially error prone. Azure offers several mechanisms for adding security measures to your applications, controlling the different security aspects for accessing your data, and controlling the services that depend on your applications.

Skills covered in this chapter:

- Skill 3.1: Implement user authentication and authorization
- Skill 3.2: Implement secure cloud solutions

Skill 3.1: Implement user authentication and authorization

When a user wants to access your application, the user must prove that he or she is the person they claim to be. Authentication is the action the user performs to prove their identity. The user proves his or her identity using information known only to the user. An authentication system must address how to protect that information so only the appropriate user can access it while nobody else—not even the authorization system—can access it. A solution for this problem is to allow the user to access their data by using two different mechanisms for proving their identity—information that only the user knows and showing something (a token) that only the user has, or using a physical characteristic of the user, such as fingerprints or retina. This approach is known as *multifactor authentication*.

Azure provides a secure mechanism for integrating authentication into your applications. You can use single-factor or multifactor authentication systems without worrying about the intricate details of implementing this kind of system.

Authenticating users before they can access your application is only part of the equation. Once your users have been authenticated, you must decide whether any user can access any part of your application or if some parts of your application are restricted. The authorization controls which actions or sections the user can perform once they have been authorized.

Authenticate and authorize users by using the Microsoft Identity platform

The authentication process requires the user to provide evidence that the user is the person they claim to be. In the real world, you can find multiple examples of authentication. For example, every time you show your driver's license to a police officer, you are actually authenticating against the police officer. In the digital world, this authentication happens by providing some information that only you know, such as a secret word (a password), a digital certificate, or any token that only you possess.

You have various options for implementing such an authentication mechanism in your application. Each implementation has pros and cons, and the appropriate authentication mechanism depends on the level of security that you require for your application.

The most basic way of authenticating a user is form-based authentication. When you use this mechanism, you must program a web form that asks the user for a username and a password. Once the user submits the form, the information in the form is compared to the values stored in your storage system. This storage system can be a relational database, a NoSQL database, or even a simple file with different formats stored on a server. If the information the user provides matches the information stored in your system, the application sends a cookie to the user's browser. This cookie stores a key or some ID for authenticating subsequent requests to access your application without repeatedly asking the user for their username and password.

One of the most significant drawbacks of using form-based authentication is the authentication mechanism's dependency on cookies. Another inconvenience is that this is stateful, requiring your server to keep an authentication session for tracking the activity between the server and the client. This dependency on cookies and authentication session management makes it more difficult to scale solutions using form-based authentication. Another point to consider is that cookies don't work well (or it's challenging to work with them) on mobile apps. Fortunately, there are alternatives to form-based authentication that are more suitable for the requirements of mobile or IoT scenarios; also, there are alternatives that can improve the scalability of your web application.

The basics of token authentication

Token-based authentication is the most extended authentication mechanism for environments and scenarios that require high scalability or do not support the use of cookies. Token-based authentication consists of a signed token that your application uses for authenticating requests and granting access to the resources in your application. The token does not contain the username and password of your user. Instead, the token stores some information about the authenticated user that your server can use for granting access to your application's resources.

When you use token-based authentication, you follow a workflow similar to the one shown in Figure 3-1:

1. An unauthenticated user connects to your web application.

2. Your web application redirects the user to the login page. This login page can be provided by your web application acting as a security server or by an external security server.

3. The security server validates the information provided by the user—typically, the username and password—and generates a JSON web token (from now on JWT).

4. The security server sends the JWT to the user. The browser or mobile app the user used to connect to your application is responsible for storing this JWT for reuse in the following requests.

5. The browsers or mobile app provides the JWT to your web application on each following request.

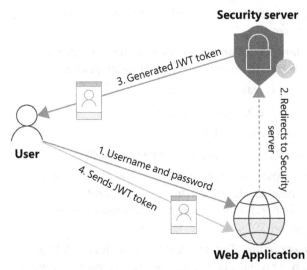

FIGURE 3-1 Basic workflow of token-based authentication

There are several token implementations, but JSON web token (JWT) is the most extended. A JWT consists of the following:

- **Header**   The header contains the name of the algorithm used for signing the token.

- **Body or Payload**   The body or payload contains different information about the token and the purpose of this token. The body contains several standard fields or claims defined in the RFC 7519 and any other custom field you might need for your application.

- **Cryptographic signature**   This is a string that validates your token and ensures that the token has not been corrupted or incorrectly manipulated.

One of the main advantages of using token-based authentication is that you can delegate the process of managing the identity of the users to external security servers. Thanks to this delegation, you can abstract from the implementation of managing and storing JWT usernames and passwords. You do that when you want to allow your users to access your application by using their Facebook, Google, or Twitter accounts. Your application trusts the identification and authentication processes made by these external security servers or identity managers, and you grant access to your application based on the information stored in the JWT provided by the security server. You still need to store some information about the user; however, there is no need to know anything about the password or any other information the user must provide to the authentication security server.

Easing the OAuth implementation

Microsoft provides the Identity platform as a group of tools that allows your applications to log in using their Microsoft identities or social accounts. The Microsoft Identity platform is compounded by the following components:

- **OAuth 2.0 and OpenID standard-compliant authentication service**   that allow your application to authenticate users using different types of identities such as:

  - Work or school accounts created in Microsoft Entra ID.

  - Personal Microsoft accounts (Skype, Xbox, Outlook.com).

  - Social or local accounts, by using Azure AD B2C

  - Social or local customer accounts by using Microsoft Entra External ID.

- **Open-source libraries**   The Microsoft Authentication Library (MSAL) is a group of open-source libraries recommended to interact with the Microsoft Identity platform. These libraries provide built-in support for the Identity platform's several features, such as conditional access, single sign-on (SSO), or built-in token caching.

- **Microsoft Identity platform endpoint**   This is the URI that provides a well-known and unified endpoint. This endpoint is OIDC-certified and ensures compatibility with the MSAL and any other standards-compliant library. The scopes are human-readable, as required by industry standards.

- **Application management portal**   This management portal is provided through the Microsoft Entra ID portal; you can register, configure, and manage your applications in this portal.

- **Application configuration API and PowerShell**   You can integrate your DevOps workflows with the Microsoft Identity platform using the PowerShell and Graph APIs to configure your application programmatically.
- **Developer content**   Microsoft provides technical documentation such as quick starts, tutorials, how-to guides, API references, and code samples to ease the learning of this platform.

Once we have a first picture of what the Microsoft Identity platform is, let's review some code for creating a simple web application that uses personal Microsoft Account identities for authenticating the users. This procedure assumes that you have a Microsoft account and an Azure subscription.

1. Open Visual Studio 2022.
2. In the Start window, click the Create A New Project button on the Get Started column on the right side of the window.
3. In the Search For Templates text box, type ***asp.net***.
4. In the Results column below the Search For Templates text box, select ASP.NET Core Web App.
5. Click the Next button on the bottom right of the window.
6. Type your project's Project and Solution name on the Configure Your New Project window.
7. Click the Next button on the bottom right of the window.
8. Select the Microsoft Identity platform option on the Authentication Type dropdown menu in the Additional Information window.
9. Click the Create button on the bottom right of the window.
10. Click Next on the Required Components window.
11. The Microsoft Identity platform shows the applications registered on your tenant. Click the Create New button on the right side of the header of the Owed applications table.
12. Type a name for your application. This name will be shown to users when they grant access to their accounts.
13. Click the Register button.
14. Click the Next button on the bottom side of the Microsoft Identity platform.
15. Click the Next button in the Additional Settings section.
16. Click the Finish button on the Summary of Changes window.
17. Once the wizard has finished, the application has been created for you on your tenant, and all the needed changes have been made to your code. Click the Close button on the bottom right of the Dependency Configuration Progress window.

At this point, if you run your application, you won't be able to log in using your personal account. This is because you are using the Microsoft Identity platform endpoint for your tenant. This is OK if your application will be available only to users in your tenant. However, if you want to make it available to other users in other tenants or to public accounts, you must use a different endpoint. The public endpoints are:

- Multi-tenant applications   *https://login.microsoftonline.com/organizations*
- Multi-tenant and personal accounts   *https://login.microsoftonline.com/common*
- Personal accounts only   *https://login.microsoftonline.com/consumers*

For our previous example to be able to use personal accounts, we need to modify the *appsettings.json* configuration file:

1. In the Visual Studio window, select the *appsettings.json* file on the Solution Explorer window.

2. In the AzureAD section, delete the Domain setting.

3. Replace the existing GUID value for the TenantID setting with the common value.

4. Save the changes to the *appsettings.json* file.

5. Press F5 to build and run your project.

6. Once the browser starts, you should be requested to log in. Use your Microsoft personal account.

7. Once you have been authenticated, the system asks you to grant permission to the application to access your basic profile. Click the Accept button.

8. Once the login process has finished, ensure that your Microsoft personal account appears at the top right of the web application.

The previous example reviewed creating a web application authenticating users from multi-tenants and personal accounts. As mentioned at the beginning of this section, one of the components of the Microsoft Identity platform is the OAuth 2.0 and OpenID standard-compliant authentication service. Now, we will review how to create your OAuth 2.0 server. The following examples will help you better understand how the OAuth 2.0 standard works. In a real-world scenario, you won't implement your own OAuth server, since the better practice is to use a trusty Identity provider such as Microsoft Entra ID, but the rest of this section shows how the exchange of different JWTs works under the hood.

Understanding the OAuth protocol

The OAuth protocol addresses the need to secure access to resources and information in your application by the third party's process. Without OAuth, if you want to grant access to an external application to your application's resources, you must use a username and password. If the third-party application is compromised, then the username and password are also compromised, and your resources are exposed. The OAuth protocol defines four different roles:

- **Resource owner**   This is the person or entity that can grant access to the resources. If the resource owner is a person, it can also be referred to as the user.

- **Resource server**   This is the server that hosts the resources that you want to share. This server must be able to accept and respond to the access codes used for accessing the resource.

- **Client** This is the third-party application that needs to access the resource. The client makes the needed requests to the resource server on behalf of the resource owner. The term "client" does not necessarily imply any specific implementation, such as a server, a desktop, or any other kind of device.

- **Authorization server** This is the server that issues the access token to the client for accessing the resources. The client must be authenticated before it can get the correct token.

Figure 3-2 shows the basic authentication flow for OAuth.

As you can see in Figure 3-2, the process of acquiring a token for accessing a protected resource consists of the following steps:

1. **Authorization request** The client requests access to the protected resource. The resource owner, based on the privileges of the client, grants access to the client for accessing the resource. The authentication of the client can be done directly by the resource owner or preferably by the authentication server.

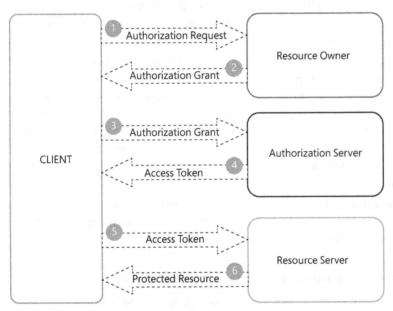

FIGURE 3-2 OAuth basic authentication flow

2. **Authentication grant** When the resource owner grants the client access to the resource, the client sends an authentication grant, which is a code or credential that represents the permission to access the resource that the resource owner has granted. The client uses this authentication grant credential to request an access token to the authorization server. There are four different mechanisms for handling this authentication:

- **Authorization code** The client instructs the resource owner to request authentication to the authentication server. Once the resource owner is authenticated, the authentication server creates an authorization code that the resource owner sends back to the client. The client uses this authorization code as the grant for requesting the access token.

- **Implicit**   Using this authentication grant flow, the authentication server does not authenticate the client. Instead, the client gets the access token without needing to authenticate to the resource server using an authentication grant. This implicit flow is a simplified authorization code flow. To improve security in this flow, the resource server uses the redirect URI provided by the client.

- **Resource owner credentials**   Instead of using an authorization code or implicit authentication, the client uses the credentials of the resource owner for authenticating against the resource server. This type of authentication grant should be used only when there is a high level of trust between the client and the resource owner.

- **Client credentials**   The client provides his or her credentials for accessing the resource. This authentication grant is useful for scenarios in which the client needs access to resources that are protected by the same authorization server as the client and are under the control of the client. This type of authentication grant is also useful if the resource server and the client arranged the same authorization for the resources and the client.

3.   **Access token**   The client requests an access token from the authorization server that allows the client to access the resource on the resource server. The client sends this access token to the resource server with each request to access the resource. This access token has an expiration date. Once the access token is expired, the token is invalid, and the client must request another access token. To ease the process of renewing the access token, the authentication server provides two different tokens: the actual access token and a refresh token. The client uses the refresh token when it needs to renew an expired access token.

4.   **Protected resource**   This is the resource that the client wants to access. The resource server protects the resource. The client must send the access token to the resource server every time it needs to access the resource.

NEED MORE REVIEW?   THE OAUTH 2.0 AUTHORIZATION FRAMEWORK

You can get more information about the details of how the OAuth 2.0 Authorization Framework works by reviewing the official RFC 6749 at *https://tools.ietf.org/html/rfc6749*.

The following example shows how to implement OAuth 2.0 authentication in your Web API application. In this example, you will create an authorization server, a resource server, and a client that can request an access token before accessing the resource. For the sake of readability, we have split the steps for implementing this example into different parts.

The following steps show how to create the authorization server:

1.   Open Visual Studio 2022.

2.   Select File > New > Project.

3.   On the Create A New Project window, on the All Languages dropdown menu, select C#.

4. In the Search For Templates text box, type **asp.net**.

5. In the result list, select ASP.NET Web Application (.NET Framework).

6. Click the Next button at the bottom right of the window.

7. In the Configure Your New Project window, type a Project Name, a Location, and a Solution Name for your project.

8. Click the Create button at the bottom right of the window.

9. Click the MVC template in the Create A New ASP.NET Web Application window.

10. Select the Individual Accounts option in the Authentication dropdown menu on the right side of the window.

11. Click the Create button on the Create A New ASP.NET Web Application window.

12. In Visual Studio, open the file at App_Start > Startup.Auth.cs, and add the following line to the beginning of the file:

```
using Microsoft.Owin.Security.OAuth;
```

13. Add the code shown in Listing 3-1 to the Startup.Auth.cs file. You need to add this code to the `ConfigureAuth()` method, after the line

```
app.UseTwoFactorRememberBrowserCookie(DefaultAuthenticationTypes.
TwoFactorRememberBrowserCookie);
```

14. Ensure that the following `using` statements exist in the Startup.Auth.cs file for avoiding compilation errors:

- `using System;`
- `using Microsoft.AspNet.Identity;`
- `using Microsoft.AspNet.Identity.Owin;`
- `using Owin;`
- `using Microsoft.Owin;`
- `using Microsoft.Owin.Security.Cookies;`
- `using Microsoft.Owin.Security.OAuth;`
- `using Microsoft.Owin.Security.Infrastructure;`
- `using AuthorizationServer.Constants;`
- `using System.Threading.Tasks;`
- `using System.Collections.Concurrent;`
- `using System.Security.Claims;`
- `using System.Security.Principal;`
- `using System.Linq;`
- `using <your_project's_name>.Models;`

LISTING 3-1 Adding OAuth Authorization Server

```
// C#. ASP.NET.
//Set up the Authorization Server
        app.UseOAuthAuthorizationServer(new OAuthAuthorizationServerOptions
        {
            AuthorizeEndpointPath = new PathString(Paths.AuthorizePath),
            TokenEndpointPath = new PathString (Paths.TokenPath),
            ApplicationCanDisplayErrors = true,
#if DEBUG
            AllowInsecureHttp = true,
#endif
            Provider = new OAuthAuthorizationServerProvider
            {
                OnValidateClientRedirectUri = ValidateClientRedirectUri,
                OnValidateClientAuthentication = ValidateClientAuthentication,
                OnGrantResourceOwnerCredentials = GrantResourceOwnerCredentials,
                OnGrantClientCredentials = GrantClientCredentials
            },

// The authorization code provider is the object in charge of creating and receiving
// the authorization code.
    AuthorizationCodeProvider = new AuthenticationTokenProvider
    {
        OnCreate = CreateAuthenticationCode,
        OnReceive = ReceiveAuthenticationCode,
    },

    // The refresh token provider is in charge in creating and receiving the
    // refresh token.
    RefreshTokenProvider = new AuthenticationTokenProvider
    {
        OnCreate = CreateRefreshToken,
        OnReceive = ReceiveRefreshToken,
    }
        });

        //Protect the resources on this server.
        app.UseOAuthBearerAuthentication(new OAuthBearerAuthenticationOptions
        {
        });
```

This code configures the OAuth Authentication Server by using the UseOAuthAuthorization-Server() method. This method accepts an OAuthAuthorizationServerOptions object for configuring several useful endpoints:

- **AuthorizeEndpointPath** The authorize endpoint is the path in the authorization server to which the client application redirects the user-agent to obtain the user or resource owner's consent to access the resource. With this consent, the client application can request an access token.

- **TokenEndpointPath** This is the path in the authorization server that the client uses to obtain an access token. If the client is configured with a client secret, the client must provide this client secret on the request for obtaining a new token.

- **AllowInsecureHttp**   This setting allows the client to make requests to the authorize and token endpoints by using HTTP URIs instead of HTTPS URIs.

- **Provider**   Your authorization server application must provide the needed delegated methods for processing the different events that arise during the OAuth authorization flow. You can do this by implementing the `OAuthAuthorizationServerProvider` interface or by using the default implementation provided by the `OAuthAuthorizationServerProvider` object. In this example, you use the `OAuthAuthorizationServerProvider` object and provide four delegate functions for the different events. Listings 3-2 to 3-5 show the different delegate methods that you use for the events managed by this provider.

- **AuthorizationCodeProvider**   When the authorization server authenticates the client, the server needs to send an authorization code to the server. This provider manages the events that arise during the management of the authentication code. Listings 3-6 and 3-7 show the delegate methods that manage the events of creating or receiving a code.

- **RefreshTokenProvider**   This object controls the events that happen when the client requests a refresh of an access token. Listings 3-8 and 3-9 show the delegate methods that control the events of creating and receiving a request of refreshing an access token.

15. Add the content from Listings 3-2 to 3-9 to the Startup.Auth.cs file. Add these methods to the Startup class. The implementation of these delegates is not suitable for production environments. For example, the validation of the client redirect URI and the authentication of the clients are based on a hard-coded value stored in the Client class. In a real-world scenario, you should have these entities stored in a database. In this example, the creation of the access token, shown in Listing 3-4, is stored in an in-memory dictionary. In a real-world scenario, you should save in a database the access tokens that you grant to the clients.

LISTING 3-2 OnValidateClientRedirectUri delegate

```
// C#. ASP.NET.
private Task ValidateClientRedirectUri(OAuthValidateClientRedirectUriContext context)
    {
        if (context.ClientId == Clients.Client1.Id)
        {
            context.Validated(Clients.Client1.RedirectUrl);
        }
        else if (context.ClientId == Clients.Client2.Id)
        {
            context.Validated(Clients.Client2.RedirectUrl);
        }
        return Task.FromResult(0);
    }
```

LISTING 3-3 OnValidateClientAuthentication delegate

```csharp
// C#. ASP.NET.
private Task
ValidateClientAuthentication(OAuthValidateClientAuthenticationContextcontext)
        {
            string clientId;
            string clientSecret;
            if (context.TryGetBasicCredentials(out clientId, out clientSecret) ||
                context.TryGetFormCredentials(out clientId, out clientSecret))
            {

                if (clientId == Clients.Client1.Id && clientSecret ==
Clients.Client1.Secret)
                {
                    context.Validated();
                }

                else if (clientId == Clients.Client2.Id && clientSecret ==
Clients.Client2.Secret)
                {
                    context.Validated();
                }
            }
            return Task.FromResult(0);
        }
```

LISTING 3-4 OnGrantResourceOwnerCredentials delegate

```csharp
// C#. ASP.NET.
private Task
GrantResourceOwnerCredentials(OAuthGrantResourceOwnerCredentialsContextcontext)
        {

            ClaimsIdentity identity = new ClaimsIdentity(new GenericIdentity(context.
UserName, OAuthDefaults.AuthenticationType), context.Scope.Select(x =>new
Claim("urn:oauth:scope", x)));

            context.Validated(identity);

            return Task.FromResult(0);
        }
```

LISTING 3-5 OnGrantClientCredentials delegate

```csharp
// C#. ASP.NET.
private Task GrantClientCredentials(OAuthGrantClientCredentialsContext context)
        {
            var identity = new ClaimsIdentity(new GenericIdentity(context.ClientId,
                OAuthDefaults.AuthenticationType), context.Scope.Select(x =>new
Claim("urn:oauth:scope", x)));
            context.Validated(identity);

            return Task.FromResult(0);
        }
```

LISTING 3-6 Authorization code for OnCreate delegate

```csharp
// C#. ASP.NET.
private void CreateAuthenticationCode(AuthenticationTokenCreateContext context)
    {
    context.SetToken(Guid.NewGuid().ToString("n") + Guid.NewGuid().
    ToString("n"));
    authenticationCodes[context.Token] = context.SerializeTicket();
 }
```

LISTING 3-7 Authorization code for OnReceive delegate

```csharp
// C#. ASP.NET.
private void ReceiveAuthenticationCode(AuthenticationTokenReceiveContext context)
   {
       string value;
       if (_authenticationCodes.TryRemove(context.Token, out value))
       {
            context.DeserializeTicket(value);
       }
    }
```

LISTING 3-8 Refresh token for OnCreate delegate

```csharp
// C#. ASP.NET.
private void CreateRefreshToken(AuthenticationTokenCreateContext context)
     {
          context.SetToken(context.SerializeTicket());
     }
```

LISTING 3-9 Refresh token for OnReceive delegate

```csharp
// C#. ASP.NET.
private void ReceiveRefreshToken(AuthenticationTokenReceiveContext context)
     {
          context.DeserializeTicket(context.Token);
     }
```

16. Add the following private property to the Startup class in the Startup.Auth.cs file:

    ```csharp
    private readonly ConcurrentDictionary<string, string> _authenticationCodes =
            new ConcurrentDictionary<string, string>(StringComparer.Ordinal);
    ```

17. In the Solution Explorer window, add a new folder to your project called Constants.

18. In the Solution Explorer window, right-click the Constants folder and select Add > New Item.

19. In the New Item window, in the tree control on the left side of the window, select Installed > Visual C# > Code.

20. Select the template named Class.

21. At the bottom of the Add New Item window, type **Clients.cs** in the Name text box.

22. Click the Add button in the bottom right of the window.

23. Replace the content of the Clients.cs file with the content in Listing 3-10. Change the namespace to match your project's name.

LISTING 3-10 Clients.cs

```csharp
// C#. ASP.NET.

namespace <YOUR_PROJECT'S_NAME>.Constants
{
    public class Clients
    {
        public readonly static Client Client1 = new Client
        {
            Id = "123456",
            Secret = "abcdef",
            RedirectUrl = Paths.AuthorizeCodeCallBackPath
        };

        public readonly static Client Client2 = new Client
        {
            Id = "78901",
            Secret = "aasdasdef",
            RedirectUrl = Paths.ImplicitGrantCallBackPath
        };
    }

    public class Client
    {
        public string Id { get; set; }
        public string Secret { get; set; }

        public string RedirectUrl { get; set; }
    }
}
```

24. In the Solution Explorer window, select your project's name and press F4.

25. In your project's properties window, ensure that the value of SSL Enabled is set to True.

26. Copy the value of the SSL URL setting.

27. Right-click the project's name and select the Properties menu item at the bottom of the contextual menu.

28. On the project's properties tab in Visual Studio, select the Web element on the left side of the window.

29. In the Servers section, paste the SSL URL value that you copied in step 28 in the Project URL text box.

30. Add a new empty C# class to the Constants folder and name it **Paths.cs**. You can repeat steps 20–24 to create a new C# class.

31. Replace the content of the file Paths.cs with the code shown in Listing 3-11.

32. Paste the value of the SSL URL that you copied in step 28 on the following constants:

   - **AuthorizationServerBaseAddress**
   - **ResourceServerBaseAddress**

- **ImplicitGrantCallBackPath**   Ensure that you don't delete the URI part. This constant should look like `<SSL URL>/Home/SignIn`.

- **AuthorizeCodeCallBackPath**   Ensure that you don't delete the URI part. This constant should look like `<SSL URL>/Manage`.

LISTING 3-11 Paths.cs

```
// C#. ASP.NET.
namespace <YOUR_PROJECT'S_NAME>.Constants
{
    public class Paths
    {
        public const string AuthorizationServerBaseAddress = "https://localhost:44317";
        public const string ResourceServerBaseAddress = "https://localhost:44317";
        public const string ImplicitGrantCallBackPath =
        "https://localhost:44317/Home/SignIn";
        public const string AuthorizeCodeCallBackPath = "https://localhost:44317/Manage";
        public const string AuthorizePath = "/OAuth/Authorize";
        public const string TokenPath = "/OAuth/Token";
        public const string LoginPath = "/Account/Login";
        public const string LogoutPath = "/Account/Logout";
        public const string MePath = "/api/Me";
    }
}
```

At this point, you need to create the API Controller that manages the requests to the Authorize and Token endpoint. When you configured the Authentication Server, you used the following code snippet for setting the endpoints that the server uses for attending OAuth requests:

```
app.UseOAuthAuthorizationServer(new OAuthAuthorizationServerOptions
        {
            AuthorizeEndpointPath = new PathString(Paths.AuthorizePath),
            TokenEndpointPath = new PathString(Paths.TokenPath),
```

If you review the value of the parameters `AuthorizePath` and `TokenPath` in your `Paths` class, you can see that their values are `/OAuth/Authorize` and `/OAuth/Token`, respectively. Now, you need to create the controller that manages the requests to these endpoints.

33. In the Solution Explorer window, right-click the Controllers folder in your project, and then choose Add > Controller.

34. In the Add Scaffold window, choose MVC 5 Controller – Empty.

35. Click the Add button.

36. In the Add Controller window, type **OAuthController**.

37. Open the OAuthController.cs file and replace the content of the file with the code shown in Listing 3-12.

LISTING 3-12 OAuthController.cs

```
// C#. ASP.NET.
using System.Security.Claims;
using System.Web;
using System.Web.Mvc;

namespace <your_project's_name>.Controllers
{
    public class OAuthController : Controller
    {

        // GET: OAuth/Authorize
        public ActionResult Authorize()
        {
            if (Response.StatusCode != 200)
            {
                return View("AuthorizeError");
            }

            var authentication = HttpContext.GetOwinContext().Authentication;
            var ticket = authentication.AuthenticateAsync("ApplicationCookie").Result;
            var identity = ticket != null ? ticket.Identity : null;
            if (identity == null)
            {
                authentication.Challenge("ApplicationCookie");
                return new HttpUnauthorizedResult();
            }

            var scopes = (Request.QueryString.Get("scope") ?? "").Split(' ');
            if (Request.HttpMethod == "POST")
            {
                if (!string.IsNullOrEmpty(Request.Form.Get("submit.Grant")))
                {

                    identity = new ClaimsIdentity(identity.Claims, "Bearer", identity.
                    NameClaimType, identity.RoleClaimType);
                    foreach (var scope in scopes)
                    {
                        identity.AddClaim(new Claim("urn:oauth:scope", scope));
                    }
                    authentication.SignIn(identity);
                }
                if (!string.IsNullOrEmpty(Request.Form.Get("submit.Login")))
                {
                    authentication.SignOut("ApplicationCookie");
                    authentication.Challenge("ApplicationCookie");
                    return new HttpUnauthorizedResult();
                }
            }

            return View();
        }
    }
}
```

38. In the Solution Explorer, right-click Views > OAuth, and then select Add > View.

39. In the Add View window, in the View Name field, type **Authorize**.

40. Click the Add button.

41. Replace the content of the file Authorize.cshtml with the code shown in Listing 3-13:

LISTING 3-13 Authorize.cshtml

```
// C#. ASP.NET.
@{
    ViewBag.Title = "Authorize";
}


@using System.Security.Claims
@using System.Web
@{
    var authentication = Context.GetOwinContext().Authentication;
    var ticket = authentication.AuthenticateAsync("ApplicationCookie").Result;
    var identity = ticket != null ? ticket.Identity : null;
    var scopes = (Request.QueryString.Get("scope") ?? "").Split(' ');
}
<!DOCTYPE html>
<html xmlns="http://www.w3.org/1999/xhtml">
<head>
    <title>@ViewBag.Title</title>
</head>
<body>
    <h1>Authorization Server</h1>
    <h2>OAuth2 Authorize</h2>
    <form method="POST">
        <p>Hello, @identity.Name</p>
        <p>A third party application wants to do the following on your behalf:</p>
        <ul>
            @foreach (var scope in scopes)
            {
                <li>@scope</li>
            }
        </ul>
        <p>
            <input type="submit" name="submit.Grant" value="Grant" />
            <input type="submit" name="submit.Login" value="Sign in as different user" />
        </p>
    </form>
</body>
</html>
```

42. Add another empty view named **AuthorizeError**.

43. Replace the content of the file AuthorizeError.cshtml with the code shown in Listing 3-14:

LISTING 3-14 AuthorizeError.cshtml

```
// C#. ASP.NET.
@{
    ViewBag.Title = "AuthorizeError";
}
@using System
@using System.Security.Claims
@using System.Web
@using Microsoft.Owin
@{
    IOwinContext owinContext = Context.GetOwinContext();
    var error = owinContext.Get<string>("oauth.Error");
    var errorDescription = owinContext.Get<string>("oauth.ErrorDescription");
    var errorUri = owinContext.Get<string>("oauth.ErrorUri");
}
<!DOCTYPE html>
<html xmlns="http://www.w3.org/1999/xhtml">
<head>
    <title>@ViewBag.Title</title>
</head>
<body>
    <h1>Katana.Sandbox.WebServer</h1>
    <h2>OAuth2 Authorize Error</h2>
    <p>Error: @error</p>
    <p>@errorDescription</p>
</body>
</html>
```

This example only provides an implementation for the Authorize endpoint for the sake of simplicity. An authorized user in your application must grant access to the resources in your application explicitly. When the user grants those privileges, the application automatically creates an in-memory OAuth token that you can use to make a request to the protected resources. In a real-world scenario, this process should be separated in the two different endpoints: Authorize and Token. You should use the Token endpoint for creating or refreshing the access token issued by the authorization server.

Now that you have created and configured your authorization server, you can create the resource server. In this example, you will create the resource server on the same application where you implemented the authorization server. In a real-world scenario, you can use the same application, or you can use a different application deployed by a different server or Azure App Service.

1.   In the Solution Explorer window, right-click the Controllers folder in your project and select Add > Controller.

2.   In the Add New Scaffolded Item window, select the Web API 2 Controller — Empty template.

3.   Click the Add button.

4.   In the Add Controller window, type **MeController** and click the Add button.

5.   Replace the content of the MeController.cs file with the code shown in Listing 3-15. This controller is quite simple and only returns the information stored in the token that you provide to the resource server when you try to access the resource.

LISTING 3-15 MeController.cs

```csharp
// C#. ASP.NET.
using System.Collections.Generic;
using System.Linq;
using System.Security.Claims;
using System.Web.Http;

namespace <your_project's_name>.Controllers
{
    [Authorize]
    public class MeController : ApiController
    {
        // GET api/<controller>
        public IEnumerable<object> Get()
        {
            var identity = User.Identity as ClaimsIdentity;
            return identity.Claims.Select(c => new
            {
                Type = c.Type,
                Value = c.Value
            });
        }
    }
}
```

6. In the Solution Explorer window, in the App_Start folder, rename the file WebApiConfig.cs to **Startup.WebApi.cs**.

7. In the Visual Studio window, select Tools > NuGet Package Manager > Manage NuGet Packages For Solution.

8. On the NuGet Package Manager tab, click Browse.

9. Type **Microsoft asp.net web api owin** and press Enter.

10. Select the Microsoft.AspNet.WebApi.Owin package.

11. On the right side of the NuGet Manager tab, select the checkbox beside your project.

12. Click the Install button.

13. On the Preview Changes window, click OK.

14. On the License Acceptance, click the I Accept button.

15. Open the Startup.WebApi.cs file and change the content of the file with the content shown in Listing 3-16.

LISTING 3-16 Startup.WebApi.cs

```csharp
// C#. ASP.NET.
using Microsoft.Owin.Security.OAuth;
using Owin;
using System.Web.Http;

namespace <your_project's_name>
{
    public partial class Startup
    {
```

```
        public void ConfigureWebApi(IAppBuilder app)
        {
            var config = new HttpConfiguration();
            // Web API configuration and services
            // Configure Web API to use only bearer token authentication.
            config.SuppressDefaultHostAuthentication();
            config.Filters.Add(new HostAuthenticationFilter(OAuthDefaults.
AuthenticationType));

            // Web API routes
            config.MapHttpAttributeRoutes();

            config.Routes.MapHttpRoute(
                name: "DefaultApi",
                routeTemplate: "api/{controller}/{id}",
                defaults: new { id = RouteParameter.Optional }
            );

            app.UseWebApi(config);
        }
    }
}
```

16. Open the Startup.cs file and add the following line at the end of the `Configuration()` method:

```
ConfigureWebApi(app);
```

Once you have implemented the resource server in your application, you should be able to make requests to the authorization server to get access to the resource published by the resource server. As you saw in the OAuth workflow, you must get authenticated by the authorization server before you can get an access token. This means that you must be logged in to the application before you can make any requests to the /OAuth/Authorize endpoint.

Now you can create your client application that makes requests to the authorization server and resource server. That client application can be the same application that you used for implementing the authorization and resource servers. You will now modify the default MVC template for making requests to the Authorization and Resource servers.

1. In the Visual Studio window, select Tools > NuGet Package Manager > Manage NuGet Packages For Solution.

2. In the NuGet Package Manager tab, click Browse.

3. Type **DotNetOpenAuth.OAuth2.Client** and press Enter.

4. Select the DotNetOpenAuth.OAuth2.Client package. This NuGet package eases the interaction with OAuth servers.

5. On the right side of the NuGet Manager tab, select the checkbox beside your project.

6. Click the Install button.

7. In the Preview Changes window, click OK.

8. Open the ManageController.cs file.

9. Add the following `using` statements to the ManageController.cs file:

- **using System;**
- **using System.Linq;**
- **using System.Threading.Tasks;**
- **using System.Web;**
- **using System.Web.Mvc;**
- **using Microsoft.AspNet.Identity;**
- **using Microsoft.AspNet.Identity.Owin;**
- **using Microsoft.Owin.Security;**
- **using AuthorizationServer.Models;**
- **using AuthorizationServer.Constants;**
- **using DotNetOpenAuth.OAuth2;**
- **using System.Net.Http;**

10. Replace the `Index()` method with the code shown in Listing 3-17.

LISTING 3-17 Index method in ManageController.cs

```
// C#. ASP.NET.
public async Task<ActionResult> Index(ManageMessageId? message)
        {
            ViewBag.StatusMessage =
            message == ManageMessageId.ChangePasswordSuccess ? "Your password has been
changed."
            : message == ManageMessageId.SetPasswordSuccess ? "Your password has been set."
            : message == ManageMessageId.SetTwoFactorSuccess ? "Your two-factor
authentication provider has been set."
            : message == ManageMessageId.Error ? "An error has occurred."
            : message == ManageMessageId.AddPhoneSuccess ? "Your phone number was added."
            : message == ManageMessageId.RemovePhoneSuccess ? "Your phone number was
removed."
            : "";

            var userId = User.Identity.GetUserId();
            var model = new IndexViewModel
            {
                HasPassword = HasPassword(),
                PhoneNumber = await UserManager.GetPhoneNumberAsync(userId),
                TwoFactor = await UserManager.GetTwoFactorEnabledAsync(userId),
                Logins = await UserManager.GetLoginsAsync(userId),
                BrowserRemembered = await AuthenticationManager.
                                    TwoFactorBrowserRememberedAsync(userId)
            };

            ViewBag.AccessToken = Request.Form["AccessToken"] ?? "";
            ViewBag.RefreshToken = Request.Form["RefreshToken"] ?? "";
            ViewBag.Action = "";
            ViewBag.ApiResponse = "";
```

```
        InitializeWebServerClient();
        var accessToken = Request.Form["AccessToken"];
        if (string.IsNullOrEmpty(accessToken))
        {

            var authorizationState =
_webServerClient.ProcessUserAuthorization(Request);
            if (authorizationState != null)
            {
                ViewBag.AccessToken = authorizationState.AccessToken;
                ViewBag.RefreshToken = authorizationState.RefreshToken;
                ViewBag.Action = Request.Path;
            }
        }

        if (!string.IsNullOrEmpty(Request.Form.Get("submit.Authorize")))
        {

            var userAuthorization =
_webServerClient.PrepareRequestUserAuthorization(
        new[] { "bio", "notes" });
            userAuthorization.Send(HttpContext);
            Response.End();
        }
        else if (!string.IsNullOrEmpty(Request.Form.Get("submit.Refresh")))
        {
            var state = new AuthorizationState
            {
                AccessToken = Request.Form["AccessToken"],
                RefreshToken = Request.Form["RefreshToken"]
            };
            if (_webServerClient.RefreshAuthorization(state))
            {
                ViewBag.AccessToken = state.AccessToken;
                ViewBag.RefreshToken = state.RefreshToken;
            }
        }
        else if (!string.IsNullOrEmpty(Request.Form.Get("submit.CallApi")))
        {
            var resourceServerUri = new Uri(Paths.ResourceServerBaseAddress);
            var client = new HttpClient(_webServerClient.CreateAuthorizingHandler
(accessToken));
            var body = client.GetStringAsync(new Uri(resourceServerUri,
Paths.MePath)).Result;
            ViewBag.ApiResponse = body;
        }

        return View(model);
    }
```

11. Add the following property to the ManageController class:

```
private WebServerClient _webServerClient;
```

12. Add the following helper method to the `ManageController` class:

```csharp
private void InitializeWebServerClient()
{
    var authorizationServerUri = new Uri(Paths.AuthorizationServerBaseAddress);
    var authorizationServer = new AuthorizationServerDescription
    {

        AuthorizationEndpoint = new Uri(authorizationServerUri, Paths.AuthorizePath),
        TokenEndpoint = new Uri(authorizationServerUri, Paths.TokenPath)
    };

    _webServerClient = new WebServerClient(authorizationServer, Clients.Client1.Id,
    Clients.Client1.Secret);
}
```

13. In the `Application_Start()` method in the Global.asax.cs file, add the following line:

```csharp
AntiForgeryConfig.SuppressXFrameOptionsHeader = true;
```

14. Add the following `using` statement to the Global.asax.cs file:

```csharp
using System.Web.Helpers;
```

15. In the Solution Explorer window, select Views > Manage > Index.cshtml.

16. Add the code shown in Listing 3-18 after the section Two-Factor Authentication in the Index.cshtml file.

LISTING 3-18 Authorization Code Grant section

```
// C#. ASP.NET.
<dt>Authorization Code Grant Client:</dt>
        <dd>
            <form id="form1" action="@ViewBag.Action" method="POST">
                <div>
                    Access Token<br />
                    <input id="AccessToken" name="AccessToken" width="604" type="text"
value="@ViewBag.AccessToken" />

                    <input id="Authorize" name="submit.Authorize" value="Authorize"
                    type="submit" />
                    <br />
                    <br />
                    Refresh Token<br />
                    <input id="RefreshToken" name="RefreshToken" width="604"
                    type="text" value="@ViewBag.RefreshToken" />
                    <input id="Refresh" name="submit.Refresh" value="Refresh"
                    type="submit" />
                    <br />
                    <br />
                    <input id="CallApi" name="submit.CallApi" value="Access Protected
                    Resource API" type="submit" />
                </div>
                <div>
                    @ViewBag.ApiResponse
                </div>
            </form>
        </dd>
```

At this point, your example application is ready for testing the implementation of the different actors that take part in the OAuth workflow. The following steps show how to test your OAuth implementation to ensure that it works correctly:

1. Open the example project in Visual Studio and press F5 to run the project.

2. A new web browser window should open with your web application. Click the Register link located at the top left of the page.

3. On the Register page, add an email address and password and confirm the password. Then click the Register button. You will use this user to grant privileges to the OAuth client for making requests to the /OAuth/Me endpoint.

4. Once you have registered the new user, you are automatically logged in and redirected to the Home page.

5. On the Home page, click your user's email link at the top left of the Home page.

6. On the Manage page, click the Authorize button, which redirects you to the Authorization Server page.

7. On the Authorization Server page, review the information provided and click the Grant button. After you grant access to the OAuth client application, you get the access and refresh token shown in Figure 3-3, which is needed to make requests to the resource server.

8. Click the Access Protected Resource API button to make a request to the /OAuth/Me endpoint. You should get all information stored in the identity claim that you use for making this request, including the scopes bio and notes.

FIGURE 3-3 OAuth Access and Refresh Token

NEED MORE REVIEW? **OAUTH AUTHORIZATION SERVER**

In this example, you reviewed how to implement the authorization and resource server, the client, and the resource owner on the same web application. Although this is a valid scenario, these roles are usually implemented in a separate application. The code we reviewed is based on the example explained in the Microsoft Docs article at *https://docs.microsoft.com/en-us/aspnet/aspnet/overview/owin-and-katana/owin-oauth-20-authorization-server*. In that article, you can review how to implement each role in separate applications.

Authenticate and authorize users and apps by using Microsoft Entra ID

In the previous section, we provided a basic introduction to what the Microsoft Identity platform is and how to authenticate your users using public accounts. In this section, we delve deep into the process of authentication and authorization when using Microsoft Entra ID, part of the Microsoft Identity platform. Before going further, let's define what authentication and authorization are:

- **Authentication** is the process of the user proving that a person, a process, or a program is who/what it claims to be. The Microsoft Identity platform uses the OpenID Connect (OIDC) protocol for this operation.

- **Authorization** is the act of granting a party permission to do something. A party can be a person, a process, or another application. The important thing is that the party must be authenticated before the authorization happens. The Microsoft Identity platform uses the OAuth 2.0 protocol for managing authorization.

> **NOTE OIDC VS OAUTH2**
>
> You might notice in the previous section that we referred to OAuth2 authentication instead of OIDC. The reason is that OIDC is built on top of OAuth2.0 and shares most of its components. In the previous section, we decided to use OAuth2 authentication for the sake of simplicity, but from now on we will use the correct terms, OIDC authentication and OAuth2 authorization.

The "Authenticate and authorize users by using the Microsoft Identity platform" section earlier in this chapter reviewed how to use OIDC authentication with a basic web application. When we reviewed the OIDC concepts in that section, you saw that in the OIDC authentication flow, a security server provides the security mechanisms for authenticating the users. Once the security server authenticates, the server emits a token that your application can validate and use for authenticating the request from your application's client. When working with the security server, you can use your own implementation of an OIDC server, or you can rely on third-party security services, such as Facebook, Google, or LinkedIn, among others.

Microsoft also provides the ability to use its services for OIDC authentication. Microsoft provides OIDC authentication through its Microsoft Entra ID identity service, formerly the Azure Active Directory. On its most basic layer, this is a free service that you can use if you want your application's users to be able to log in using Microsoft Outlook.com accounts for personal accounts or Microsoft Entra ID accounts for professional accounts.

Before your application can use the Microsoft Entra ID service to authenticate your users, you need to register the application in your Microsoft Entra ID tenant. When registering your application, there are some points you must consider before proceeding to the registration:

- **Supported account types**   You need to consider whether the users of your application would be
  - **Users from your organization only**   Any person that has a user account in your Microsoft Entra ID tenant would be able to use your application.
  - **Users from any organization**   Use this option when you want any user with a professional or educational Microsoft Entra ID account to be able to log in to your application.
  - **Users from any organization or Microsoft accounts**   Use this option if you want your users to log in to your application by using professional, educational, or any of the freely available Microsoft accounts.
- **Platform**   The OIDC authentication is not limited to web applications. You can also use this type of authentication with mobile platforms, such as iOS or Android, or desktop platforms, such as macOS, Console, IoT, Windows, or UWP.

The following procedure shows how to register a web application in Microsoft Entra ID:

1. Open the Azure portal (*https://portal.azure.com*),
2. In the Search Resources, Services, and Docs text box at the middle-top of the Azure portal, type **Microsoft Entra ID**.
3. In the result list, in the Services section, select Microsoft Entra ID.
4. On the Microsoft Entra ID page, in the Manage section, select App Registrations.
5. In the App Registrations blade, click the New Registration button at the top left of the panel.
6. In the Register An Application blade, type the name of your application in the Name text box.
7. In the Supported Account Types option control, select Accounts In This Organizational Directory Only.
8. Click the Register button at the bottom left of the blade.

The previous procedure shows how to make a simple app registration. Now you need to configure your app registration according to your app needs. One of the most critical sets of settings that you need to configure correctly are the Authentication settings, shown in Figure 3-4. You use the Authentication settings for managing the authentication options for your application. In this case, you configure the redirect URLs used by Microsoft Entra ID for authenticating your application's requests. If the redirect URL provided by your application doesn't match any of the URLs configured in this section, the authentication fails.

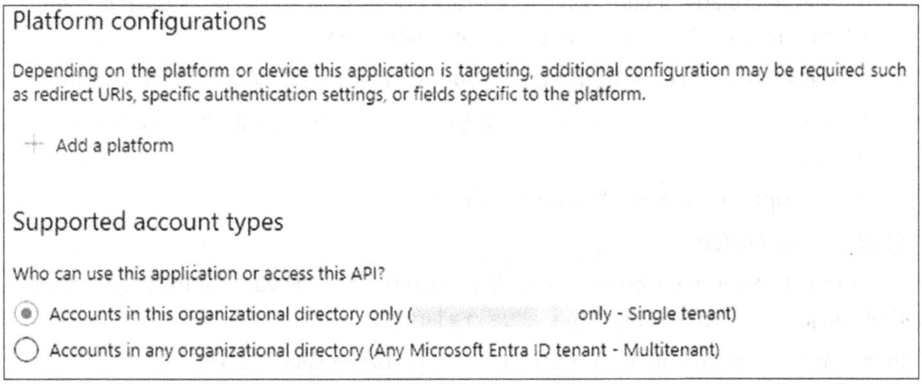

FIGURE 3-4 Authentication settings

The other two critical sets of settings that you need to consider are Certificates & Secrets and API Permissions. Certificates & Secrets enables you to manage the certificates and secrets that your application needs to use to provide the application's identity when requesting a token. You use the API Permissions for configuring the needed permission for calling other APIs, either from Microsoft, your organization, or other third-party APIs.

The following example shows how to create a simple web application that uses Microsoft Entra ID authentication. Although you could register the app for this example directly from the wizard in Visual Studio 2022, we prefer to show you how to make an app registration directly from the Azure portal. In this example, you will use the app that you registered in the previous procedure. If you didn't follow that procedure, you should review and follow it before proceeding with the following example:

1. Open Visual Studio 2022.

2. On the Start Window, click the Create A New Project button on the Get Started column on the right side of the window.

3. In the Search For Templates text box, type *asp.net*.

4. In the results column below the Search For Templates text box, select ASP.NET Core Web App.

5. Click the Next button on the bottom right of the window.

6. Type your project's Project and Solution name on the Configure Your New Project window.

7. Click the Next button on the bottom right of the window.

8. Select the None option on the Authentication type dropdown menu in the Additional Information window.

9. Click the Create button on the bottom right of the window.

10. Open the Azure portal (*https://portal.azure.com*) and navigate to the app that you registered in the previous example.

11. In the Overview blade of your app in the Azure portal, copy the value of the parameter Application (client) ID. You need this value for a later step.

12. In the Manage section on the left side of your App blade, select Certificates & Secrets.

13. On the Certificates & Secrets blade, click the New Client Secret button in the Client Secrets tab.

14. Type a description in the text box for this client secret.

15. Click the Add button.

16. In the Client Secrets area, on the list of client secrets, copy the value of the client secret that you just created. You need this value in a later step.

17. In the Manage section on the left side of your App blade, click Owners.

18. Click the Add Owners button on the top left of the Owners blade.

19. Type the name of your user in the Search text box.

20. Select the checkbox beside the correct user.

21. Click the Select button.

> **NOTE   APPLICATION OWNER**
>
> Adding an application owner is not required to configure your application's Microsoft Entra ID authentication, but it eases the process. If you don't configure the owner, you won't be able to see your application on the list of owned applications while configuring your project in Visual Studio.

22. In the Solution Explorer window in Visual Studio 2022, right-click the Connected Services node.

23. Select Add Connected Service in the contextual menu.

24. In the Connected Services windows, select the Microsoft Identity platform option.

25. In the Required Components windows, review the information and click the Next button on the bottom right of the window.

26. Ensure that you are logged in to your tenant in the Microsoft Identity platform window. You should be able to see the account you are using for connecting to your tenant in the top right of the window.

27. In the Microsoft Identity platform window, in the Tenants dropdown menu, select your tenant's name. You can find this information in the Azure portal, on the Overview blade of your Microsoft Entra ID tenant.

28. Select your application on the Owned Applications table in the Microsoft Identity platform window.

29. Click the Finish button.

30. On the Configuration Settings area, select Use Settings From An Existing Azure AD Application To Configure Your Project.

31. In the Client ID text box, paste the value that you copied in step 13.

32. Leave Redirect URI blank.

33. Click the Next button at the bottom right of the window.

34. In the Directory Access section, check the Read Directory Data option.

35. In the Client Secret text box, copy and paste the client secret that you created in step 18.

36. Click the Finish button.

37. In your Visual Studio 2023 window, press F5 to run your project.

Once you execute the web application, a generic Microsoft login page should appear in your browser. You must provide a valid user account from your tenant to log in. At this point, your application uses the Microsoft Entra ID for authenticating users. Additionally, you can also read information from your tenant.

When you add the Microsoft Identity platform connected service, the wizard makes some changes to your code and your application that you should understand. The wizard adds some properties to the AzureAd section in the *appsettings.json* file. These properties represent relevant settings needed for connecting to your Microsoft Entra ID tenant:

- **ClientId**   This is the ID representing your registered application in your Microsoft Entra ID tenant.

- **Instance**   Provides the instance that you will use for authentication. In most situations, you use general public instances. You only need to change this value if your tenant is hosted in isolated instances such as Government, China, or Germany.

- **Domain**   This is your Microsoft Entra ID tenant, where you registered your app.

- **TenantId**   This is the ID representing the tenant where you registered your app.

- **CallbackPath**   This is the URL where Microsoft redirects the user once the authentication process finishes successfully. This value must match the value configured in your app registration in the Azure portal.

- **ClientSecret**   The client secret is similar to the password that your application uses for authenticating against the Microsoft Entra ID service before it can interact with the APIs protected by the identity service.

In addition to the changes made to your code, the wizard automatically registers the callback path as redirect URIs on the Authentication section of your registered application on Microsoft Entra ID.

As with any other authorization system in C#, you must add the [Authorized] attribute to any resource you want to protect. In this case, the wizard adds this attribute to any existing controller in your application. Finally, the most critical piece of code is the one used for configuring the OIDC authentication and OAuth2 authorization. Listing 3-19 shows the code snippet added to your Program.cs file for connecting your application with Microsoft Entra ID.

LISTING 3-19 Program.cs extension

```
// C#. ASP.NET.
builder.Services.AddAuthentication(OpenIdConnectDefaults.AuthenticationScheme)
    .AddMicrosoftIdentityWebApp(builder.Configuration.GetSection("AzureAd"));

builder.Services.AddAuthorization(options =>
{
    options.FallbackPolicy = options.DefaultPolicy;
});

// Add services to the container.
builder.Services.AddRazorPages()
    .AddMicrosoftIdentityUI();
```

The AddAuthentication extension method adds the OIDC authentication middleware to your application using the settings configured in the AzureAd section in the *appsettings.json* file. The AddAuthorization extension method adds the OAuth2 authorization middleware. When you configure authentication and authorization, all requests to your application are inspected to ensure that an authenticated user makes the request and has sufficient permissions to access the resource.

EXAM TIP

When registering a new application in your Microsoft Entra ID tenant, you must consider which will be your target user. If you need any user from any Microsoft Entra ID organization to be able to log in to your application, you need to configure a multi-tenant app. In those multi-tenant scenarios, the app registration and management are always performed in your tenant and not in any other external tenant.

Create and implement shared access signatures

Until now, all the protection and access control mechanisms reviewed in this section concerned protecting the information managed directly by your application. These mechanisms are good if your application manages and presents the information to the user. However, they are only appropriate for some services that can also store information managed by your application. If your application uses Azure Storage accounts for storing some reports, images, or documents in a table, and you want to grant third parties access to that information, none of the previously reviewed mechanisms are appropriate for that scenario.

When working with storage, you must control who and how much time a process, person, or application can access your data. Azure Storage allows you to control this access based on several levels of protection:

- **Shared Key Authorization** You use one of the two access keys configured at the Azure Storage account level to construct the correct request for accessing the Azure Storage account resources. You need to use the Authorization Header to use the access key in your request. The access key provides access to the entire Azure Storage account and all its containers, such as blobs, files, queues, and tables. You can consider Azure Storage account keys to be like the root password of the Azure Storage account.

- **Shared Access Signatures** You use Shared Access Signatures (SAS) to narrow the access to specific containers inside the Storage Account. The advantage of using SAS is that you don't need to share the Azure Storage account's access key. You can also configure a higher level of granularity when setting access to your data.

The drawback of using shared access keys is that if either of the two access keys is exposed, the Azure Storage account and all the containers and data in the Azure Storage account are also exposed. The access keys also allow you to create or delete elements in the Azure Storage account.

Shared access signatures provide you with a mechanism for sharing access with clients or applications to your Azure Storage account without exposing the entire account. You can configure each SAS with a different level of access to each of the following:

- **Services** You can configure SAS for granting access only to the services that you require, such as blob, file, queue, or table.

- **Resource types** You can configure access to a service, container, or object. For the Blob service, this means that you can configure the access to API calls at the service level, such as list containers. If you configure the SAS token at the container level, you can make API calls like getting or setting container metadata or creating new blobs. If you decide to configure the access at the object level, you can make API calls such as creating or updating blobs in the container.

- **Permissions** Configure the action or actions that the user is allowed to perform in the configured resources and services.

- **Date expiration** You can configure the period for which the configured SAS is valid for accessing the data.

- **IP addresses** You can configure a single IP address or a range of IP addresses allowed to access your storage.

- **Protocols** You can configure whether the access to your storage is performed using HTTPS only or HTTP and HTTPS protocols. You cannot grant access to the HTTP-only protocol.

Azure Storage uses the values of previous parameters for constructing the signature that grants access to your storage. You can configure three different types of SAS:

- **User delegation SAS**   This type of SAS applies only to Blob Storage. You use a Microsoft Entra ID user account to secure the SAS token.

- **Account SAS**   Account SAS controls access to the entire Storage Account. You can also control access to operations at the service level, such as getting service stats or getting or setting service properties. You must use the storage account key to secure this kind of SAS.

- **Service SAS**   Service SAS delegates access to only specific services inside the Storage Account. You must use the storage account key to secure this kind of SAS.

You must construct an SAS token for access regardless of the SAS type. You append this SAS token to the URL you use to access your storage resource. One of the parameters of an SAS token is the signature. The Azure Storage Account service uses this signature to authorize access to the storage resources. How you create this signature depends on the SAS type you are using.

For user delegation SAS, you need to use a user delegation key created using Microsoft Entra ID credentials. The user creating this delegation key must be granted the `Microsoft.Storage/storageAccounts/blobServices/generateUserDelegationKey/action` Role-Base Access Control permission.

For service or account SAS, you must use the Azure Storage Account key to create the signature you must include in the SAS token. For constructing the SAS URI for an Account SAS, you must use the parameters shown in Table 3-1.

TABLE 3-1 Account SAS URI parameters

Parameter Name	URI Parameter	Required	Description
api-version	api-version	NO	You can set the version of the storage service API that processes your request.
SignedVersion	sv	YES	Sets the version of the signed storage service used to authenticate your request. This version should be 2015-04-05 or later.
SignedServices	ss	YES	Sets the services to which you grant access. You can grant access to more than one service by combining the allowed values: ■ **Blob** You need to use the value (b) in the SAS URI. ■ **Queue** You need to use the value (q) in the SAS URI. ■ **Table** You need to use the value (t) in the SAS URI. ■ **File** You need to use the value (f) in the SAS URI.

Parameter Name	URI Parameter	Required	Description
Signed-ResourceTypes	Srt	YES	Sets the resource type to which you grant access. You can configure more than one resource type simultaneously by combining more than one of the allowed values: ■ **Service** You need to use the value (s) in the SAS URI. ■ **Container** You need to use the value (c) in the SAS URI. ■ **Object** You need to use the value (o) in the SAS URI.
SignedPermission	sp	YES	Configures the permissions that you grant to the resource types and services configured on previous parameters. Not all permissions apply to all resource types and services. The following list shows only the permissions that apply to the Blob service: ■ **Read** You need to use the value (r) in the SAS URI. ■ **Write** You need to use the value (w) in the SAS URI. ■ **Delete** You need to use the value (d) in the SAS URI. ■ **List** You need to use the value (l) in the SAS URI. ■ **Add** You need to use the value (a) in the SAS URI. ■ **Create** You need to use the value (c) in the SAS URI. If you set a permission that is meaningful only for a service or resource type that you didn't set on the previous parameters, the permission is silently ignored.
SignedStart	st	NO	Sets the time and date at which the SAS token is valid. It must be expressed in UTC using ISO 8601 format: ■ YYYY-MM-DD ■ YYYY-MM-DDThh:mmTZD ■ YYYY-MM-DDThh:mm:ssTZD
SignedExpiry	se	YES	Sets the time and date in which the SAS token becomes invalid. It must be expressed in UTC using ISO 8601 format.
SignedIP	sip	NO	Sets the IP or range of IP addresses from which the storage service accepts requests. When using ranges of IPs, the limits are included in the range.
SignedProtocol	spr	NO	Sets the protocol allowed to request the API. Correct values are ■ HTTPS only (https) ■ HTTP and HTTPS (https, http)
Signature	sig	YES	This is an HMAC-SHA256–computed string encoded using Base64 that the API uses for authenticating your request. You calculate the signature based on the parameters that you provided in the SAS URI. This signature must be valid to process your request.

Use the following procedure for constructing and testing your own account SAS token:

1. Sign in to the Azure management portal (*http://portal.azure.com*).

2. In the search box at the top of the Azure portal, type the name of your Storage Account.

3. On the Storage Account blade, select Shared Access Signature in the Security + Networking section.

4. In the Shared Access Signature panel, deselect the File, Table, and Queue checkboxes under Allowed Services, as shown in Figure 3-5. Leave the Blob checkbox selected.

5. Ensure that all options in Allowed Resource Types and Allowed Permissions are checked, as shown in Figure 3-5.

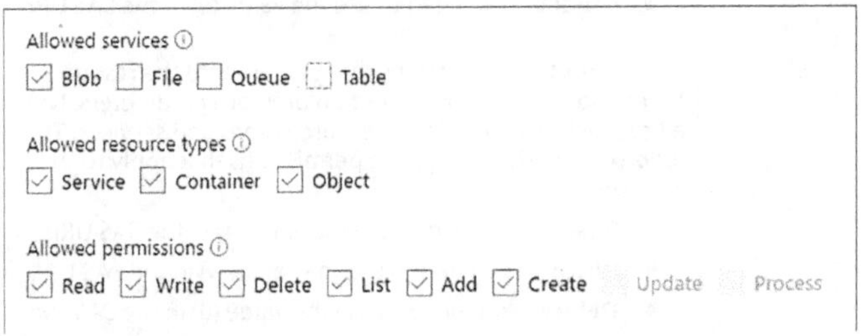

Allowed services ⓘ
☑ Blob ☐ File ☐ Queue ☐ Table

Allowed resource types ⓘ
☑ Service ☑ Container ☑ Object

Allowed permissions ⓘ
☑ Read ☑ Write ☑ Delete ☑ List ☑ Add ☑ Create ☐ Update ☐ Process

FIGURE 3-5 Configuring the Account SAS policy

6. In the Start And Expiry Date/Time section, set a date for a start and ending date and time during which the Azure Storage Account accepts requests using this token.

7. Ensure that Allowed IP addresses have no value in the text box, and HTTPS Only is selected in the Allowed Protocols section.

8. In the Signing Key dropdown menu, make sure that you have selected the Key1 value.

9. Click the Generate SAS And Connection String button at the bottom of the panel.

10. Copy the Blob Service SAS URL. Now you can test your SAS token, using a tool such as Postman, curl, a web browser, or Microsoft Azure Storage Explorer.

11. Open Microsoft Azure Storage Explorer. If you don't have this tool installed, you can download it from *https://azure.microsoft.com/en-us/features/storage-explorer/*.

12. In the Microsoft Azure Storage Explorer window, on the left side of the window, click the button with a plug icon. This button opens the Connect dialog box.

13. Select the Use A Shared Access Signature (SAS) URI option in the Connect dialog box.

14. Click the Next button on the bottom side of the dialog box.

15. In the Attach With SAS URI, type a name for your connection in the Display Name text box.

16. In the URI text box, paste the URL you copied in step 10.

17. Click the Next button.

18. Click the Connect button.

Once the connection is created, you should be able to view your Blob Storage service and create new containers or blobs inside the containers.

If you need to narrow the access to your resources and limit it only to tables or entities, you can create a Service SAS. This type of SAS token is quite similar to an Account SAS; you need to create a URI that you append to the URL that you use to request your Blob Storage service. Account and Service SAS share most of the URI parameters, although some parameters are specific to the service, and you need to consider them when creating your Service SAS token. Table 3-2 shows the parameters that you need to set for creating a Blob Service SAS. Other Azure Storage services require different parameters.

TABLE 3-2 BLOB Service SAS URI parameters

Parameter Name	URI Parameter	Required	Description
SignedVersion	Sv	YES	Sets the version of the signed storage service used to authenticate your request. This version should be 2015-04-05 or later.
SignedResource	sr	YES	Sets the type of shared resource: ■ **Blob** You need to use the value (b) in the SAS URI. ■ **Container** You need to use the value (c) in the SAS URI.
SignedPermission	Sp	YES	Configures the permissions that you grant to the shared resource. You need to omit this parameter if you decide to use a Stored Access Policy.
SignedStart	st	NO	Sets the time and date at which the SAS token is valid. It must be expressed in UTC using ISO 8601 format: ■ YYYY-MM-DD ■ YYYY-MM-DDThh:mmTZD ■ YYYY-MM-DDThh:mm:ssTZD If you use an API version 2012-02-12 or later, the difference between signedstart and signedexpiry cannot be greater than one hour unless you are using a container policy.
SignedExpiry	se	YES	Sets the time and date in which the SAS token becomes invalid. It must be expressed in UTC using ISO 8601 format. You need to omit this parameter if you decide to use a Stored Access Policy.
SignedIP	sip	NO	Sets the IP or range of IP addresses from which the storage service accepts requests. When using ranges of IPs, the limits are included in the range. You need to omit this parameter if you decide to use a Stored Access Policy.
SignedProtocol	spr	NO	Sets the protocol allowed to request the API. Valid values are ■ HTTPS only (https) ■ HTTP and HTTPS (https, http)
SignedIdentifier	Si	NO	Relates the SAS URI that you are constructing with a Stored Access Policy on your Storage Account. Using Stored Access Policies provides a greater level of security.
Signature	sig	YES	This is an HMAC-SHA256 computed string encoded using Base64 that the API uses for authenticating your request. You calculate the signature based on the parameters that you provided in the SAS URI. This signature must be valid to process your request.

Parameter Name	URI Parameter	Required	Description
Cache-Control	rscc	NO	Requires version (sv) set to 2013-08-15 or later for Blob service and 2015-02-21 or later for File service.
Content-Disposition	rscd	NO	Requires version (sv) set to 2013-08-15 or later for Blob service and 2015-02-21 or later for File service.
Content-Encoding	rsce	NO	Requires version (sv) set to 2013-08-15 or later for Blob service and 2015-02-21 or later for File service.
Content-Language	rscl	NO	Requires version (sv) set to 2013-08-15 or later for Blob service and 2015-02-21 or later for File service.
Content-Type	rsct	NO	Requires version (sv) set to 2013-08-15 or later for Blob service and 2015-02-21 or later for File service.

The following example shows how to create a Shared Access Signature for a blob container. This SAS token grants access to the blob container and all blobs stored inside the blob container. For this example, you need an Azure Storage Account with a blob container that is configured with the private access level:

1. Open the Azure portal (*https://portal.azure.com*).

2. In the search text box at the top of the Azure portal, type the name of your Azure Storage Account.

3. In the Results list, select the name of your Azure Storage Account.

4. On your Azure Storage Account's blade, select StorageExplorer (preview) in the navigation menu on the left side of the blade.

On the Storage Explorer panel shown in Figure 3-6, select the Blob Containers node.

FIGURE 3-6 Storage services in the Storage Explorer

5. On the right side of the Storage browser panel, click the three dots on the right side of the container that you want to grant access to.

6. In the contextual menu over your blob container, select Generate SAS.

7. In the Generate SAS panel shown in Figure 3-7, configure the Start Time, Expiry Time, and Permissions that you want to grant to the SAS token.

8. Click the Generate SAS token and URL button at the bottom of the panel.

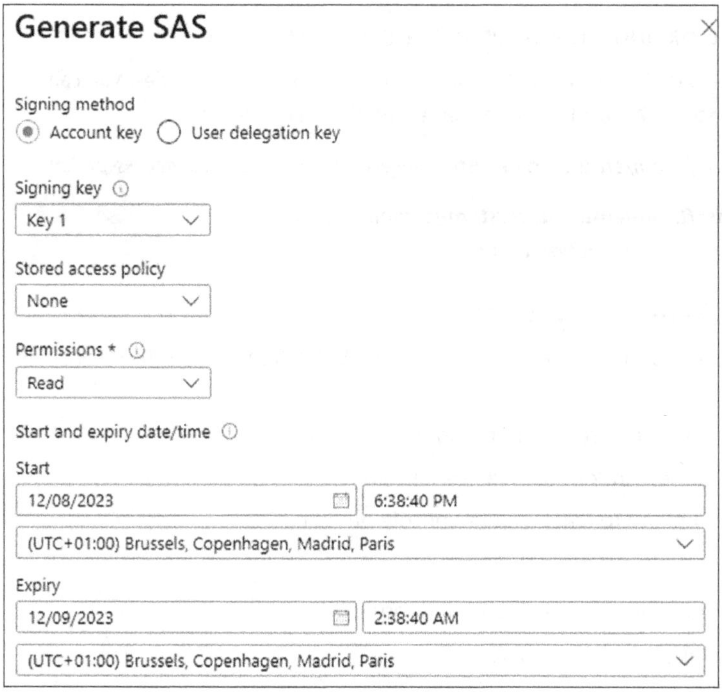

Generate SAS

Signing method
◉ Account key ○ User delegation key

Signing key ⓘ

| Key 1 | ∨ |

Stored access policy

| None | ∨ |

Permissions * ⓘ

| Read | ∨ |

Start and expiry date/time ⓘ

Start

| 12/08/2023 | 🗓 | 6:38:40 PM |

| (UTC+01:00) Brussels, Copenhagen, Madrid, Paris | ∨ |

Expiry

| 12/09/2023 | 🗓 | 2:38:40 AM |

| (UTC+01:00) Brussels, Copenhagen, Madrid, Paris | ∨ |

FIGURE 3-7 Creating a Shared Access Signature

9. On the Generate SAS, copy the Blob SAS URL of the newly generated SAS. You can share this SAS URL with any third party needing access to this specific blob.

You can use these steps to create an SAS token for a single blob in a container. Just navigate using the Storage Explorer to the blob you want to share, right-click the blob, and select Generate SAS in the contextual menu.

Working with Stored Access Policies

As you can imagine, one drawback of using this approach is that anyone who has access to the SAS URL can access the information protected by that SAS. You can improve the security of the SAS tokens by creating a Stored Access Policy and attaching the policy to the SAS token. Stored Access Policies allow you to define access policies that are associated and stored with the table that you want to protect. When you define a Stored Access Policy, you provide an identifier to the policy. Then you use this identifier when you construct the Service SAS token. You need to include this identifier when you construct the signature that authenticates the token and is part of the SAS itself.

The advantage of using a Stored Access Policy is that you define and control the validity and expiration of the policy without needing to modify the Service SAS token. Using a Stored

Access Policy also improves security by hiding the details of the Access Policy from the user, since you provide the name of the Stored Access Policy. You can associate up to five different stored access policies.

> **NEED MORE REVIEW?** **WORKING WITH STORED ACCESS POLICIES**
>
> Working with Stored Access Policies is similar to working with ad-hoc access policies. You can review how to work with Stored Access Policies by reviewing the following articles:
>
> - *https://docs.microsoft.com/en-us/rest/api/storageservices/define-stored-access-policy*
>
> - *https://docs.microsoft.com/en-us/azure/storage/common/ storage-stored-access- policy-define-dotnet*

Working with SAS tokens from your code

The following example shows how to create a user delegation SAS token using a .NET Core console application:

1. Open Visual Studio Code and create a folder for your project.

2. In the Visual Studio Code Window, open a new terminal.

3. Use the following command to create a new console project:

   ```
   dotnet new console
   ```

4. Use the following command to install NuGet packages:

   ```
   dotnet add package <NuGet_package_name>
   ```

5. Install the following NuGet packages:

   - Azure.Storage.Blobs

   - Azure.Identity

6. Open the Program.cs file and replace the content with the code shown in Listing 3-20.

LISTING 3-20 Program.cs

```csharp
// C#. ASP.NET.
using System;
using Azure.Storage.Blobs;
using Azure.Storage.Blobs.Models;
using Azure.Storage.Sas;
using Azure;
using Azure.Identity;

namespace ch3_1_3
{
    class Program
    {
        static void Main(string[] args)
        {
            string storageAccount = "az204testing";
```

```
            DateTimeOffset startTimeKey = DateTimeOffset.UtcNow;
            DateTimeOffset endTimeKey = DateTimeOffset.UtcNow.AddDays(7);
            DateTimeOffset startTimeSAS = startTimeKey;
            DateTimeOffset endTimeSAS = startTimeSAS.AddDays(1);

            Uri blobEndpointUri = new
Uri($"https://{storageAccount}.blob.core.windows.net");

            var defaultCredentials = new DefaultAzureCredential(true);

            BlobServiceClient blobClient = new
BlobServiceClient(blobEndpointUri,defaultCredentials);

            //Get the key. We will use this key for creating the SAS
            UserDelegationKey key = blobClient.GetUserDelegationKey
(startTimeKey,endTimeKey);

            System.Console.WriteLine($"User Key Starts on: {key.SignedStartsOn}");
            System.Console.WriteLine($"User Key Expires on: {key.SignedExpiresOn}");
            System.Console.WriteLine($"User Key Service: {key.SignedService}");
            System.Console.WriteLine($"User Key Version: {key.SignedVersion}");

            //We need to use the BlobSasBuilder for creating the SAS
            BlobSasBuilder blobSasBuilder = new BlobSasBuilder()
            {
                StartsOn = startTimeSAS,
                ExpiresOn = endTimeSAS
            };

            //We set the permissions Create, List, Add, Read, and Write
            blobSasBuilder.SetPermissions("clarw");

            string sasToken = blobSasBuilder.ToSasQueryParameters
            (key, storageAccount).ToString();

            System.Console.WriteLine($"SAS Token: {sasToken}");
        }
    }
}
```

> **NOTE** **AUTHORIZATIONPERMISSIONMISMATCH**
>
> If you get an exception while running the code in Listing 3-20, and the exception message is something similar to "This request is not authorized to perform this operation using this permission" with the error code AuthorizationPermissionMismatch, don't worry; there is nothing wrong with your code. This exception happens because the user you are using for running this code doesn't have sufficient privileges to get a user delegation key. You can solve this issue by granting the correct permissions to your user.

As you can see in the piece of code in bold in Listing 3-20, you use the GetUserDelegation-Key() method for getting a user delegation key for your Azure Storage Account. The user you are using for getting this key needs to be assigned the Microsoft.Storage/storageAccounts/blobServices/generateUserDelegationKey/action permission; otherwise, you get an exception.

Once you have your user delegation key, you use the `BlobSasBuilder` class to create an object that constructs the SAS token for you. Using the instance of the `BlobSasBuilder` class, you can configure the permissions you need for accessing the container. In this case, you use the `SetPermission()` method with the parameter `clarw` that matches the permissions shown in Table 3-1. In this example, we received an SAS token for the Azure Blob Storage Account because we didn't set any container name.

You get the actual SAS token using the `ToSasQueryParameters()` method from the `BlobSasBuilder` class. You need to provide the user delegation key that you obtained previously to this method for getting the SAS token.

Once you get your SAS token, you can use it to access your Azure Storage Account. The code in Listing 3-21 shows how to interact with your Azure Storage Account, using the SAS token you created in Listing 3-20. If you want to test this code, replace the content of the Program.cs file you created in the previous example with the content in Listing 3-21. Before replacing your code, you need to add the System.IO NuGet Package by running the following command in your Visual Studio Code terminal window:

```
dotnet add package System.IO
```

LISTING 3-21 Program.cs extension

```csharp
// C#. ASP.NET.
using System;
using Azure.Storage.Blobs;
using Azure.Storage.Blobs.Models;
using Azure.Storage.Sas;
using Azure;
using Azure.Identity;
using System.IO;

namespace ch3_1_2
{
    class Program
    {
        static void Main(string[] args)
        {
            string storageAccount = "az204testing";
            string containerName = "az204-blob-testing";
            string blobName = System.IO.Path.GetRandomFileName();

            DateTimeOffset startTimeKey = DateTimeOffset.UtcNow;
            DateTimeOffset endTimeKey = DateTimeOffset.UtcNow.AddDays(7);
            DateTimeOffset startTimeSAS = startTimeKey;
            DateTimeOffset endTimeSAS = startTimeSAS.AddYears(1);

            Uri blobEndpointUri = new
Uri($"https://{storageAccount}.blob.core.windows.net");

            var defaultCredentials = new DefaultAzureCredential(true);

            BlobServiceClient blobClient = new
BlobServiceClient(blobEndpointUri,defaultCredentials);
```

```
            //Get the key. We will use this key for creating the SAS
            UserDelegationKey key = blobClient.GetUserDelegationKey
(startTimeKey,endTimeKey);

            Console.WriteLine($"User Key Starts on: {key.SignedStartsOn}");
            Console.WriteLine($"User Key Expires on: {key.SignedExpiresOn}");
            Console.WriteLine($"User Key Service: {key.SignedService}");
            Console.WriteLine($"User Key Version: {key.SignedVersion}");

            //We need to use the BlobSasBuilder for creating the SAS
            BlobSasBuilder blobSasBuilder = new BlobSasBuilder()
            {
                BlobContainerName = containerName,
                BlobName = blobName,
                Resource = "b",
                StartsOn = startTimeSAS,
                ExpiresOn = endTimeSAS,
                Protocol = Azure.Storage.Sas.SasProtocol.Https
            };

            //We set the permissions Create, List, Add, Read, and Write
            blobSasBuilder.SetPermissions(BlobSasPermissions.All);

            string sasToken = blobSasBuilder.ToSasQueryParameters
(key, storageAccount).ToString();

            Console.WriteLine($"SAS Token: {sasToken}");

            //We construct the full URI for accessing the Azure Storage Account
            UriBuilder blobUri = new UriBuilder()
            {
                Scheme = "https",
                Host = $"{storageAccount}.blob.core.windows.net",
                Path = $"{containerName}/{blobName}",
                Query = sasToken
            };

            //We create a random text file
            using (System.IO.StreamWriter sw = System.IO.File.CreateText(blobName))
            {
                sw.Write("This is a testing blob for uploading using user delegated
SAS tokens");
            }

            BlobClient testingBlob = new BlobClient(blobUri.Uri);
            testingBlob.Upload(blobName);

            //Now we download the blob again and print the content.

            Console.WriteLine($"Reading content from testing blob {blobName}");

            Console.WriteLine();
            BlobDownloadInfo downloadInfo = testingBlob.Download();
            using (StreamReader sr = new StreamReader(downloadInfo.Content, true))
            {
```

```
            string line;
            while ((line = sr.ReadLine()) != null)
            {
                Console.WriteLine(line);
            }
        }

        Console.WriteLine();
        Console.WriteLine("Finished reading content from testing blob");
    }
  }
}
```

We have put the essential parts in bold in Listing 3-21. When you need to use the SAS token for working Azure Storage accounts, you need to construct the correct SAS token for the element you are working with. This means if you are going to work with a container, then you need to create a SAS token for that container and get a reference to the container using the `BlobContainerClient`. Once you have the reference to the container, you can keep working with other child elements without needing to create a new SAS token for each element inside the container.

In the example in Listing 3-21, we create a random text file with some content that we uploaded to the container and then downloaded again. Then we created an SAS token for uploading the random text file. Notice that we created the SAS token pointing to a blob that doesn't even exist. Once we have the correct SAS token, with the correct permissions, we create a `BlobClient` object using the URI pointing to the final location in the Azure Blob Storage account inside the container. We use the SAS token as the query parameter of the URI. Once we have our `BlobClient` object representing the blob, we can perform all the needed operations without creating a new SAS token for the same blob, as long as the token has not expired.

NEED MORE REVIEW? **SHARED ACCESS SIGNATURES**

If you want to read more about how to work with Shared Access Signatures, not only with the Azure Blob Storage service, but with other Azure Storage services, such as Tables, Queue, or Files, you can review the article at *https://docs.microsoft.com/en-us/rest/api/storageservices/delegate-access-with-shared-access-signature*.

EXAM TIP

If you plan to work with user delegation SAS, you need to consider that this type of SAS is available only for Azure Blob Storage and Azure Data Lake Storage Gen2. You cannot use either Stored Access Policies when working with user delegation SAS.

Implement solutions that interact with Microsoft Graph

If you use an Azure subscription, you might also have a Microsoft 365 account. In that case, you might need to access some information in your Microsoft 365 account programmatically—for example, if you want to develop an application that gets some information from your tenant or need to make some bulk operations on all the users' accounts in your Microsoft 365 tenant. For these cases and any others that might require working programmatically with the Microsoft 365 platform, you are provided with a single point of connection.

Microsoft provides the Microsoft Graph service for accessing the different services in the Microsoft 365 platform. You can access these services by using the REST API that Graph exposes or by using a client library SDK specific to the language you are using. The services available through Microsoft Graph are grouped into the following categories:

- **Microsoft 365 core services**   Outlook/Exchange, People (Outlook contacts), Planner, SharePoint, Teams, To Do, Viva Insights, Bookings, Calendar, Delve, Excel, Microsoft 365 compliance, eDiscover, Microsoft Search, OneDrive, and OneNote.

- **Enterprise Mobility + Security services**   Advanced Thread Analytics, Advanced Thread Protection, Microsoft Entra ID, Identity Manager, and Intune.

- **Windows services**   Activities, devices, notifications, and Universal Print.

- **Dynamics 365 Business Central services**

The Microsoft Identity platform eases the use of these services by providing a unified programmability model that you can use to access the services mentioned. You can also import data from external data sources to Microsoft Graph by using connectors. These Microsoft Graph connectors bring information from external services such as Google Drive, Jira, Salesforces, or any of the hundreds of connectors available in the connectors gallery. You can also create your custom connector for bringing information from your on-premises or custom Line of Business application to Microsoft Graph. Once you connect an external data source, the information is indexed and available through the Microsoft Search service.

The following example shows how to authenticate a console application to Microsoft Graph. This is the baseline for more complex scenarios such as a Web API, daemon, or service. All these types of applications share one feature: they need to interact with Microsoft Graph without asking the user for credentials interactively. In those scenarios, you need to use the Client Credential flow.

NEED MORE REVIEW?   **AUTHENTICATION FLOWS**

Different types of applications require different authentication flows. The type of authentication flow depends on whether your user's application needs to sign in using the Microsoft Identity platform or whether it's a service application that needs to run in the background. Your application's audience also affects the authentication flow that you can use. You can review all these details by reading the following Microsoft article: *https://learn.microsoft.com/ en-us/entra/identity-platform/v2-oauth2-client-creds-grant-flow.*

Before digging into the code, we must register our application using Microsoft Entra ID. The process is very similar to registering a web application. Use the following procedure for registering the console application:

1. Open the Azure portal (*https://portal.azure.com*).

2. In the Search Resources, Services, and Docs text box at the top-middle of the Azure portal, type **Microsoft Entra ID**.

3. In the results list, in the Services section, select Microsoft Entra ID.

4. On the Microsoft Entra ID page, in the Manage section, select App Registrations.

5. In the App Registrations blade, click the New Registration button on the top left of the panel.

6. In the Register An Application blade, type the name of your application in the Name text box.

7. In the Supported Account Types option control, select Accounts In This Organizational Directory Only.

8. Click the Register button at the bottom left of the blade.

9. In the overview panel of your registered application, copy the Application (client) ID value. You will need this value later in the code.

10. Copy the Directory (tenant) ID value. You will need this value later in the code.

11. Select the Certificates & Secrets option in the Manage section.

12. Click the New Client Secret button on the middle left of the Certificates & Secrets blade.

13. Enter a Description for this secret.

14. Leave the Expires dropdown menu with the recommended value.

15. Click the Add button at the bottom left of the Add A Client Secret panel.

16. Copy the secret Value. You will need this value later in the code. If you forget to copy this value now and close this blade, you won't be able to get the secret value again.

17. Select the API Permissions setting in the Manage section.

18. Click the Add A Permission button.

19. On the Request API Permissions panel, select Microsoft Graph.

20. Click the Application Permission button. You cannot use Delegated Permissions because our application won't have a logged user that makes requests.

21. Type **User.** in the search text box.

22. Expand the User node and select the User.Read.All permission checkbox, as shown in Figure 3-8.

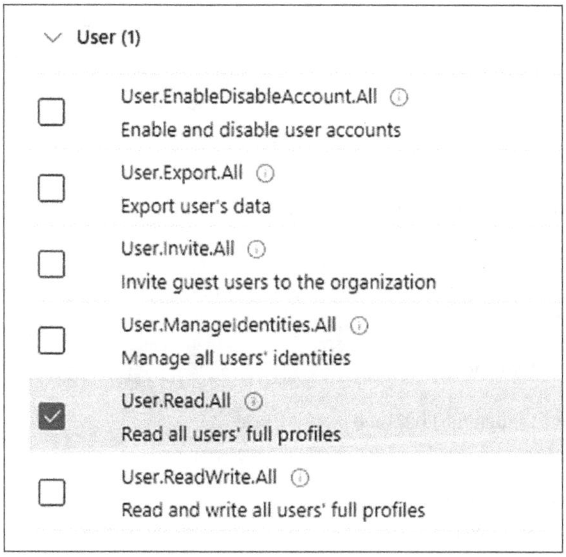

FIGURE 3-8 Delegated Graph Permissions

23. Click the Add Permissions button on the bottom left of the Requests API Permissions panel.

24. Select the Grant Admin Consent For <Your tenant's name> on the API Permissions blade.

At this point, you are ready to write the code that uses the application you registered in the previous procedure. Use the following procedure for creating a console application that lists all the users in your tenant:

1. Open a terminal and create a new console application using the following command:

```
dotnet new console
```

2. Add the package `Microsoft.Identity.Web.GraphServiceClient` using the following command in the same directory where you created the console application. This package contains the `Microsoft.Graph` and `Azure.Identity` packages.

```
dotnet add package Microsoft.Identity.Web.GraphServiceClient
```

3. Open the project in your favorite editor. In this example, we will use Visual Studio Code.

4. Replace the content of the **Program.cs** file with the one shown in Listing 3-22.

5. Replace the string <YOUR CLIENT ID> with the value you copied in step 9.

6. Replace the string <YOUR TENANT ID> with the value you copied in step 10.

7. Replace the string <YOUR CLIENT SECRET> with the value you copied in step 16.

8. Press F5 to run the code. You should get a list of all users and their assigned email addresses in your tenant.

LISTING 3-22 Program.cs

```csharp
// C#. .NET Core
using Microsoft.Graph;
using Microsoft.Graph.Models;
using Microsoft.Identity.Web;
using Azure.Identity;

var scopes = new[] { "https://graph.microsoft.com/.default" };

var clientId = "<YOUR CLIENT ID>";
var tenantId = "<YOUR TENANT ID>";
var clientSecret = "<YOUR CLIENT SECRET>";

var options = new ClientSecretCredentialOptions
{
    AuthorityHost = AzureAuthorityHosts.AzurePublicCloud,
};

var clientSecretCredential = new ClientSecretCredential(
    tenantId, clientId, clientSecret, options);

var graphClient = new GraphServiceClient(clientSecretCredential, scopes);

try
{
        var users = await graphClient.Users
                .GetAsync(requestConfiguration => {
                        requestConfiguration.QueryParameters.Top = 10;
                        requestConfiguration.QueryParameters.Select = new string[]
{"displayName", "mail"};
                        requestConfiguration.Options.WithAppOnly();
                        });

        if (users == null)
        {
                Console.WriteLine("We could not retrieve the user's list.");
                return;
        }

        Console.WriteLine($"{users!.Value.Count} users");
        var pageIterator = PageIterator<User,UserCollectionResponse>.CreatePageIterator(
                graphClient, users,
                (user) => {
                        Console.WriteLine($"{user.DisplayName}, {user.Mail}");
                        return true;
                }
        );
        await pageIterator.IterateAsync();
}
catch (ServiceException ex)
{
        Console.WriteLine("We could not retrieve the user's list: " + $"{ex}");
}
```

This example is simple but still has some interesting points that help us understand how to work with the Microsoft Graph SDK. Remember that this code uses client credentials flow authentication. This type of authentication is used for daemons or services that run in the background. When using this flow authentication, you can only use one scope, the resource identifier of the resource we want to access, followed by the `.default` suffix. In this case, the resource identifier is `https://graph.microsoft.com`. You will get an error if you try to use more than one scope in this authentication flow. All the application permissions, or scopes, are configured by the administrator. In this example, we granted these permissions in steps 19–24.

Then you create a `ClientSecretCredential` object with the tenant ID, client ID, client secret, and the URL of the Azure instance you want to access. You use this object for creating the `GraphServiceClient` that you will use to communicate with Microsoft Graph. Other authentication flows will use other Credential objects such as `InteractiveBrowserCredential` for interactive flow or `DeviceCodeCredential` for device flow.

Once we initialize the `GraphServiceClient` object, we query Microsoft Graph for all users in the tenant. In this case, we make some adjustments to the query. For example, since we are using the client credentials flow and won't have any interactive login activity, we instruct the `GraphServiceClient` to only use application authentication by using the method `.WithAppOnly()`. As we request all the users in the tenant, which can be a huge number of records, Microsoft Graph uses pagination automatically for returning the results. We configure the page size to 10 elements using the `Top` query parameter. In a real-world example, you could increase the size of this page to 999 elements. Finally, we get only a subset of all the properties available for the User object. In this example, we used the `Select` query parameter to choose only the `displayName` and `mail` attributes of the User object.

You might notice that the `users` object only contains 10 elements, which matches the page size. Microsoft Graph returns only the first page of the results and attaches the `@odata.nextlink` attribute to the result. If this attribute is null, there are no more elements in the response, but if this attribute has a value, then this attribute points to the next page of results. You have two options when retrieving all the elements in the response: you can use the `OdataNextLink` attribute (the C# version of the @odata.nextlink attribute) and build your own logic to get all the elements in the result, or you can use the `PageIterator` object to get all the pages of the response. In our example, we used the second approach.

NEED MORE REVIEW? **DEPENDENCY INJECTION AND PRODUCTION ENVIRONMENTS**

The previous example is sufficient for showing how to work with Microsoft Graph but lacks some important features that you need to consider when working in a real-world application. The following Microsoft article shows how to use dependency injection with client credentials flow: *https://learn.microsoft.com/en-us/entra/identity-platform/quickstart-console-app-netcore-acquire-token.*

EXAM TIP

Choosing the correct authentication flow is critical when working with OIDC in general and Microsoft Graph in particular. Each authentication flow includes details that impact how you grant access to resources in Microsoft Graph. Setting the wrong scope for the wrong flow will result in authentication failures.

Skill 3.2: Implement secure cloud solutions

The previous skill reviewed how to protect access to the data by authenticating and authorizing users who try to access the information managed in your application. This protection is only a portion of the mechanisms you should implement to protect your data. You also need to ensure that all the configuration needed for running your application in the different environments is managed securely. The reason for also securing the configuration is that the configuration has the needed passwords, certificates, and secrets for accessing the information your application manages.

When you encrypt your data, you need to use encryption and decryption keys or secrets for accessing and protecting the data. Storing these secrets and encryption keys is as important as encrypting the data. Losing an encryption or decryption key is similar to losing your house keys. The Azure Key Vault allows you to securely store these encryption/decryption keys and other secrets or certificates that your applications might require in a secured encryption store in Azure. In conjunction with Managed Identities, the Azure Key Vault services allow you to securely store your secrets without needing to store a password, certificate, or any credentials for accessing your secrets.

> **This skill covers how to**
> - Secure app configuration data by using App Configuration or Azure Key Vault
> - Develop code that uses keys, secrets, and certificates stored in Azure Key Vault
> - Implement Managed Identities for Azure resources

Secure app configuration data by using App Configuration or Azure Key Vault

Most of today's medium to large applications are based on distributed architectures. Independently of whether the infrastructure that executes your application is based on virtual machines, containers, serverless computing, or any other type of computing, you need to share the configuration between the elements that execute the same component of your application. For example, if your application runs on an Internet Information Services (IIS) cluster behind a load balancer, all the virtual machines hosting the IIS service share the same configuration for running your application.

In this kind of scenario, Azure App Configuration becomes a handy tool. Azure App Configuration allows you to store all the necessary configurations for your cloud application in a single repository. Other Azure services also allow you to manage configuration for your apps, but they have some crucial differences that you should consider:

- **Azure App Service settings** As you know, you can create settings for your Azure App Service. These settings apply to the instance that you are configuring. You can even create different settings values for different deployment slots. On the other hand, the Azure App Configuration service is a centralized configuration service that allows you to share the same configuration between different Azure App Service instances. You also need to consider that the Azure App Configuration service is not limited to the Azure App Service. You can also use it with containerized applications or with applications running inside virtual machines.

- **Azure Key Vault** Azure Key Vault allows you to securely store passwords, secrets, and any other setting your application might need. The encryption is performed using hardware-level encryption, among other interesting features such as certificate rotation or granular access policies. Although Azure App Configuration encrypts the value of your configuration, Azure Key Vault still provides higher levels of security. You can use the Azure Key Vault in conjunction with Azure App Configuration by creating references in Azure App Configuration to items stored in the Azure Key Vault.

When working with Azure App Configuration, you must deal with two different components: the App Configuration store and the SDK. The Azure App Configuration store is where you store your configuration. When you configure your Azure App Configuration store, you can choose between two different pricing tiers: Free and Standard. The main difference between the two pricing tiers is the number of stores you can create in a subscription. In the Free tier, you are limited to one store per subscription, whereas you don't have such a limitation in the Standard tier. Other differences between the two tiers are the maximum size of the store: 10 MB in the Free tier versus 1 GB in the Standard tier, or the size of the key history: 7 days in the Free tier versus 30 days in the Standard tier. You can switch from the Free tier to the Standard tier at any time, but you cannot switch back to the Free tier from the Standard tier.

The following procedure shows how to create an Azure App Configuration:

1. Open the Azure portal (*https://portal.azure.com*).
2. Click the Create A Resource button in the Azure Services section at the top of the Azure portal.
3. In the New blade, type **app configuration** in the Search The Marketplace text box.
4. In the result list below the text box, select App Configuration.
5. In the App Configuration blade, click the Create button.
6. In the App Configuration blade, select the subscription where you want to deploy your App Configuration store using the Subscription dropdown menu.
7. In the Resource Group dropdown menu, select the resource group where you want to deploy your App Configuration store. Alternatively, you can create a new resource group by clicking the Create New link below the Resource Group dropdown menu.

8. In the App Configuration blade, type a name for the App Configuration store in the Resource Name text box. The name must contain only alphanumeric ASCII characters or the hyphen (-) character, and it must be between 5 and 50 characters.

9. Select a location in the Location dropdown menu.

10. In the Pricing Tier dropdown menu, select Free.

11. Click the Review + Create button at the bottom of the blade.

12. Click the Create button.

Once you have created your Azure App Configuration store, you can create the key-value pairs for storing your configuration. Before you create your first key-value pair, you should review how keys work inside the App Configuration store.

A key is an identifier associated with a value stored in the App Configuration store. You use the key for retrieving a value from the store. Keys are case sensitive, so "appSample204" and "APPSAMPLE204" are different keys. This is important because some languages or frameworks are case insensitive for settings, so you should not use case sensitivity for differencing keys. When naming a key, you can use any Unicode character, except the asterisk (*), the comma (,), and the back slash (\). If you need to include any of these reserved characters, you need to prepend the back slash (\) escape character. As a best practice, you should consider using namespace when naming your keys. By using a separator character between the different levels, you can create a hierarchy of settings inside your store. Since the Azure App Configuration service doesn't analyze or parse your keys, it is entirely up to you to choose the namespace that best fits your needs. Some examples of keys using namespaces are

```
AppSample:Devel:DbConnection
AppSample:AUS:WelcomeMessage
```

You can also add a label attribute to a key. By default, the label attribute is null. You can use the label for making values different using the same key. This is especially useful when used for deployment environments: The following three examples are different keys because the labels are different:

```
Key = AppSample:DBConnection [nd] Label = Develop
Key = AppSample:DBConnection [nd] Label = Stage
Key = AppSample:DBConnection [nd] Label = Production
```

When creating a new key-value pair, you have a limit of 10,000 for the size of the pair. This limit applies to the size of the key, plus the size of the optional label, plus the size of the value. You should also keep in mind that the same limitations that apply to the string that you use for the key are the same for value. That is, you can use any Unicode character for the value, except asterisk (*), comma (,), and back slash (\). If you need to include any of these reserved characters, you need to prepend the back slash (\) escape character.

NEED MORE REVIEW? **FEATURE MANAGEMENT AND DYNAMIC CONFIGURATION**

You can take advantage of Azure App Configuration for implementing more advanced features such as feature management or dynamic configuration. The following articles provide more insight about these features:

- **Feature Management** *https://docs.microsoft.com/en-us/azure/azure-app-configuration/quickstart-feature-flag-aspnet-core*

- **Enable Dynamic configuration** *https://docs.microsoft.com/en-us/azure/azure-app-configuration/enable-dynamic-configuration-aspnet-core*

After you've reviewed the basics of the Azure App Configuration, you can review how to use this service in your code. The following example is based on the code in Chapter 2 in the section "Interact with data using the appropriate SDK." In this example, you will modify the code for using an Azure App Container store instead of using an AppSettings JSON file:

1. Open Visual Studio Code and create a folder for your project.

2. In the Visual Studio Code window, open a new terminal.

3. Use the following command to create a new console project:

    ```
    dotnet new console
    ```

4. Use the following command to install NuGet packages:

    ```
    dotnet add package <NuGet_package_name>
    ```

5. Install the following NuGet packages:

    - Azure.Storage.Blobs

    - Azure.Storage.Common

    - Azure.Identity

    - Microsoft.Extensions.Configuration

    - Microsoft.Extensions.Configuration.AzureAppConfiguration

6. Create a C# class file and name it **AppSettings.cs**.

7. Replace the contents of the AppSettings.cs file with the contents of Listing 3-23. Change the name of the namespace to match your project's name.

8. Create a C# class file and name it **Common.cs**.

9. Replace the contents of the Common.cs file with the contents of Listing 3-24.

10. Change the name of the namespace to match your project's name.

11. Replace the contents of the **Program.cs** file with the contents of Listing 3-25. Change the name of the namespace to match your project's name.

LISTING 3-23 AppSettings.cs

```csharp
// C#. ASP.NET.
using System;
using Microsoft.Extensions.Configuration;

namespace ch3_2_1
{
    public class AppSettings
    {
        public string SourceSASConnectionString { get; set; }
        public string SourceAccountName { get; set; }
        public string SourceContainerName { get; set; }
        public string DestinationSASConnectionString { get; set; }
        public string DestinationAccountName { get; set; }
        public string DestinationContainerName { get; set; }

        public static AppSettings LoadAppSettings()
        {
            var builder = new ConfigurationBuilder();
            builder.AddAzureAppConfiguration(Environment.GetEnvironmentVariable
("ConnectionString"));

            var config = builder.Build();
            AppSettings appSettings = new AppSettings();
            appSettings.SourceSASConnectionString =
config["TestAZ204:StorageAccount: Source:ConnectionString"];
            appSettings.SourceAccountName =
config["TestAZ204:StorageAccount:Source:AccountName"];
            appSettings.SourceContainerName =
config["TestAZ204:StorageAccount:Source:ContainerName"];
            appSettings.DestinationSASConnectionString =
config["TestAZ204:StorageAccount:Destination:ConnectionString"];
            appSettings.DestinationAccountName =
config["TestAZ204:StorageAccount:Destination:AccountName"];
            appSettings.DestinationContainerName =
config["TestAZ204:StorageAccount:Destination:ContainerName"];
            return appSettings;
        }
    }
}
```

LISTING 3-24 Common.cs

```csharp
// C#. ASP.NET.
using Azure.Storage.Blobs;

namespace ch3_2_1
{
    public class Common
    {

        public static BlobServiceClient CreateBlobClientStorageFromSAS(string
SASConnectionString)
        {
            BlobServiceClient blobClient;
```

```
        try
        {
            blobClient = new BlobServiceClient(SASConnectionString);
        }
        catch (System.Exception ex)
        {

            Console.WriteLine("An error happened while connecting to the Blob
Storage service. Error: " + $"{ex}");
        }

        return blobClient;

    }
  }
}
```

LISTING 3-25 Program.cs

```
// C#. ASP.NET.
using System.Threading.Tasks;
using System;
using Azure.Storage.Blobs;

namespace ch3_2_1
{
    class Program
    {
        static void Main(string[] args)
        {
            Console.WriteLine("Copy items between Containers Demo!");
            Task.Run(async () => await StartContainersDemo()).Wait();
        }

        public static async Task StartContainersDemo()
        {
            string sourceBlobFileName = "Testing.zip";
            AppSettings appSettings = AppSettings.LoadAppSettings();

            //Get a cloud client for the source Storage Account
            BlobServiceClient sourceClient =
Common.CreateBlobClientStorageFromSAS(appSettings.SourceSASConnectionString);

            //Get a reference for each container
            var sourceContainerReference =
sourceClient.GetBlobContainerClient(appSettings.SourceContainerName);
            var destinationContainerReference =
sourceClient.GetBlobContainerClient(appSettings.DestinationContainerName);

            //Get a reference for the source blob
            var sourceBlobReference = sourceContainerReference.
                                GetBlobClient(sourceBlobFileName);
            var destinationBlobReference = destinationContainerReference.
                                GetBlobClient(sourceBlobFileName);
```

```
        //Move the blob from the source container to the destination container
await destinationBlobReference.StartCopyFromUriAsync(sourceBlobReference.Uri);
        }
    }
}
```

Listings 3-24 and 3-25 are mostly the same files you can find in the example in Chapter 2 in the section "Interact with data using the appropriate SDK." The file AppSettings.cs shown in Listing 3-23 contains all the magic for working with the App Configuration service. As with any regular .NET Core application, you must create a `ConfigurationBuilder` object to manage the application's configuration. Once you get your builder, you use the `AddAzureAppConfiguration()` extension method for connecting to the App Configuration store. Finally, you use the `Build()` method from the builder object to load all the settings in the App Configuration store. Once you have loaded all the settings, you can access each key-value pair by just using the correct key, as you can see in Listing 3-25.

At this point, if you try to run this example, you will get some exceptions because you are not providing the connection string needed for accessing your Azure App Configuration store. You did not define any key-value pair in your App Configuration store, so you would get null values even if you could access the store. Use the following steps to get the connection string needed for accessing the App Configuration store and define each of the needed key-value pairs:

1. Open the Azure portal (*https://portal.azure.com*).

2. In the Search Resources, Services, and Docs text box at the top of the Azure portal, type the name of your App Configuration store.

3. In your App Configuration Store blade, select Access Keys in the Settings section.

4. In the Access Keys blade, copy one of the connection strings by clicking the blue icon on the right side next to the Connection String text box.

5. In your Visual Studio Code window, open a new terminal and type the following command. Replace the text *<your_connection_string>* with the value that you copied in step 4:

    ```
    setx ConnectionString "<your_connection_string>"
    ```

6. Restart your Visual Studio Code window. You need to perform this step to ensure that the environment variable that you defined in the previous step is available for your code.

7. In the Azure portal, in your App Configuration store blade, click Configuration Explorer in the Operations section on the left side of the blade.

8. In the Configuration Explorer, click the Create button at the top left of the blade.

9. In the Create panel, shown in Figure 3-9, type the name of the key in the Key text box. Use one of the keys shown in Listing 3-23.

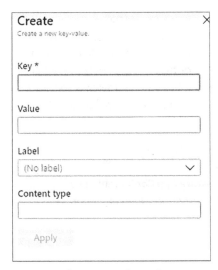

Create ✕
Create a new key-value.

Key *

Value

Label
(No label) ⌄

Content type

Apply

FIGURE 3-9 Create a new key-value

10. In the Value text box, provide the value for the corresponding key. Remember that you are using values from the example in Chapter 2 in the section "Interact with data using the appropriate SDK." The correct values are specific to your scenario, but you can use Listing 2-23 for reference.

11. Click the Apply button.

12. Repeat steps 8 to 10 until you create a key-value pair for each setting in Listing 3-22. Here is the complete list for your reference:

- TestAZ204:StorageAccount:Source:ConnectionString
- TestAZ204:StorageAccount:Source:AccountName
- TestAZ204:StorageAccount:Source:ContainerName
- TestAZ204:StorageAccount:Destination:ConnectionString
- TestAZ204:StorageAccount:Destination:AccountName
- TestAZ204:StorageAccount:Destination:ContainerName

13. In your Visual Studio Code window, press F5 to run your project. At this point, your code should be able to connect to your Azure App Configuration store and retrieve all the needed settings.

This example shows you the basics for working with Azure App Configuration but also shows some drawbacks that you should consider for production environments. In this example, you defined an environment variable for storing the connection string for connecting to the App Configuration store. Although this could be a valid configuration for testing or developing environments, there are security implications that you should consider for production environments. You should consider using Managed Service Identity for production environments instead of connection strings.

Another security improvement you should consider is storing connection strings directly as a key-value in your App Configuration store. For this kind of sensitive information, you should store it as a secret in an Azure Key Vault and create an Azure Key Vault Reference in your App Configuration store pointing to the right secret. For the sake of brevity, we didn't include the procedure of how to create Key Vault references, but you can review a complete reference in the article at *https://docs.microsoft.com/en-us/azure/azure-app-configuration/ use-key-vault-references-dotnet-core*.

> **NEED MORE REVIEW? BEST PRACTICES**
>
> You can review some best practices when working with Azure App Configuration by reading the article at *https://docs.microsoft.com/en-us/azure/azure-app-configuration/ howto-best-practices*.

EXAM TIP

When defining your key-value pair, remember that you are limited to a maximum length of 10,000. Remember also that keys are case sensitive, so "AppSetting" and "appsetting" are treated as different keys.

Develop code that uses keys, secrets, and certificates stored in Azure Key Vault

Azure Key Vault is Microsoft's service for securely storing secret keys and certificates in a centralized, secure store. By using Azure Key Vault, your developers no longer need to store this sensitive information on their computers while developing an application. Thanks to the identity-based access control, you only need to configure a policy for granting access to the secure store's needed service or user principals. Another advantage is that you can apply fine-grained access control, allowing access to specific secrets only to the needed application or user.

The next example shows how to use the KeyVault API to create, read, update, or delete the different elements you store in the Azure Key Vault. You need an empty Azure App Service and an Azure Key Vault configured in your Azure subscription to run this example.

1. Open the Azure portal (*https://portal.azure.com*).
2. In the search text box on top of the Azure portal, type the name of your Azure Web App.
3. Select the name of your Azure Web App in the result list below the text box.
4. On the Azure Web App Service blade, select the Identity menu item in the Settings section.
5. In the Status switch control, click the On option.
6. Click Save.

7. In the Enable System Assigned Managed Identity dialog box, click Yes.

8. Once you enable the system-assigned managed identity, you get the Principal or Object ID associated with your Azure App Service.

9. In the search text box at the top of the Azure portal, type the name of your Azure Key Vault. Select the name of your Azure Key Vault in the result list. If you don't already have an Azure Key Vault and need to create a new one, you can use the procedure at *https://docs.microsoft.com/en-us/azure/key-vault/quick-create-portal*.

10. Click Access Control (IAM) in the navigation menu on the Key Vault blade.

11. On the Access Control (IAM) blade, click the Add button on the top left, and then Add role assignment.

12. Select the Key Vault Certificates Officer role on the Add Role Assignment blade.

13. Select the Members tab on the top side of the Add Role Assignment blade.

14. Click the Select Members button.

15. Type the name of your web app in the Select text box.

16. Select your web app from the results list.

17. Type the username you use to connect to your Azure Subscription.

18. Select your username in the results list.

19. Click the Select button at the bottom of the Select Members panel.

20. Double-click the Review + Assign button at the bottom left of the Add Role Assignment blade.

21. Repeat steps 12 to 20 to add the roles of *Key Vault Crypto Officer* and *Key Vault Secrets Officer*.

22. Open Visual Studio 2022.

23. In the Welcome window of Visual Studio 2022, in the Get Started column, click Create A New Project.

24. On the Create A New Project window, on the All Languages dropdown menu, select C#.

25. In the Search For Templates text box type **asp.net**.

26. In the result list, select ASP.NET Web Application (.NET Framework).

27. Click the Next button at the bottom right of the window.

28. On the Configure Your New Project, type a Project Name, a Location, and a Solution Name for your project.

29. Click the Create button at the bottom right of the window.

30. On the Create A New ASP.NET Web Application window, select the MVC template in the template list in the middle of the left side of the window. MVC stands for Model-View-Controller.

31. On the right side of the Create A New ASP.NET Web Application window, in the Authentication section, ensure that the Authentication is set to None.

32. Click the Create button at the bottom right of the window.

33. In the Visual Studio window, select Tools > NuGet Package Manager > Manage NuGet Packages For Solution.

34. On the NuGet Package Manager tab, click Browse.

35. Type **Azure.Identity** and press Enter.

36. Click the Azure.Identity package.

37. On the right side of the NuGet Manager tab, select the checkbox next to your project.

38. Click the Install button.

39. In the Preview Changes window, click OK.

40. In the License Acceptance window, click the I Accept button.

41. Repeat steps 35 through 40 and install the following packages:

   - Azure.Security.KeyVault.Secrets
   - Azure.Security.KeyVault.Certificates
   - Azure.Security.KeyVault.Keys

42. Open the HomeController.cs file in the Controllers folder.

43. Replace the content of the `Index()` method with the content of Listing 3-26. You might need to add the following namespaces to the HomeController.cs file:

   - Azure.Identity
   - Azure.Security.KeyVault.Secrets
   - Azure.Security.KeyVault.Certificates
   - Azure.Security.KeyVault.Keys

LISTING 3-26 Creating, deleting, updating, and reading Key Vault items

```
// C#. ASP.NET.
public ActionResult Index()
        {
                string keyVaultName = "<YOUR_VAULT's_NAME>";
                string vaultBaseURL = $"https://{keyVaultName}.vault.azure.net";

                // Manage secrets in the Key Vault.
                //Get a secret client for accessing the Key Vault.
                var secretClient = new SecretClient(new Uri(vaultBaseURL),
new DefaultAzureCredential());
                // Create a new secret
                string secretName = "secret-az204";
                _ = secretClient.SetSecret(secretName, "This is a secret testing value");
                // Get the secret
                var secret = secretClient.GetSecret(secretName);
                // Update an existing secret
                _ = secretClient.SetSecret(secretName, "Updated the secret testing value");
```

```
            // Delete the secret
            _ = secretClient.StartDeleteSecret(secretName);

            // Manage certificates in the Key Vault
            //Get a certificate client for accessing the Key Vault.
            var certificateClient = new CertificateClient(new Uri(vaultBaseURL),
new DefaultAzureCredential());
            string certName = "cert-az204";
            // Create a new self-signed certificate
            var policy = new CertificatePolicy("self", "CN=AZ204KEYVAULTDEMO")
            {
                ContentType = CertificateContentType.Pkcs12,
                KeyType = CertificateKeyType.Rsa,
                KeySize = 2048,
                Exportable = true
            };
            _ = certificateClient.StartCreateCertificate(certName, policy);
            // Creating a new certificate in the Key Vault takes some time
            // before it's ready.
            // We added some wait time here for the sake of simplicity.
            Thread.Sleep(10000);
            KeyVaultCertificateWithPolicy certificate =
certificateClient.GetCertificate(certName);
            // Update properties associated with the certificate.
            CertificatePolicy updatePolicy = new CertificatePolicy
            {
                KeyUsage =
                {
                    CertificateKeyUsage.CrlSign,
                    CertificateKeyUsage.NonRepudiation
                }
            };
            _ = certificateClient.UpdateCertificatePolicy(certName, updatePolicy);
            Thread.Sleep(10000);


            certificate = certificateClient.GetCertificate(certName);
            // Disable the certificate.
            CertificateProperties certificateProperties = new
CertificateProperties(certName)
            {
                Enabled = false
            };
            _ = certificateClient.UpdateCertificateProperties(certificateProperties);
            Thread.Sleep(10000);
            // Delete the self-signed certificate.
            _ = certificateClient.StartDeleteCertificate(certName);

            // Manage keys in the Key Vault
            //Get a key client for accessing the Key Vault.
            var keyClient = new KeyClient(new Uri(vaultBaseURL), new
DefaultAzureCredential());
            string keyName = "key-az204";
            var ecKey = new CreateEcKeyOptions(keyName)
            {
```

```
            CurveName = KeyCurveName.P256K,
            KeyOperations =
            {
                KeyOperation.Sign,
                KeyOperation.Verify
            }
        };

        _ = keyClient.CreateEcKey(ecKey);
        // Get the key
        KeyVaultKey key = keyClient.GetKey(keyName);
        // Update keys in the Key Vault
        key.Properties.ExpiresOn = DateTime.UtcNow.AddYears(1);
        KeyVaultKey updatedKey = keyClient.UpdateKeyProperties(key.Properties,
key.KeyOperations);

        // Delete keys from the Key Vault
        DeleteKeyOperation operation = keyClient.StartDeleteKey(keyName);
        // Purge the deleted key
        while (!operation.HasCompleted)
        {
            Thread.Sleep(2000);
            operation.UpdateStatus();
        }
        keyClient.PurgeDeletedKey(keyName);

        return View();
    }
```

At this point, you should be able to run the example. Because you didn't make any modifications to any view, you should not be able to see any changes in your Azure Key Vault. To see how this code creates, reads, modifies, and deletes the different item types in your Azure Key Vault, you should set some breakpoints:

1. Add a breakpoint to the following lines:

```
string secretName = "secret-az204";
string certName = "cert-az204";
string keyName = "key-az204";
```

2. Open your Azure Key Vault in the Azure portal, as shown in step 9 of the previous procedure.

3. On your Azure Key Vault blade, select Secrets in the Settings section in the navigation menu.

4. In Visual Studio, press F5 to debug your project.

5. When you hit the breakpoint, press F10 and go back to the Azure portal to see the results. Use the Refresh button to see the changes in your Azure Key Vault.

> ***NOTE*** **FORBIDDEN ACCESS**
>
> **If you get a Forbidden Access Error while you are debugging your application in Visual Studio, ensure that you have granted the correct role for the user account that you have configured in your Visual Studio for connecting with your Azure subscription. Also ensure that the account you are using for developing is correctly authenticated in Microsoft Entra ID. Check your development account in Tools > Options > Azure Service Authentication. If there is a Re-Authenticate link below your development account, click the link to authenticate again.**

When you work with the KeyVault API, you need to create a client object for the service you want to use, Secrets, Keys, or Certificates responsible for communicating with the Azure Key Vault services. As described in the example in the "Implement Managed Identities for Azure resources" section that follows, you need to get an access token for authenticating your service or user principal to the Azure Key Vault. The following code snippet shows how to perform this authentication:

```
var secretClient = new SecretClient(new Uri(vaultBaseURL), new
DefaultAzureCredential());
var certificateClient = new CertificateClient(new Uri(vaultBaseURL), new
DefaultAzureCredential());
var keyClient = new KeyClient(new Uri(vaultBaseURL), new DefaultAzureCredential());
```

Now you can use the `secretClient`, `certificateClient`, or `keyClient` variables for working with the different item types. The KeyVault API provides specialized synchronous and asynchronous methods for each item type. You should use the `SetSecretAsync()` method to create a new secret in your Azure Key Vault. The following code snippet shows how to create a new secret:

```
_ = secretClient.SetSecret(secretName, "This is a secret testing value");
```

If you try to create a new secret, key, or certificate using the same name of an object already in the vault, you are creating a new version of that object, as shown in Figure 3-10. The only exception to this rule is if you have enabled soft deletion in your Azure Key Vault and you try to create a new secret using the same name as a deleted object. In that situation, you get a collision exception. You can select each version to review the object's properties for that version.

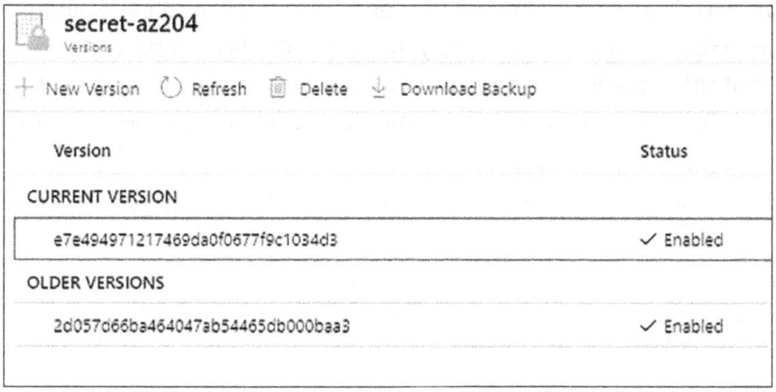

FIGURE 3-10 A secret object with different versions

Most of the methods in the KeyVault API that work with items require the vault URL and the name of the item that you want to access. In this example, you define a variable with the correct value at the beginning of the `Index()` method, as shown in the following code snippet:

```
string keyVaultName = "<YOUR_VAULT's_NAME>";
string vaultBaseURL = $"https://{keyVaultName}.vault.azure.net";
```

These methods are usually overloaded for accepting an object identifier instead of the vault base URL and the object's name. The identifier has the following form:

```
https://{keyvault-name}.vault.azure.net/{object-type}/{object-name}/{object-version}
```

Where:

- *keyvault-name* is the name of the key vault where the object is stored.
- *object-type* is the type of object that you want to work with. This value can be secrets, keys, or certificates.
- *object-name* is the name that you give the object in the vault.
- *object-version* is the version of the object that you want to access.

Creating a key or certificate uses a slightly different approach from the one that you used for creating a secret. Keys and certificates are more complex objects and require some additional configuration for creating them. The following code snippet extracted from Listing 3-26 shows how to create a new self-signed certificate in the Azure Key Vault:

```
// Create a new self-signed certificate
        var policy = new CertificatePolicy("self", "CN=AZ204KEYVAULTDEMO")
        {
            ContentType = CertificateContentType.Pkcs12,
            KeyType = CertificateKeyType.Rsa,
            KeySize = 2048,
            Exportable = true
        };

            _ = certificateClient.StartCreateCertificate(certName, policy);
```

You need to create a `CertificatePolicy` object before you can create the certificate. A certificate policy is an object that defines the properties of how to create a certificate and any new version associated with the certificate object. You use this certificate policy object as a parameter of the `StartCreateCertificate()` method. Suppose you need to modify any property of an existing certificate. In that case, you need to define a new certificate policy and update the policy using the `UpdateCertificatePolicy()` method, as shown in the following code snippet:

```
// Update properties associated with the certificate.
        CertificatePolicy updatePolicy = new CertificatePolicy
        {
            KeyUsage =
            {
                CertificateKeyUsage.CrlSign,
                CertificateKeyUsage.NonRepudiation
```

```
        }
    };

    _ = certificateClient.UpdateCertificatePolicy(certName, updatePolicy);
```

Deleting an object from the key vault is quite straightforward; you only need to provide the vault base URL and the object's name to the `StartDeleteSecret()`, `StartDeleteCertificate()`, or `StartDeleteKey()` method. All these methods return their corresponding `DeleteSecretOperation`, `DeleteCertificateOperation`, and `DeleteKeyOperation` to track the status of the delete operation. Azure Key Vault also supports soft-delete operations on the protected objects or the vault itself. This option is enabled by default. When you soft delete an object or a vault, the Azure Key Vault provider automatically marks them as deleted but holds the object or vault for a default period of 90 days. This means you can recover the deleted object later if needed.

> **NEED MORE REVIEW?** **MORE DETAILS ABOUT KEYS, SECRETS, AND CERTIFICATES**
>
> You can find more information about the details of the different object types that are available in the Azure Key Vault service by reviewing the article at *https://docs.microsoft.com/en-us/azure/key-vault/about-keys-secrets-and-certificates*.

EXAM TIP

The kind of information that you usually store in an Azure Key Vault is essential information that must be kept secret, such as passwords, connection strings, private keys, and so on. When configuring the access to your Key Vault, carefully review the access level you grant to the security principal. As a best practice, you should always apply the principle of least privilege. You grant access to the different levels in a Key Vault by creating Access Policies.

Implement Managed Identities for Azure resources

When designing your application, you usually identify the different services or systems on which your application depends. For example, your application might need to connect to an Azure SQL database for storing data or might need to connect to Azure Event Hub for reading messages from other services. In all these situations, there is a common need to authenticate with the service before you can access it. In the Azure SQL database case, you need to use a connection string; if you need to connect to an Azure Event Hub, you need to use a combination of event publishers and Shared Access Signature (SAS) tokens.

The drawback of this approach is that you need to store a security credential, token, or password to be able to authenticate to the service that you want to access. This is a drawback because you might find that this information is stored on developers' computers or is checked in to the source control by mistake. You can address most of these situations by using the Azure Key Vault, but your code still needs to authenticate to Azure Key Vault to get the information for accessing the other services.

Fortunately, Microsoft Entra ID provides the Managed Identities for Azure resources (formerly known as Managed Service Identity) that removes the need to use credentials for authenticating your application to any Azure service that supports Microsoft Entra ID authentication. This feature automatically creates a managed identity that you can use for authenticating to any service that supports Microsoft Entra ID authentication without needing to provide any credentials.

You can work with two different types of managed identities:

- **System-assigned managed identities**   Azure automatically enables these identities when you create an Azure service instance, such as an Azure virtual machine (VM) or an Azure data lake store. Azure creates an identity associated with the new instance and stores it to the Microsoft Entra ID tenant associated with the subscription where you created the service instance. If you decide to delete the service instance, then Azure automatically deletes the managed instance associated with the service instance stored in the Microsoft Entra ID tenant.

- **User-assigned managed identities**   You can create your managed identities in the Microsoft Entra ID tenant associated with your Azure subscription. You can associate this type of managed identity to one or more service instances. The life cycle of the managed identity is independent of the service instance. This means that if you delete the service instance, the user-assigned managed identity remains in the Microsoft Entra ID tenant. You must remove the managed identity manually.

Usually, you use the system-assigned managed identities when your workload is contained within the same Azure resource, or you need to independently identify each of the service instances, like Virtual Machines. On the other hand, if you need to grant access to a workload distributed across different resources or you need to pre-authorize a resource as part of a provisioning flow, you should use user-assigned managed identities.

When working with managed identities, keep in mind these three concepts:

- **Client ID**   This is a unique identifier generated by Microsoft Entra ID. This ID associates the application and the service principal during its initial provisioning.

- **Principal ID**   This is the ID of the service principal associated with the managed identity. A service principal and a managed identity are tightly coupled, but they are different objects. The service principal is the object that you use to grant role-based access to an Azure resource.

- **Azure Instance Metadata Service (IMDS)**   When you use managed identities in an Azure VM, you can use the IMDS to request an OAuth Access Token from your application deployed within the VM. The IMDS is a REST endpoint that you can access from your VM using a non-routable IP address (169.254.169.254).

The following example shows how to create a system-assigned identity in an Azure App Service and how to use this managed identity from your code to access an Azure Key Vault. For this example, you must have an empty Azure App Service, an Azure Key Vault, and at least one item in the Azure Key Vault. You also need to have your Visual Studio connected to the Azure subscription where you have configured the Azure Key Vault.

1. Open the Azure portal (*https://portal.azure.com*).

2. In the search text box at the top of the Azure portal, type the name of your Azure Web App. If you don't have an Azure Web App, you can create a new Azure Web App by following the procedure at *https://docs.microsoft.com/en-in/azure/app-service/app-service-web-get-started-dotnet*.

3. On the Azure Web App Service blade, select the Identity menu item in the Settings section.

4. On the Status switch control, click the On option.

5. Click the Save button.

6. In the Enable System Assigned Managed Identity dialog box, click the Yes button.

7. Once you enable the system-assigned managed identity, you get the Principal or Object ID, as shown in Figure 3-11.

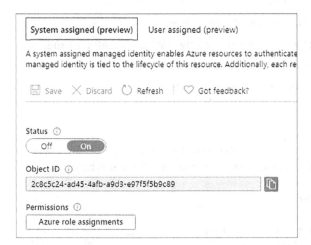

FIGURE 3-11 System assigned managed identity

8. Open Visual Studio 2022.

9. In the Welcome window of Visual Studio 2022, in the Get Started column, select Create A New Project.

10. In the Create A New Project window, in the All Languages dropdown menu, select C#.

11. In the Search For Templates text box, type **asp.net**.

12. In the results list, click ASP.NET Web Application (.NET Framework).

13. Click the Next button at the bottom right of the window.

14. In the Configure Your New Project, type a Project Name, a Location, and a Solution Name for your project.

15. Click the Create button at the bottom right of the window.

16. In the Create A New ASP.NET Web Application window, select the MVC template on the template list in the middle of the left side of the window. MVC stands for Model-View-Controller.

17. On the right side of the Create A New ASP.NET Web Application window, in the Authentication section, ensure that the Authentication is set to None.

18. Click the Create button at the bottom right of the window.

19. In the Visual Studio window, select Tools > NuGet Package Manager > Manage NuGet Packages For Solution.

20. On the NuGet Package Manager tab, click Browse.

21. Type **Azure.Identity** and press Enter.

22. Select the Azure.Identity package.

23. On the right side of the NuGet Manager tab, select the checkbox next to your project.

24. Click the Install button.

25. In the Preview Changes window, click OK.

26. In the License Acceptance window, click the I Accept button.

27. Repeat steps 21 through 26 and install the Azure.Security.KeyVault.Secrets package.

28. Open the HomeController.cs file in the Controllers folder.

29. Add the following statements to the HomeController.cs file:

```
using Azure.Security.KeyVault.Secrets;
using Azure.Identity;
```

30. Replace the content of the Index() method with the content of Listing 3-27. The crucial pieces of code related to accessing the Azure Key Vault are highlighted in bold.

LISTING 3-27 Getting a secret from the key vault

```
// C#. ASP.NET.
string keyVaultName = "<PUT_YOUR_KEY_VAULT_NAME_HERE>";
string secretName = "<PUT_YOUR_SECRET_NAME_HERE>";

//Create a Key Vault client for accessing the items in the vault.
        var secretClient = new SecretClient(new
Uri($"https://{keyVaultName}.vault.azure.net/"),
new DefaultAzureCredential());
        var secret = secretClient.GetSecret(secretName);
        ViewBag.KeyVaultName = keyVaultName;
        ViewBag.keyName = secretName;
        ViewBag.secret = secret.Value.Value;
return View();
```

As you can see, this code is quite similar to the code in Listing 3-26. This is because you used managed identities to get access to the Azure Key Vault in the example in Listing 3-26. The DefaultAzureCredentials() method manages all the authentication processes for you. This method tries several authentication methods, including Environment variables, Workload,

Managed Identities, SharedToken, Visual Studio and Visual Studio Code Credentials, Azure CLI, Azure PowerShell, Azure Developer CLI, and Interactive web browser. Once one of the methods returns a valid credential, your code uses that token for authenticating any request to Azure or Microsoft Graph. Even if you get a valid access token, you still need to grant the appropriate role to your Azure App Service application in the Azure Key Vault.

1. Open the Views > Home > Index.cshtml file.
2. Append the content of Listing 3-28 to the end of the file.

LISTING 3-28 Adding secret information to the home page

```
// C#. ASP.NET.
<div class="row">
    <div class="col-lg-12">
        <dl class="dl-horizontal">
            <dt>Key Vault Name: </dt>
            <dd>@ViewBag.keyVaultName</dd>
            <dt>Key Name: </dt>
            <dd>@ViewBag.keyName</dd>
            <dt>Key Secret: </dt>
            <dd>@ViewBag.secret</dd>
        </dl>

    </div>
</div>
```

At this point, you could run your project and see the results. Depending on the roles assigned in your Azure Key Vault, your Azure user might already have access to the secrets stored in the key vault. In that case, you should be able to access the secret stored in the Azure Key Vault. If you get an exception when running the web application, chances are good that you don't have roles assigned in the Azure Key Vault. The following steps show how to grant access to your Azure App Service application in the Azure Key Vault.

1. Open the Azure portal (*https://portal.azure.com*).
2. Type the name of your Azure Key Vault in the search text box at the top of the Azure portal. If you don't already have an Azure Key Vault and need to create a new one, you can follow the procedure at *https://docs.microsoft.com/en-us/azure/key-vault/quick-create-portal*.
3. Select Access Control (IAM) from the navigation menu on the Key Vault blade.
4. On the Access Control (IAM) blade, click the Add button at the top left, and then Add role assignment.
5. Select the *Key Vault Secrets Officer* role on the Add Role Assignment blade.
6. Select the Members tab at the top of the Add Role Assignment blade.
7. Click the Select Members button.
8. Type the name of your web app in the Select text box.
9. Select your web app from the results list.
10. Type the username you use to connect to your Azure subscription.

11. Select your username in the results list.

12. Click the Select button at the bottom of the Select Members panel.

13. Double-click the Review + Assign button at the bottom left of the Add Role Assignment blade.

14. In the Visual Studio window, right-click your project's name in the Solution Explorer window.

15. In the contextual menu, select Publish.

16. In the Publish window, ensure that Azure is selected on the right side of the window.

17. Click Next.

18. In the Specific Target section, ensure that Azure App Service (Windows) is selected.

19. Click Next.

20. In the App Service window, in the tree view at the bottom of the window, look for your App Service and select it. At this point, if you are not able to see your App Service, chances are good that you created a Linux App Service plan. In that case, you can create a new App Service Plan from this wizard. Remember to grant the *Key Vault Secrets Officer* role to the new App Service Plan.

21. Click the Finish button.

22. Click the Close button.

23. Click the Publish button.

At this point, Visual Studio starts publishing your web application to the selected Azure App Service. When the publishing operation finishes, you should be able to see your web application showing the content of the secret stored in your Key Vault.

EXAM TIP

You can configure two different types of managed identities: system-assigned and user-assigned. System-assigned managed identities are tied to the service instance. If you delete the service instance, the system-assigned managed identity is automatically deleted as well. You can assign the same user-assigned managed identities to several service instances.

Chapter summary

- Authentication is the act of proving that a user is who they claim to be.
- A user authenticates by providing some information that only the user knows.
- There are several mechanisms of authentication that provide different levels of security.
- Some of the authentication mechanisms are form-based, token-based, or certificate-based.
- Using form-based authentication requires your application to store your users' passwords.

- Form-based authentication requires HTTPS to make the authentication process more secure.

- Using token-based authentication, you can delegate the authorization to third-party authentication providers.

- You can add social logins to your application by using token-based authentication.

- Multifactor authentication is an authentication mechanism that requires the users to provide more than one piece of information that only the user knows.

- You can easily implement multifactor authentication by using Microsoft Entra ID.

- There are four main actors in OIDC authentication: client, resource server, resource owner, and authentication server.

- The resource owner needs to authenticate the client before sending the authorization grant.

- The access token grants access to the resource hosted on the resource server.

- The authorization grant or authorization code grants the client the needed rights to request an access token to the authorization server.

- The client uses the refresh token to get a new access token when it expires without needing to request a new authorization code.

- The JSON web token is the most extended implementation of OAuth tokens.

- Shared Access Signatures (SAS) is an authentication mechanism for granting access to Azure Storage Accounts without sharing account keys.

- Shared Access Signatures (SAS) tokens must be signed.

- There are three types of SAS token: user delegation, account, and service SAS.

- User delegation SAS tokens are signed using a key assigned to a Microsoft Entra ID user.

- Account and Service SAS are signed using the Azure Storage account key.

- You can hide the details of the SAS tokens from the URL by using Stored Access Policies.

- Shared access signature tokens provide fine-grained access control to your Azure storage accounts.

- You can create a SAS token for service, container, and item levels.

- You need to register applications in Microsoft Entra ID to be able to authenticate users using your tenant.

- There are three account types supported for authentication: accounts only in the organizational directory, accounts in any organizational directory, and Microsoft accounts.

- You need to provide a return URL for authenticating your application when requesting user authentication.

- You need to configure a secret or a certificate when your application needs to access information in other APIs.

- A security principal is an entity to which you can grant privileges.

- Security principals are users, groups, service principals, and managed identities.

- A permission is an action that a security principal can make with a resource.
- A role definition, or role, is a group of permissions.
- A scope is a level where you can assign a role.
- A role association is a relationship between a security principal, a role, and a scope.
- There are four scopes: management groups, subscription, resource group, and resources.
- You can centralize the configuration of your distributed application using Azure App Configuration.
- Azure App Configuration stores the information using key-value pairs.
- Values in the Azure App Configuration are encrypted.
- Azure Key Vault provides better security than the Azure App Configuration service.
- The size limit for an Azure App Configuration is 10,000, including the key, label, and value.
- You can create references from Azure App Configuration items to Azure Key Vault items.
- Azure Key Vault allows you to store three types of objects: keys, secrets, and certificates.
- You should use managed identities authentication for accessing the Azure Key Vault.
- You need to define a certificate policy before creating a certificate in the Azure Key Vault.
- If you import a certificate into the Azure Key Vault, a default certificate policy is automatically created for you.

Thought experiment

In this thought experiment, demonstrate your skills and knowledge of the topics covered in this chapter. You can find answers to this thought experiment in the next section.

You are developing a web application for your company. The application is in the early stages of development. This application is an internal application that will be used only by the employees of the company. Your company uses Microsoft 365 connected with your company's Active Directory domain. The application needs to use information from Microsoft 365. Answer the following questions about the security implementation of this application:

1. The employees need to be able to access the application using the same username and password they use for accessing Microsoft 365. What should you do?

2. You are using Azure App Services for developing the application. You need to ensure that the web application can access other Azure services without using credentials in your code. What should you do?

3. You need to ensure that the configuration of your application is stored in central storage. You also need to provide the best security for sensitive information such as connection strings and passwords. What should you do?

Thought experiment answers

This section contains the solutions to the thought experiment. Each answer explains why the answer choice is correct.

1. You should use OIDC authentication with Microsoft Entra ID. If you want your application to be able to use Microsoft Entra ID OIDCE authentication, you need to register your application in your Azure tenant. Because your application needs access to information in Microsoft 365, you also need to create a client secret before you can access the Microsoft Graph API. When you connect Microsoft 365 with an Active Directory (AD) domain, users in the AD domain can authenticate to Microsoft 365 using the same username and password they use in the AD domain. Microsoft 365 uses a Microsoft Entra ID tenant for managing the identities of the users in the subscription. Your organization has already configured the synchronization between AD and Microsoft 365 and Microsoft Entra ID. By using OIDC authentication with Microsoft Entra ID, your users should be able to access your application using the same username and passwords that they use in the AD domain.

2. You should use the Managed Service Identity (MSI) authentication. Using this feature, Azure authenticates services based on a service principal configured in a service instance. You can use MSI authentication with services that support Microsoft Entra ID authentication, such as Azure Key Vault or Azure SQL Databases. You need to enable a system-assigned or user-assigned managed identity on your Azure App Service. Using MSI, the Azure SQL Database authenticates the identity assigned to your Azure App Service without you needing to provide a password.

3. You should create an Azure App Configuration store. This is the appropriate service for securely storing your app configuration settings in centralized storage. Although the Azure App Configuration store provides secure storage by encrypting the value of the key-value pairs representing your settings, you should use Key Vault references in your Azure App Configuration store for sensitive information that requires a higher level of security. Azure Key Vault uses hardware-based encryption for storing keys, secrets, and certificates.

CHAPTER 4

Monitor, troubleshoot, and optimize Azure solutions

Providing a good experience for your users is one of the key factors for the success of your application. Several factors affect the user's experience, such as a good user interface design, ease of use, good performance, and low failure rate. You can ensure that your application will perform well by assigning more resources, but if there are not enough users using your application, you might be wasting resources and money.

To ensure that your application is working correctly, you should deploy a monitoring mechanism that helps you gather information about your application's behavior. This is especially important during peak usage periods or failures. Azure provides several tools that help you monitor, troubleshoot, and improve the performance of your application.

Even more important is to observe how your application and your infrastructure behave. In general terms, monitoring is collecting information and detecting failures based on a set of rules you previously configured on your monitoring platform. Observability is the ability to understand what's happening inside your application and infrastructure, thanks to the output data. Analyzing this output data, an observability solution can help you identify situations that deviate from your application's normal behavior.

Skills covered in this chapter:

- Skill 4.1: Implement caching for solutions
- Skill 4.2: Troubleshoot solutions by using Application Insights

Skill 4.1: Implement caching for solutions

Any web application you implement delivers two types of content: dynamic and static.

- **Dynamic content** is the type of content that changes depending on user interaction. An example of dynamic content is a dashboard with several graphs or a list of user movements in a banking application.
- **Static content** is the same for all application users. Images and PDFs are examples of static content (as long as they are not dynamically generated) that users can download from your application.

If the users of your application access it from several locations across the globe, you can improve the application's performance by delivering the content from the location nearest to the user. For static content, you can improve the performance by copying the content to different cache servers distributed across the globe. Using this technique, users can retrieve the static content from the nearest location with lower latency, which improves the performance of your application.

For dynamic content, you can use caching software to store the most accessed data. This means your application returns the information from the cache, which is faster than reprocessing the data or getting it from the storage system.

> **This skill covers how to**
> - Configure cache and expiration policies for Azure Cache for Redis
> - Implement secure and optimized application cache patterns including data sizing, connections, encryption, and expiration
> - Implement Azure Content Delivery Network endpoints and profiles

Configure cache and expiration policies for Azure Cache for Redis

Redis is an open-source cache system that allows you to work *as if in* an in-memory data structure store, database cache, or message broker. The Azure Redis Cache or Azure Cache for Redis is a Redis implementation managed by Microsoft. Redis is available in two different flavors, open-source (OSS Redis) and Redis Enterprise, a commercial product from Redis Inc. Microsoft offers these two flavors as a managed service. Azure Redis Cache has five service tiers that provide different levels of features:

- **Basic** This is the tier with the fewest features and less throughput and higher latency. You should use this tier only for development or testing purposes. No Service Level Agreement (SLA) is associated with the Basic tier. This service tier runs the OSS Redis flavor in a single virtual machine (VM).

- **Standard** This tier offers a two-node, primary-secondary replicated Redis cache managed by Microsoft. This tier is associated with a high-availability SLA of 99.9 percent. This service runs the OSS Redis flavor in two virtual machines in a replicated configuration.

- **Premium** This is a high-performance Redis cluster managed by Microsoft. This tier offers the complete group of features with the highest throughput and lower latencies. The Redis cluster is also deployed on more powerful hardware. This tier has a high-availability SLA of 99.9 percent. This service runs on the OSS Redis flavor deployed on virtual machines more powerful than Basic and Standard layers.

- **Enterprise** This layer uses the Redis Enterprise flavor from Redis Inc. This tier offers enterprise modules such as RedisSearch, RedisBloom, RedisJSON, and RedisTimeSeries. This tier's availability is also higher than the Premium, Standard, and Basic layers. The SLA for this layer is 99.99 percent.

- **Enterprise Flash** This layer offers cost-effective data storage using nonvolatile memory for cache data, instead of DRAM. Since this layer reduces the overall cost per GB, it is best suited for large cache requirements.

> **NOTE** **SCALING THE AZURE REDIS CACHE SERVICE**
>
> You can scale up your existing Azure Redis cache service to a higher tier, but you cannot scale down your current tier to a lower one.

You can work with Azure Cache for Redis using different languages and frameworks, such as ASP.NET, .NET, .NET Core, Node.js, Java, or Python. Before you can add caching features to your code using Azure Redis Cache, you need to create your Azure Cache for Redis database using the following procedure:

1. Open the Azure portal (*https://portal.azure.com*).

2. Click the Create A Resource button.

3. In the Search Services and Marketplace text box, type **azure redis**.

4. Select the Create dropdown menu on the Azure Cache for Redis rectangle in the results area, as shown in Figure 4-1. Then select the Azure Cache for Redis option.

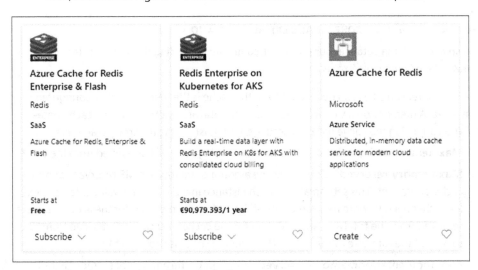

FIGURE 4-1 Creating a new Azure Cache for Redis resource

5. Type a DNS Name for your Redis resource on the New Redis Cache blade.

6. Select the Subscription, Resource Group, and Location from the appropriate dropdown menu that best fits your needs.

7. In the Pricing tier dropdown menu, select the Basic C0 tier.

8. Click the Review + Create button at the bottom of the New Redis Cache blade.

9. Click the Create button.

Deploying your new Azure Cache for Redis takes a few minutes to complete. Once the deployment is complete, you need to get the access keys for your instance of the Azure Cache for Redis. You use this information in your code to connect the Redis service in Azure. The next section will review how to work with Azure Cache for Redis in your code.

As with any cache system, data stored in Azure Cache for Redis has a finite lifetime. When the end-of-life time assigned to the data stored in your cache is reached, the data is deleted from your cache database. This lifetime is configured through the memory policies. This policy controls which data should be evicted or removed from the cache when the cache database is full. Data in Redis is always stored using the key-value pattern. This means that you need to refer to the key when accessing or managing the data stored in your cache database. This principle also applies to data eviction.

Data can be evicted from the cache for two reasons: the time-to-live (TTL) associated with the date is reached or because of a memory management policy. When you create a new key-value in your cache, the data has no TTL assigned. This means your data will be kept in the database forever or until you manually delete it. You can set the TTL of a key by using the EXPIRE Redis command. This command sets the TTL in seconds for a key. After the TTL is reached, the key is automatically deleted from the cache. When you set a TTL, the *expire* field of the key is set to *true*.

> **NEED MORE REVIEW? MORE DETAILS EXPIRE COMMAND**
>
> You can review all the details about the EXPIRE command by reading the Redis article at *https://redis.io/commands/expire/*.

The second reason a key can be evicted from the cache is the memory policy configured for the database. A memory policy controls how keys (or data) are evicted from the cache database. When adjusting the cache memory settings, you must deal with three parameters:

- **Maxmemory policy** Controls how to select the keys that will be evicted from the cache.

- **Maxmemory-reserved** Configures the amount of memory in MB reserved for non-cache operations. This setting affects each instance in a cluster. This value affects workloads that need to write large amounts of data. Memory reserved for these operations is removed from the total available memory for the cache. You can set the value from 10% to 60% of the total size of the cache. The reserved space is shown in MB.

- **Maxfragmentationmemory-reserved** Configures the amount of memory in MB per instance in the cluster reserved for managing memory fragmentation. Making a reservation for memory fragmentation ensures a more consistent behavior in scenarios where the memory is full or close to full. Memory reserved for these operations is removed from the total available memory for the cache. You can set the value from 10% to 60% of the total size of the cache. The reserved space is shown in MB.

When selecting the *maxmemory* policy, there are three main types of algorithms for choosing the key that will be removed from the cache: Random, LRU, and LFU. Random algorithms pick a random key from the database and delete it. LRU stands for Least Recently Used. This algorithm calculates the idle time of a key and removes those keys with higher idle times. The idle time is the difference between now and the last time the key was accessed.

LFU stands for Least Frequently Used. The algorithm assigns a frequency counter to the key. This counter tracks the number of times the key has been accessed. The frequency counter is affected by a decay period that reduces the frequency counter according to the last time the key was accessed. This way, a key that has been frequently used in the past but is no longer used will become a candidate to be deleted from the database.

Bearing in mind the type of algorithms, the available policies are:

- **Volatile-lru**   This is the default policy. This will remove the least recently used keys with the *expire* field set to true.

- **Allkeys-lru**   Removes any key using the LRU algorithm, independently of whether or not the *expire* field is set.

- **Volatile-random**   Removes a random key with the *expire* field set to true.

- **Allkeys-random**   Removes any random key, independently of whether or not the *expire* field is set.

- **Volatile-lfu**   Removes the least frequently used keys with the *expire* field set to true.

- **Allkeys-lfu**   Removes any key using the LFU algorithm, independently of whether or not the *expire* field is set.

- **Noeviction**   No key is removed from the database. If the database is full and you try to add a new key, you will get an error.

Remember that when you create a new key, this key does not set any expire value. This could lead to a situation where the volatile-lru, volatile-lfu, or volatile-random policies cannot find a candidate key to evict from the cache. In that situation, these policies behave as the noeviction policy.

NEED MORE REVIEW?   **MORE DETAILS ON KEY EVICTION**

You can review the details of how the LRU and LFU algorithms are implemented in Redis by reading the article at *https://redis.io/docs/reference/eviction/*.

Implement secure and optimized application cache patterns including data sizing, connections, encryption, and expiration

When working with Azure Cache for Redis, you can use different implementation patterns that solve different issues depending on the architecture of your application:

- **Cache-Aside**   In most situations, your application stores the data that it manages in a database. Accessing data in a database is a relatively slow operation because it depends on the time to access the disk storage system. A solution would be to load the database in memory, but this approach is costly; in most cases, the database simply doesn't fit on the available memory. One solution to improve the performance of your application in these scenarios is to store the most accessed data in the cache. When the back-end system changes the data in the database, the same system can also update the data in the cache, which makes the change available to all clients.

- **Content caching** Most web applications use webpage templates that use common elements, such as headers, footers, toolbars, menus, stylesheets, images, and so on. These template elements are static elements (or at least don't change often). Storing these elements in Azure Cache for Redis relieves your web servers from serving these elements and improves the time your servers need to generate dynamic content.

- **User session caching** This pattern is a good idea if your application needs to register too much information about the user history or data that you need to associate with cookies. Storing too much information in a session cookie hurts the performance of your application. You can save part of that information in your database and store a pointer or index in the session cookie that points that user to the information in the database. If you use an in-memory database, such as Azure Cache for Redis, instead of a traditional database, your application benefits from the faster access times to the data stored in memory.

- **Job and message queuing** You can use Azure Cache for Redis to implement a distributed queue that executes long-lasting tasks that may negatively affect the performance of your application.

- **Distributed transactions** A transaction is a group of commands that need to complete or fail together. Any transaction needs to ensure that the data is always in a stable state. If your application needs to execute transactions, you can use Azure Cache for Redis for implementing these transactions.

If you are using any of the .NET languages, you can use the StackExchange.Redis client for accessing your Azure Cache for Redis resource. You can also use this Redis client for accessing other Redis implementations. When reading or writing values in the Azure Cache for Redis, you must create a ConnectionMultiplexer object. This object creates a connection to your Redis server. The ConnectionMultiplexer class is designed to be reused as much as possible.

For this reason, you should store this object and reuse it across all your code, whenever it is possible to reuse. Creating a connection is a costly operation. For this reason, you should not create a ConnectionMultiplexer object for each read or write operation to the Redis cache. Once you have created your ConnectionMultiplexer object, you can use any of the available operations in the StackExchange.Redis package. Following are the basic operations that you can use with Redis:

- **Use Redis as a database** You get a database from Redis, using the GetDatabase() method, for writing and reading values from the database. You use the StringSet() or StringGet() methods for writing and reading.

- **Use Redis as a messaging queue** You get a subscriber object from the Redis client, using the GetSubscriber() method. Then you can publish messages to a queue, using the Publish() method, and read messages from a queue, using the Subscribe() method. Queues in Redis are known as *channels*.

The following procedure shows how to connect to an Azure Cache for Redis database and read and write data to and from the database using an ASP.NET application:

1. Open Visual Studio 2022.
2. In the Welcome window of Visual Studio 2022, in the Get Started column, select Create A New Project.
3. In the Create A New Project window, in the All Languages dropdown menu, select C#.
4. In the Search For Templates text box, type **asp.net**.
5. In the result list, select ASP.NET Web Application (.NET Framework).
6. Click the Next button at the bottom right of the window.
7. On the Configure Your New Project window, type a Project Name, a Location, and a Solution Name for your project.
8. Click the Create button at the bottom right of the window.
9. In the Create A New ASP.NET Web Application window, select the MVC template on the template list in the middle-left side of the window. MVC stands for Model-View-Controller.
10. On the right side of the Create A New ASP.NET Web Application window, in the Authentication section, ensure that the Authentication is set to None.
11. Click the Create button at the bottom right of the window.
12. In the Visual Studio window, select Tools > NuGet Package Manager > Manage NuGet Packages For Solution.
13. On the NuGet Package Manager tab, click Browse.
14. Type **StackExchange.Redis** and press Enter.
15. Click the StackExchange.Redis package.
16. On the right side of the NuGet Manager tab, click the checkbox next to your project.
17. Click the Install button.
18. In the Preview Changes window, click OK.
19. In the License Acceptance window, click the I Accept button.
20. Open the Azure portal (*https://portal.azure.com*).
21. In the search text box at the top-middle of the portal, type the name of your Azure Cache for Redis that you created in the previous example.
22. In the results list, select your Azure Cache for Redis.
23. On the Azure Cache for Redis blade, select Access Keys in the Settings section in the navigation menu on the left side of the blade.

24. On the Access Keys blade, copy the value of the Primary Connection String (StackExchange.Redis). You need this value in the next steps.

25. In the Visual Studio window, open the Web.config file.

26. In the `<appSettings>` section, add the following code:

```
<add key="CacheConnection " value="<value_copied_in_step_24>"/>
```

> **NOTE SECURITY BEST PRACTICE**
>
> In real-world development, you should avoid putting connection strings and secrets on files that could be checked with the rest of your code. To avoid this, you can put the `<appSettings>` section with the keys containing the sensible secrets or connection strings in a separate file outside the source code control folder. Then add the file parameter to the `<appSettings>` tag pointing to the external `appSettings` file path. You can also use the Azure App Configuration in conjunction with the Azure Key Vault for storing your connection strings.

27. Open the HomeController.cs file in the Controllers folder.

28. Add the following `using` statements to the HomeController.cs file:

```
using System.Configuration;
using StackExchange.Redis;
```

29. Add the code in Listing 4-1 to the `HomeController` class.

LISTING 4-1 HomeController RedisCache method

```
// C#. ASP.NET.
public ActionResult RedisCache()
{
    ViewBag.Message = "A simple example with Azure Cache for Redis on ASP.NET.";

    var lazyConnection = new Lazy<ConnectionMultiplexer>(() =>
    {

    string cacheConnection = ConfigurationManager.AppSettings["CacheConnection"].
ToString();
    return ConnectionMultiplexer.Connect(cacheConnection);
    });
        // You need to create a ConnectionMultiplexer object for accessing the Redis
        // cache.
        // Then you can get an instance of a database.
        IDatabase cache = lazyConnection.Value.GetDatabase();

        // Perform cache operations using the cache object...

        // Run a simple Redis command
        ViewBag.command1 = "PING";
        ViewBag.command1Result = cache.Execute(ViewBag.command1).ToString();

        // Simple get and put of integral data types into the cache
        ViewBag.command2 = "GET Message";
        ViewBag.command2Result = cache.StringGet("Message").ToString();
```

```
    // Write a new value to the database.
    ViewBag.command3 = "SET Message \"Hello! The cache is working from ASP.NET!\"";
    ViewBag.command3Result = cache.StringSet("Message", "Hello! The cache is working
from ASP.NET!").ToString();

    // Get the message that we wrote on the previous step
    ViewBag.command4 = "GET Message";
    ViewBag.command4Result = cache.StringGet("Message").ToString();

    // Get the client list, useful to see if the connection list is growing...
    ViewBag.command5 = "CLIENT LIST";

    ViewBag.command5Result = cache.Execute("CLIENT", "LIST").ToString().
Replace("id=", "\rid=");
    lazyConnection.Value.Dispose();

    return View();

}
```

30. In the Solution Explorer, right-click Views > Home folder and select Add > View from the contextual menu.

31. In the Add View window, type **RedisCache** for the View Name. Leave other fields with their default values.

32. Click the Add button.

33. Open the RedisCache.cshtml file.

34. Replace the content of the RedisCache.cshtml file with the content of Listing 4-2.

LISTING 4-2 RedisCache View

```
// C#. ASP.NET.
@{
    ViewBag.Title = "Azure Cache for Redis Test";
}

<h2>@ViewBag.Title.</h2>
<h3>@ViewBag.Message</h3>
<br /><br />
<table border="1" cellpadding="10">
    <tr>
        <th>Command</th>
        <th>Result</th>
    </tr>
    <tr>
        <td>@ViewBag.command1</td>
        <td><pre>@ViewBag.command1Result</pre></td>
    </tr>
    <tr>
        <td>@ViewBag.command2</td>
        <td><pre>@ViewBag.command2Result</pre></td>
    </tr>
    <tr>
        <td>@ViewBag.command3</td>
        <td><pre>@ViewBag.command3Result</pre></td>
```

```
    </tr>
    <tr>
        <td>@ViewBag.command4</td>
        <td><pre>@ViewBag.command4Result</pre></td>
    </tr>
    <tr>
        <td>@ViewBag.command5</td>
        <td><pre>@ViewBag.command5Result</pre></td>
    </tr>
</table>
```

35. Press F5 to run your project locally.

36. In the web browser running your project, append the *Home/RedisCache* URI to the URL. Your result should look like Figure 4-2.

Command	Result
PING	PONG
GET Message	
SET Message "Hello! The cache is working from ASP.NET!"	True
GET Message	Hello! The cache is working from ASP.NET!
CLIENT LIST	id=9774 addr=127.0.0.1:35187 fd=8 name=PORTAL_CONSOLE age=152 id=9853 addr=83.56.0.194:61343 fd=18 name=DEV-CS age=1 idle=0 id=9854 addr=83.56.0.194:61344 fd=14 name=DEV-CS age=1 idle=1

FIGURE 4-2 Example results

EXAM TIP

You can use Azure Cache for Redis for static content and the most accessed dynamic data. You can use it for in-memory databases or message queues using a publication/subscription pattern.

NEED MORE REVIEW?   MORE DETAILS ABOUT REDIS

You can review features, patterns, and transactions of the Redis cache system by reading the following articles:

- *https://stackexchange.github.io/StackExchange.Redis/Basics*
- *https://stackexchange.github.io/StackExchange.Redis/Transactions*
- *https://stackexchange.github.io/StackExchange.Redis/KeysValues*

The code in Listing 4-1 is very basic code that shows how to connect to an Azure Cache for Redis service, but this code does not implement any best practices. As you can see in that code, we create a `ConnectionMultiplexer` object to connect to the Redis cache. The problem with this code is that it creates and disposes of a `ConnectionMultiplexer` object, even when using lazy initialization, every time the RedisCache is invoked. Instead, you should consider using a `ConnectionMultiplexer` singleton.

Even working with a singleton pattern, you may face situations for which the `Connection-Multiplexer` object is unable to reconnect to Redis after a transient failure. To avoid these situations, you should monitor `RedisConnectionExceptions` and `RedisSocketExceptions` and call the `ForceReconnectAsync()` method to recover from a transient connection error.

When working with Redis, you need to adjust two timeout values to your needs. These timeout values are connection and command timeout. The connection timeout is the time that your application (the client) waits to establish a connection with the Redis server. Don't set this value to less than 5 seconds. Reducing this value too much may lead to situations where the connection attempt fails when there is high resource pressure, such as high server CPU usage or high client CPU usage. Low connection time values may lead to a connect-fail-retry loop.

The other timeout value is the command timeout. This value represents the amount of time the client waits for a response from the Redis server. The initial recommendation is to set this value to 5 seconds, but this would greatly depend on the size of your database. Setting this value too low may lead to the connection seeming unstable. Setting this value too high may lead to your application waiting too long to see whether the command will time out.

In the same way that setting the connection timeout to a too-small value could lead to a connect-fail-retry loop and longer outages, reconnecting many client instances simultaneously may extend the time a client needs to establish a successful connection. Consider implementing a reconnect strategy and let the `ConnectionMultiplexer` handle the reconnection. In this scenario, you should also set the `abortConnect` connection string property to false.

Another topic you should consider when working with Azure Cache for Redis is the size of the data you store in your database. Redis works better with smaller values. Any data size over 100 KB is considered a large value. If you need to work with large values, consider splitting the value into smaller chunks and creating more keys.

NEED MORE REVIEW?   **MORE ABOUT BEST PRACTICES WHEN USING REDIS**

You can find more details about some of the best practices we reviewed in this section by reading the following Microsoft articles:

- *https://learn.microsoft.com/en-us/azure/architecture/best-practices/caching*

- *https://learn.microsoft.com/en-us/azure/azure-cache-for-redis/cache-best-practices-development*

- *https://learn.microsoft.com/en-us/azure/azure-cache-for-redis/cache-best-practices-memory-management*

- *https://learn.microsoft.com/en-us/azure/azure-cache-for-redis/cache-best-practices-performance*

Implement Azure Content Delivery Network endpoints and profiles

A Content Delivery Network (CDN) is a group of servers distributed in different locations across the globe that can deliver web content to users. Because the CDN has servers distributed in several locations, when a user makes a request to the CDN, the CDN delivers the content from the server nearest to the user.

The main advantage of using Azure CDN with your application is that Azure CDN caches your application's static content. When a user makes a request to your application, the CDN stores the static content, such as images, documents, and stylesheet files. When a second user from the same location as the first user accesses your application, the CDN delivers the cached content, relieving your web server from delivering the static content. You can use third-party CDN solutions such as Verizon or Akamai with Azure CDN.

To use Azure CDN with your solution, you must configure a profile. This profile contains the list of endpoints in your application that would be included in the CDN. The profile also configures the behavior of content delivery and access of each configured endpoint. When you configure an Azure CDN profile, you choose between using Microsoft's CDN or using CDNs from Verizon or Akamai.

You can configure as many profiles as you need for grouping your endpoints based on different criteria, such as internet domain, web application, or any other criteria. Keep in mind that Azure CDN pricing tiers are applied at the profile level so that you can configure different profiles with different pricing characteristics. As with any CDN solution in the real world, you need a web application to run the procedures and demonstrations throughout this skill.

The following procedure shows how to create a basic web application in Visual Studio and publish it in an Azure Web App. You can use this Azure Web App in all the examples in the rest of this skill:

1. Open Visual Studio 2022 on your computer.
2. In the Visual Studio home window, click the Continue Without Code link at the bottom of the Get Started column.
3. Select the Tools menu and choose Get Tools And Features. Verify that the ASP.NET And Web Development In The Web & Cloud section is checked.
4. In the Visual Studio window, select File > New > Project to open the New Project window.
5. In the Create a New Project window, select C# in the dropdown menu below the Search For Templates text box at the top right of the window.
6. In the All Project Types dropdown menu, select Web.
7. In the list of templates on the right side of the window, select ASP.NET Core Web Application.
8. Click the Next button at the bottom right of the Create A New Project window.

9. In the Configure Your New Project window, complete the following steps:

   A. Select a name for the project.

   B. Enter a path for the location of the solution.

   C. In the Solution dropdown menu, select Create A New Solution.

   D. Enter a name for the solution.

10. Click the Next button in the bottom right of the Configure Your New Project window.

11. In the Additional Information ASP.NET Core Web Application window, ensure that the .NET 6.0 option is selected in the Framework dropdown menu.

12. Deselect the Configure For HTTPS option.

13. Click the Create button in the bottom right of the Additional Information ASP.NET Core Web Application window.

14. On the Overview Tab that opens in Visual Studio, select the Publish option on the left side once the new project has been created.

15. In the Publish window, in the Target tab, select the Azure option.

16. Click the Next button.

17. In the Specific Target tab, select Azure App Service (Windows) and click the Next button.

18. In the Azure App Service tab, click the Create New button on the right side of the window.

19. In the Create App Service window, add a new Azure account. This account must have enough subscription privileges for creating new resource groups, app services, and an App Service plan.

20. Once you have added a valid account, you can configure the settings for publishing your web application. In the App Name text box, enter a name for the App Service. By default, this name matches the name that you gave to your project.

21. In the Subscription dropdown menu, select the subscription in which you want to create the App Service.

22. In the Resource Group dropdown menu, select the resource group you want to create the App Service and the App Service plan. If you need to create a new resource group, you can do so by clicking the New link on the right side of the dropdown menu.

23. Click the New link to open the Configure Hosting Plan window to the right of the Hosting Plan dropdown menu.

24. In the Configure Hosting Plan window, type a name for the App Service plan in the App Service Plan text box.

25. Select a region from the Location dropdown menu.

26. Select a virtual machine size from the Size dropdown menu.

27. Click the OK button in the bottom right of the window. This closes the Configure Hosting Plan window.

28. At the bottom right of the Create App Service window, click the Create button. This starts the creation of the needed resources to publish the App Service.

29. Ensure that the newly created App Service is selected in the App Service section in the Publish window, and then click the Finish button on the bottom right of the window.

30. Click the Publish button on the top right of the Publish tab in Visual Studio.

31. Once the publishing process has finished, Visual Studio opens your default web browser with the URL of the newly deployed App Service. This URL will have the structure *https://<your_app_service_name>.azurewebsites.net*.

Once you have created your testing Azure Web App, you can use the URL that you got from step 31 in the previous procedure with the rest of the procedures in this skill. The following procedure shows how to create an Azure CDN profile with one endpoint for caching content from a web application:

1. Open the Azure portal (*https://portal.azure.com*).

2. Click the Create A Resource button in the Azure Services section.

3. On the New blade, in the Search Services And Marketplace text box, type **CDN**.

4. In the results list, select the Front Door and CDN Profiles box.

5. On the Front Door and CDN Profiles blade, click the Create button.

6. Keep the default options on the Compare Offerings blade and click the Continue To Create A Front Door button.

7. Select an existing Resource Group in the dropdown menu on the Create A Front Door profile blade. Alternatively, you can create a new resource group by clicking the Create New link below the Resource Group dropdown menu.

8. Type a Name for the profile in the corresponding text box.

9. In the Pricing Tier option, select Standard.

10. Type an Endpoint Name. This will be part of the URL you need to access your application.

11. Select App Service from the Origin Type dropdown menu.

12. Select your app service from the Origin Host Name dropdown menu.

13. Click the Review + Create button at the bottom of the CDN profile blade.

14. Click the Create button.

15. Click the Go To Resource button on the deployment blade. Alternatively, in the Search text box at the top of the Azure portal, you can type the name for your Front Door and CDN profile.

16. Select the Front Door Manager option in the Settings section, shown in Figure 4-3, to review the endpoint you created while creating the profile.

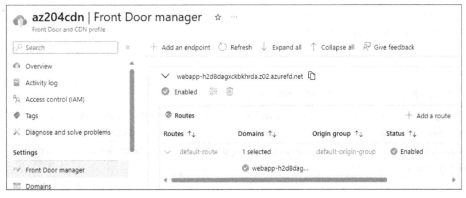

FIGURE 4-3 CDN profile

The propagation of the content through the CDN depends on the type of CDN that you configured. For Standard CDN, the propagation usually completes in 10 minutes. Once the propagation of the CDN completes, you can access your web application by using the endpoint that you configured in the previous procedure: *https://<your_endpoint's_name>-<hash>.z01. azurefd.net*.

Once you have configured the endpoint, you can apply some advanced options to adjust the CDN to your needs:

- **Custom DNS domain** By default, when using the CDN, your users access your application by using the URL *https://<your_endpoint's_name>-<hash>.z01.azurefd.net*. This URL would not be appropriate for your application. You can assign more appropriate DNS domains to the CDN endpoint, such as *https://app.contoso.com*, which allows your users to access your web application using a URL related to your business and your DNS domain name.

- **Compression** You can configure the CDN endpoint to compress some MIME types. This compression is made on the fly by the CDN when the content is delivered from the cache. Compressing the content allows you to deliver smaller files, improving the overall performance of the application.

- **Caching rules** You can control how the content is stored in the cache by setting different rules for different paths or content types. By configuring a cache rule, you can modify the cache expiration time, depending on the conditions you configure. Caching rules are only available for profiles from Verizon's Azure CDN Standard and Akamai's Azure CDN Standard.

- **Geo-filtering** You can block or allow a web application's content to specific countries across the globe.

- **Optimization** You can configure the CDN for optimizing the delivery of different types of content. Depending on the type of profile, you can optimize your endpoint for
  - General web delivery
  - Dynamic site acceleration

- General media streaming
- Video-on-demand media streaming
- Large file downloads

> **NEED MORE REVIEW? HOW CACHING WORKS**
>
> Caching web content involves working with HTTP headers, setting the appropriate expiration times, or deciding which files should be included in the cache. You can review the details of how caching works by reading the article at *https://docs.microsoft.com/en-us/azure/cdn/cdn-how-caching-works*.

Skill 4.2: Troubleshoot solutions by using Application Insights

Knowing how your application behaves during regular operation is essential, especially for production environments. You need to get information about the number of users, resource consumption, transactions, and other metrics that can help you troubleshoot your application if an error occurs. Adding custom metrics to your application is also important when creating alerts that warn you when your application is not behaving as expected.

Azure provides features for monitoring the consumption of resources assigned to your application. Also, you can monitor the transactions and any other metrics that you may need, which allows you to fully understand how your application behaves under conditions that are usually difficult to simulate or test. You can also use these metrics for efficiently creating auto-scale rules to improve the performance of your application.

> **This skill covers how to**
>
> - Configure an app or service to use Application Insights
> - Monitor and analyze metrics, logs, and traces
> - Implement Application Insights Web Test and Alerts

Configure an app or service to use Application Insights

Microsoft provides you with the ability to monitor your application while it is running by using Application Insights. This tool integrates with your code, allowing you to monitor what is happening inside your code while it is executing in a cloud, on-premises, or in a hybrid environment. You can also enable Application Insights for applications that are already deployed in Azure without modifying the already deployed code.

By adding a small instrumentation package, you can measure several aspects of your application. These measures, known as telemetry, are automatically sent to the Application Insights component deployed in Azure. Based on the information sent from the telemetry streams from your application to the Azure portal, you can analyze your application's performance and create alerts and dashboards, which help you better understand how your application is behaving. Although Application Insights must be deployed in the Azure portal, your application can be executed in Azure, in other public clouds, or in your on-premises infrastructure. When you deploy the Application Insights instrumentation in your application, it monitors the following points:

- **Request rates, response times, and failure rates**   You can view which pages your users request more frequently, distributed across time. You may find that your users tend to visit specific pages at the beginning of the day, whereas other pages are visited more at the end of the day. You can also monitor the time that your server takes for delivering the requested page or even if there were failures when delivering the page. You should monitor the failure rates and response times to ensure that your application is performing correctly and your users have a pleasant experience.

- **Dependency rates, response times, and failure rates**   If your application depends on external services (such as Azure Storage Accounts), Google, or Twitter security services for authenticating your users, or any other external service, you can monitor how these external services are performing and how they are affecting your application.

- **Exceptions**   The instrumentation keeps track of the exceptions raised by servers and browsers while your application is executing. You can review the details of the stack trace for each exception via the Azure portal. You can also view statistics about exceptions that arise during your application's execution.

- **Page views and load performance**   Measuring the performance of your server's page delivery is only part of the equation. Using Application Insights, you can also get information about the page views and load performance reported from the browser's side.

- **AJAX calls**   This measures the time taken by AJAX calls made from your application's webpages. It also measures the failure rates and response time.

- **User and session counts**   You can keep track of the number of users who are connected to your application. Just as the same user can initiate multiple sessions, you can track the number of sessions connected to your application. This allows you to clearly measure the threshold of concurrent users supported by your application.

- **Performance counters**   You can get information about the performance counters of the server machine (CPU, memory, and network usage) from which your code is executing.

- **Hosts diagnostics**   Hosts diagnostics can get information from your application if it is deployed in a Docker or Azure environment.

- **Diagnostic trace logs** Trace log messages can be used to correlate trace events with the requests made to the application by your users.

- **Custom events and metrics** Although the out-of-the-box instrumentation offered by Application Insights offers much information, some metrics are too specific to your application to be generalized and included in the general telemetry. For those cases, you can create custom metrics to monitor your server and client code. This allows you to monitor user actions, such as shopping cart checkouts or game scoring.

Application Insights are not limited to .NET languages. There are instrumentation libraries available for other languages, such as Java, JavaScript, or Node.js. There are also libraries available for other platforms such as Android or iOS. You can use the following procedure to add Application Insights instrumentation to your ASP.NET application. To run this example, you must meet these prerequisites:

- An Azure Subscription.

- Visual Studio 2022. If you don't have Visual Studio, you can download the Community edition for free from *https://visualstudio.microsoft.com/free-developer-offers/*.

- Install the following workloads in Visual Studio:
    - ASP.NET and web development, including the optional components.
    - Azure development.

In this example, you will create a new MVC application from a template and then add the Application Insights instrumentation. You can use the same procedure to add instrumentation to any of your existing ASP.NET applications:

1. Open Visual Studio 2022.

2. In the home window in Visual Studio, click the Create A New Project button in the Get Started section on the right side of the window.

3. In the Create A New Project window, in the Search box, type **asp.net**.

4. Select the ASP.NET Web Application (.NET Framework) template.

5. Click the Next button in the bottom right of the window.

6. Type a name for your project and solution in the Project Name and Solution Name boxes, respectively.

7. Select the Location where your project will be stored.

8. Click the Create button at the bottom right of the window.

9. On the Create A New ASP.NET Web Application window, select the MVC template.

10. Click the Create button at the bottom right of the window.

11. In the Solution Explorer window, right-click the name of your project.

12. In the contextual menu, shown in Figure 4-4, select Add > Application Insights Telemetry.

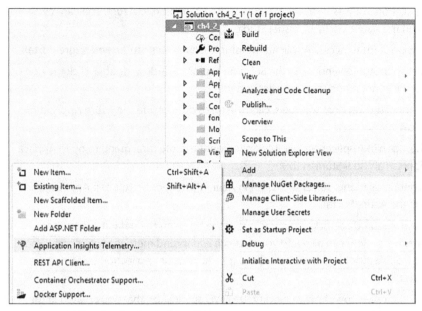

FIGURE 4-4 Adding Application Insights Telemetry

13. In the Connect to dependency menu, select Azure Application Insights.

14. Click the Next button.

15. On the Application Insights Configuration page, click the Get Started button at the bottom.

16. On the Connect to Azure Application Insights page, ensure that the correct Azure Account and Azure Subscription are selected in the dropdown menus.

17. Click the Create New button on the middle right side of the window.

18. In the Application Insights Create New dialog box, type a name for the new Application Insights instance.

19. In the Application Insights Create New dialog box, select the Subscription, Resource Group, Location, and Azure Log Analytics workspace where you want to create the new Application Insight resource.

20. Click the Create button.

21. On the Connect To Azure Application Insights window, click the Next button.

22. Click the Finish button.

23. Click the Close button when the Dependency Configuration process finishes.

At this point, Visual Studio starts adding the needed packages and dependencies to your project. Visual Studio also automatically configures the Instrumentation Key, which allows your application to connect to the Application Insights resource created in Azure. Now, your project is connected with the Application Insights instance deployed in Azure. As soon as you run your project, the Application Insights instrumentation sends information to Azure. You can review this information in the Azure portal or Visual Studio.

Use the following steps to access Application Insights from Visual Studio and Azure portal:

1. From the Visual Studio window, in the Solution Explorer window, double-click the Connected Services node under your project's name.

2. On the Connected Services windows, click the three dots beside the Azure Application Insights row.

3. Select the Open In Application Insights option on the contextual menu to open Application Insights in a Visual Studio tab.

4. On the contextual menu, select the Open In Azure Portal option to open Application Insights in the Azure Portal.

Apart from the standard metrics that come out of the box with the default Application Insights instrumentation, you can also add your custom events and metrics to your code. You can analyze and troubleshoot logic and workflows specific to your application using custom events and metrics.

The following example shows how to modify the MVC application that you created in the previous example for adding custom events and metrics:

1. Open the project that you created in the previous example.

2. Open the HomeController.cs file.

3. Add the following using statements at the beginning of the file:

```
using Microsoft.ApplicationInsights;
using System.Diagnostics;
```

4. Replace the content of the HomeController class in the HomeController.cs file with the content in Listing 4-3.

LISTING 4-3 HomeController class

```
// C#. ASP.NET.
public class HomeController : Controller
    {
        private TelemetryClient telemetry;
        private double indexLoadCounter;

        public HomeController()
        {
            //Create a TelemetryClient that can be used during the life of the
            // Controller.
            telemetry = new TelemetryClient();

            //Initialize some counters for the custom metrics.
            //This is a fake metric just for demo purposes.
            indexLoadCounter = new Random().Next(1000);
        }
```

```
public ActionResult Index()
{
    //This example is trivial since ApplicationInsights already registered the
    // load of the page.
    //You can use this example for tracking different events in the
    // application.
    telemetry.TrackEvent("Loading the Index page");
    //Before you can submit a custom metric, you need to use the GetMetric
    //method.

    telemetry.GetMetric("CountOfIndexPageLoads").TrackValue(indexLoadCounter);


    //This trivial example shows how to track exceptions using Application
    //Insights.
    //You can also send trace messages to Application Insights.
    try
    {
        Trace.TraceInformation("Raising a trivial exception");
        throw new System.Exception(@"Trivial Exception for testing Tracking
        Exception feature in Application Insights");
    }
    catch (System.Exception ex)
    {
        Trace.TraceError("Capturing and managing the trivial exception");
        telemetry.TrackException(ex);
    }


    //You need to instruct the TelemetryClient to send all in-memory data to
    // the ApplicationInsights.
    telemetry.Flush();
    return View();
}

public ActionResult About()
{
    ViewBag.Message = "Your application description page.";


    //This example is trivial since ApplicationInsights already registers the
    //load of the page.
    //You can use this example for tracking different events in the
    // application.
    telemetry.TrackEvent("Loading the About page");

    return View();
}

public ActionResult Contact()
{
    ViewBag.Message = "Your contact page.";
    //This example is trivial since ApplicationInsights already registers the
load
    //of the page.
    //You can use this example for tracking different events in the
```

```
        // application.
        telemetry.TrackEvent("Loading the Contact page");

        return View();
    }
}
```

5. In Solution Explorer, open the ApplicationInsights.config file.

6. In the `<Add Type="Microsoft.ApplicationInsights.Extensibility.PerfCounterCollector. PerformanceCollectorModule, Microsoft.AI.PerfCounterCollector">` XML item, add the following child XML item:

    `<EnableIISExpressPerformanceCounters>true</EnableIISExpressPerformanceCounters>`

> **NOTE CONTROLLERS CONSTRUCTORS**
>
> In the previous example, we used a private property in the constructor for creating and initial-izing a TelemetryClient object. In a real-world application, you should use dependency injec-tion techniques for properly initializing the Controller class. There are several frameworks, such as Unity, Autofac, or Ninject, that can help you implement the dependency injection pattern in your code.

At this point, you can press F5 and run your project to see how your application is sending information to Application Insights. If you review the Application Insights Search tab, you can see the messages, shown in Figure 4-5, that your application is sending to Application Insights.

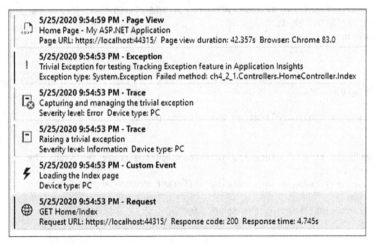

5/25/2020 9:54:59 PM - Page View
Home Page - My ASP.NET Application
Page URL: https://localhost:44315/ Page view duration: 42.357s Browser: Chrome 83.0

5/25/2020 9:54:53 PM - Exception
Trivial Exception for testing Tracking Exception feature in Application Insights
Exception type: System.Exception Failed method: ch4_2_1.Controllers.HomeController.Index

5/25/2020 9:54:53 PM - Trace
Capturing and managing the trivial exception
Severity level: Error Device type: PC

5/25/2020 9:54:53 PM - Trace
Raising a trivial exception
Severity level: Information Device type: PC

5/25/2020 9:54:53 PM - Custom Event
Loading the Index page
Device type: PC

5/25/2020 9:54:53 PM - Request
GET Home/Index
Request URL: https://localhost:44315/ Response code: 200 Response time: 4.745s

FIGURE 4-5 Application Insights messages

You send messages to Application Insights by using the `TelemetryClass` class. This class provides you with the appropriate methods for sending the different types of messages to Application Insights. You can send custom events by using the `TrackEvent()` method. You use this method for tracking meaningful events to your application, such as when the user creates a new shopping cart in an eCommerce web application, or the user wins a game in a mobile app.

If you need to keep track of the value of certain variables or properties in your code, you can combine GetMetric() and TrackValue() methods. The GetMetric() method retrieves a metric from the azure.applicationinsight namespace. If the metric doesn't exist on the namespace, the Application Insights library automatically creates a new one. Once you have a reference to the correct metric, you can use the TrackValue() method to add a value to that metric. You can use these custom metrics for setting alerts or autoscale rules. Use the following steps for viewing the custom metrics in the Azure portal:

1. From the Visual Studio window, double-click the Connected Services node under your project's name in the Solution Explorer window.

2. On the Connected Services windows, click the three dots beside the Azure Application Insights row.

3. In the contextual menu, select the Open In Azure Portal option to open Application Insights in the Azure portal.

4. On the Application Insights blade, select Metrics in the Monitoring section of the navigation menu on the left side of the blade.

5. On the Metrics blade, on the toolbar above the empty graph, on the Metric Namespace dropdown menu, select azure.applicationsight.

6. In the Metric dropdown menu, select CountOfIndexPageLoad. This is the custom metric that you defined in the previous example.

7. In the Aggregation dropdown menu, select Count. The values for your graph will be different but should look similar to Figure 4-6.

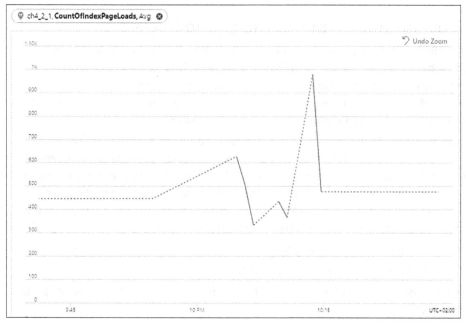

FIGURE 4-6 Custom metric graph

You can also send log messages to Application Insights by using the integration between System.Diagnostics and Application Insights. Any message sent to the diagnostics system using the Trace class appears in Application Insights as a Trace message. In this same line, use the TraceException() method for sending the stack trace and the exception to Application Insights. The advantage of doing this is that you can easily correlate exceptions with the operations that were performing your code when the exception happened.

EXAM TIP

Remember that Application Insights is a solution for monitoring the behavior of an application on different platforms, written in different languages. You can use Application Insights with web applications, native applications, or mobile applications written in .NET, Java, JavaScript, or Node.js. There is no requirement to run your application in Azure. You only need to use Azure to deploy the Application Insights resource that you use for analyzing the information sent by your application.

NEED MORE REVIEW? CREATING CUSTOM EVENTS AND METRICS

You can create more complex metrics and events than the ones that we reviewed here. For complex operations, you can track all the actions inside an operation to correctly correlate all the messages generated during the execution of the operation. You can learn more about how to create custom events and metrics by reading the article at *https://docs.microsoft.com/en-us/azure/azure-monitor/app/api-custom-events-metrics*.

Monitor and analyze metrics, logs, and traces

Azure Monitor is a tool composed of several elements that help you monitor and better understand the behavior of your solutions. Application Insights is a tool for collecting information from your solutions. Once you have the collected information, you can use the Analyze tools for reviewing the data and troubleshooting your application. You can use Metric Analytics or Log Analytics depending on the information you need to analyze.

You can use Metric Analytics to review the standard and custom metrics sent from your application. A metric is a numeric value related to some aspect at a particular point in time of your solution. CPU usage, free memory, and the number of requests are all examples of metrics. You can also create your own custom metrics. Because metrics are lightweight, you can use them to monitor scenarios in near real-time. You analyze metric data by representing the values of the metrics in a time interval using different types of graphs.

Use the following steps for reviewing graphs:

1. Open the Azure portal (*https://portal.azure.com*).

2. In the Search Resources, Services, And Docs text box on the top side of the Azure portal, type **monitor**.

3. Select Monitor in the Services section in the result list.

4. On the Monitor blade, select Metrics in the navigation menu on the left side of the blade.

5. On the Metrics blade, the Select A Scope panel should appear automatically.

6. On the Select A Scope panel, in the scope tree, select the subscription or resource groups that contain the Azure App Service containing the metrics you want to add to the graph.

7. In the Resource Type dropdown menu, below the scope tree, select only the App Services resource type.

8. In the App Service dropdown, select one of your App Services.

9. Click the Apply button at the bottom of the panel.

10. On the Metrics blade, select the Average Response Time metric in the Metric dropdown menu.

11. Click the Add Metric button at the top of the graph. You can add several metrics to the same graph, which means you can analyze different metrics that are related among them.

12. Repeat step 10 for adding the Connections metric. Figure 4-7 shows the metrics added to the graph.

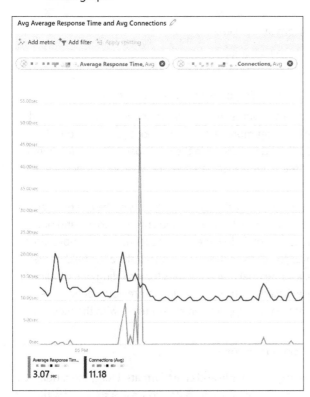

FIGURE 4-7 Configuring metrics for a graph

You use Log Analytics for analyzing the trace, logs, events, exceptions, and any other message sent from your application. Log messages are more complex than metrics because they can contain much more information than a simple numeric value. You can analyze log messages by using queries for retrieving, consolidating, and analyzing the collected data. Log Analytics for Azure Monitor uses a version of the Kusto query language. You can construct your queries to get information from the data stored in Azure Monitor. To do so, complete the following steps:

1. Open the Azure portal (*https://portal.azure.com*).
2. In the Search Resources, Services, And Docs text box at the top of the Azure portal, type **monitor**.
3. Select Monitor in the Services section in the result list.
4. On the Monitor blade, select Logs in the navigation menu on the left side of the blade.
5. On the Logs blade, click the Get Started button.
6. On the Logs blade, the Select A Scope panel should appear automatically.
7. On the Select A Scope panel, in the scope tree, navigate to the resources containing the logs you want to query. Click the checkbox next to the resource. You can select only resources of the same type. For this example, the resource type should be Application Insights.
8. Click the Apply button at the bottom of the panel.
9. On the Logs blade, type **traces** in the text area.
10. Click the Run button.
11. Review the result of your query in the section below the query text area.

This simple query returns all the trace error events stored in your Application Insights workspace. You can use more complex queries to get more information about your solution. The available fields for the queries depend on the data loaded in the workspace. The data schema manages these fields. Figure 4-8 shows the schema associated with a workplace that stores data from Application Insights.

Once you get the results from a query, you can easily refine the results of the query by adding where clauses to the query. The easiest way to add new filtering criteria is to expand one of the records in the table view in the results section below the query text area. If you move your mouse over each of the fields in a record, you can see three small dots before the field of the record. If you click the three-dots icon, a contextual menu appears for including or excluding the value of the field in the where clause. Based on the example in the previous section, the following query would get all traces sent from the application except those with the message Raising a trivial exception.

```
traces | where message <> "Raising a trivial exception"
```

You can review the results of this query in both table and chart formats. Using the different visualization formats, you can get a different insight into the data. Figure 4-9 shows how the results from the previous query are plotted into a pie chart.

FIGURE 4-8 Workspace schema

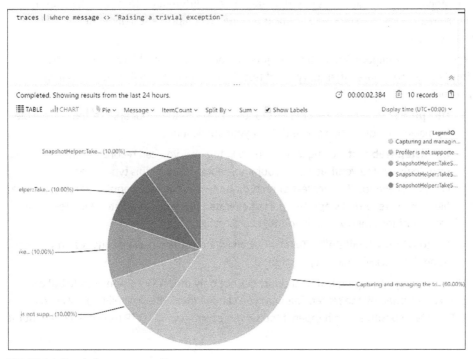

FIGURE 4-9 Rendering query results

EXAM TIP

When you try to query logs from the Azure Monitor, remember that you must enable the diagnostics logs for the Azure App Services. If you get the message, *We didn't find any logs* when you try to query the logs for your Azure App Service, that could mean that you need to configure the diagnostic settings in your App Service.

Implement Application Insights Web Test and Alerts

As a result of analyzing the data sent from your application to the Azure Monitor using Application Insights, you may find some situations that you need to monitor more carefully. Using Azure Monitor, you can set alerts based on the value of different metrics or logs. For example, you can create an alert to receive a notification when your application generates an HTTP return code 502.

You can also configure Application Insights to monitor the availability of your web application. You can configure different types of tests for checking the availability of your web application:

- **URL ping test**   This is a simple test for checking whether your application is available by making a request to a single URL for your application.

- **Multistep web test**   Using Visual Studio Enterprise, you can record the steps that you want to use as the verification for your application. You use this type of test for checking complex scenarios. The process of recording the steps in a web application generates a file with the recorded steps. Using this generated file, you can create a web test in Application Insights; then you upload the recording file.

- **Custom Track Availability Test**   You can create your own availability test in your code using the TrackAvailability() method.

When creating a URL ping test, you can check not only the HTTP response code but also the content returned by the server. This way, you can minimize the possibility of false positives. These false positives can happen if the server returns a valid HTTP response code, but the content is different due to configuration errors. Use the following procedure for creating a URL ping test on your Application Insights that checks the availability of your web application:

1. Open the Azure portal (*https://portal.azure.com*).

2. In the Search Resources, Services, And Docs text box at the top of the Azure portal, type **monitor**.

3. Select Monitor in the Services section in the result list.

4. On the Monitor blade, select Applications in the Insights section.

5. On the Applications blade, select the name of the Application Insights resource where you want to configure the alert.

6. On the Applications Insights blade, select Availability in the Investigate section of the navigation menu on the left side of the blade.

7. On the Availability blade, select Add Classic Test at the top left of the blade.

8. On the Create Test blade, shown in Figure 4-10, type a name for the test in the Test Name text box.

FIGURE 4-10 Creating a URL test

9. Ensure that URL Ping is selected in the SKU dropdown menu.

10. In the URL text box, type the URL of the application you want to test.

11. Expand the Test Location section. Select the locations from which you want to perform the URL ping test.

12. Leave the other options as they are.

13. Click the Create button at the bottom of the panel.

When you configure the URL ping test, you cannot configure the alert directly during the creation process. You need to finish the creation of the test, and then you can edit the alert for defining the actions that you want to perform when the alert fires.

Use the following procedure for configuring an alert associated with the URL ping test that you configured previously:

1. On the Availability blade, click the ellipsis beside the newly created alert.

2. In the contextual menu, select the Open Rules (Alerts) Page option.

3. On your alert Rules Management blade, in the Condition column, ensure that there is a default condition with the name *Failed locations >= 2*.

4. Click the name of your newly created alert.

5. On the Metric Alert Rule blade, select the Action Groups option in the Alert Rule Configuration section.

6. On the Configured Actions panel, click the Create Action Group button.

7. On the Create Action Group panel, select a resource group to save this action group. Alternatively, you can create a new resource group by clicking the Create New link below the Resource Group dropdown menu.

8. Type a name in the Action Group Name text box. This name must be unique in the resource group that you selected in the previous step.

9. Type a descriptive name in the Display Name text box.

10. Click the Next: Notifications button at the bottom of the panel.

11. In the Notifications section, in the Notification Type dropdown menu, select Email/SMS Message/Push/Voice.

12. On the Email/SMS/Push/Voice panel, select the Email checkbox.

13. Type an email address in the text box below the Email checkbox.

14. Click the OK button at the bottom of the panel.

15. Type a name in the Name text box, next to the Notification Type dropdown menu.

16. Click the Next: Actions button at the bottom of the panel.

17. Leave the Actions section as is. You can use this section for configuring actions such as calling an Azure Function, creating a ticket in an ITSM system, or starting an Azure Automation Runbook.

18. Click the Review & Create button.

19. Click the Create button.

20. On your alert Rules Management blade, ensure that the newly created Action Group has been correctly added to the list of Action Groups attached to the alert.

21. Click the Save button on the top left of your alert Rules Management blade.

Now you can test whether the URL ping test is working correctly by temporarily shutting down your testing application. After five minutes, you should receive an email message at the email address you configured in the alert action associated with the URL ping test.

EXAM TIP

Remember that you need a Visual Studio Enterprise license for creating multistep web tests. You use Visual Studio Enterprise for the definition of the steps that are part of the test, and then you upload the test definition to Azure Application Insights.

NEED MORE REVIEW? AZURE MONITOR ALERTS

Apart from creating alerts when a web test fails, you can also create alerts based on other conditions that depend on the events information stored in Application Insights. You can review the details about how to create these alerts by reviewing the article at *https://docs.microsoft. com/en-us/azure/azure-monitor/platform/alerts-log*.

EXAM TIP

Remember to test your retry strategy carefully. Using the wrong retry strategy could lead your application to exhaust the resources needed for executing your code. A wrong retry strategy can potentially lead to infinite loops if you don't use circuit breakers.

Chapter summary

- Your application must be able to manage transient faults.
- You must determine the type of fault before retrying the operation.
- You should not use immediate retry more than once.
- You should use random starting values for the retry periods.
- You should use the built-in SDK mechanism when available.
- You should test your retry count and interval strategy.
- You should log transient and nontransient faults.
- You can improve the performance of your application by adding a cache to your application.
- Azure Cache for Redis allows the caching of dynamic content.
- Using Azure Cache for Redis, you can create in-memory databases to cache the most-used values.
- Azure Cache for Redis allows you to use messaging queue patterns.
- Content Delivery Networks (CDNs) store and distribute static content in servers distributed across the globe.

- CDNs reduce the latency by serving the content from the server nearest to the user.
- You can invalidate the content of the cache by setting a low TTL (Time-To-Live).
- You can invalidate the content of the cache by removing all or part of the content from the cache.
- Application Insights gets information from your application and sends it to Azure.
- You can use Application Insights with different platforms and languages.
- Application Insights is part of the Azure Monitor service.
- Application Insights generates two types of information: metrics and logs.
- Application Insights allows you to create web tests to monitor the availability of your application.
- You can configure alerts and trigger different actions associated with web tests.

Thought experiment

In this thought experiment, demonstrate your skills and knowledge of the topics covered in this chapter. You can find answers to this thought experiment in the next section.

Your company has a Line-of-Business (LOB) application that has been developed by your team. This LOB application is an eCommerce application that has more usage during holiday periods. The LOB application needs to get some information from external systems. You are receiving some complaints about the stability and performance of the application. Answer the following questions about the troubleshooting and the performance of the application:

1. After reviewing the metrics of your application in the Azure Monitor, you find that you don't have enough detail about the performance of the internal application workflows. What should you do to get information about the internal workflows?

2. After reviewing the metrics of your application in the Azure Monitor, you find that some of the stability issues are due to the external systems. You need to minimize the effect on the user experience. Which strategy should you use?

3. You need to ensure that the purchase process is working correctly. You decide to configure a web test in Application Insights. Which type of test should you configure?

Thought experiment answers

This section contains the solutions to the thought experiment. Each answer explains why the answer choice is correct.

1. You should integrate Application Insights instruments with your code. Once you integrate the Application Insights with your code, you can track custom events in your code. You can define operations inside your code to track complex operations compounded of several tasks. This allows you to get more information about the internal workflows

executed in the application. Performing Application Insights agent-based monitoring doesn't provide enough information.

2. When dealing with the user experience, you should consider implementing a retry strategy consisting of a small number of retries with a short retry interval. Using this kind of strategy allows you to minimize the time that your users need to wait for your application to recover from a transient fault. You can also consider using an immediate retry as the first retry. If this first retry fails, then you should switch to another retry strategy. There is no one-fits-all strategy, so you need to test your strategy to ensure that you provide the best user experience.

3. The process of a purchase in a web application is a complex testing scenario. In this scenario, you must use a multistep web test. Using Visual Studio Enterprise, you need to record the steps needed for performing a purchase in your web application. Once you have generated the file with the recorded steps, you can create a web test in Application Insights to monitor the purchase process.

CHAPTER 5

Connect to and consume Azure services and third-party services

Today, companies use different systems for different tasks that are usually performed by different departments. Although these separate systems work to solve a specific need, they usually act as independent actors in a large scenario. These independent actors manage information about the company that other independent actors can potentially duplicate.

When a company realizes that independent actors are managing their data, they usually try to make all the independent actors or systems work together and share information between them. This situation is independent of using cloud services or on-premises services. To make the independent actors work together, you must make connections between each actor or service that needs to communicate with the others.

You can use different services and techniques to achieve this interconnection. Azure provides some useful services that allow different services to work together without making big changes to the interconnected services.

Skills covered in this chapter:

- Skill 5.1: Implement API Management
- Skill 5.2: Develop event-based solutions
- Skill 5.3: Develop message-based solutions

Skill 5.1: Implement API Management

Most of the applications and solutions that you can currently find or develop offer an API for accessing the features available in the solution. In business environments, it is quite common that those solutions need to communicate with each other using their respective APIs. Sometimes, you need to expose your solutions to your clients to offer your services. In those situations, you must ensure that you offer a consistent and secure API. Implementing the necessary mechanism for achieving an enterprise-grade level of security, consistency, and flexibility is not easy. This task is even harder if you also need to publish several of your services under a common API.

Microsoft provides the Azure API Management (APIM) service. This service allows you to create an enterprise-grade API for your existing back-end services. Using APIM, you can securely publish your back-end applications, providing your customers with a platform protected against DOS attacks or JWT token validations.

In October 2023, Microsoft released version 2 of the Basic and Standard tiers: Basic v2 and Standard v2. The main features of the v2 tiers are faster deployment and scaling so that you can deploy new APIM instances in just a few minutes, private networking so you can connect your exposed APIM instance with your internal VNETs, and scaling so that you can use up to 10 scale units to meet the needs of your APIM instance workloads.

> **This skill covers how to**
> - Create an APIM instance
> - Create and document APIs
> - Configure authentication for APIs
> - Implement policies for APIs

Create an APIM instance

The API Management service allows you to expose a portion (or all) of the APIs offered by your back-end systems. By using the APIM service, you can unify all your back-end APIs in a common interface that you can offer to external users, such as clients or partners, as well as internal or external developers. In general, the APIM service is a façade of the APIs that you configure in your APIM instance. Thanks to this façade feature, you can customize the front-end API offered by the APIM instance without changing the back-end API.

When exposing your back-end systems, you are not limited to REST API back ends. You can use a back-end service that uses a SOAP API and then publish this SOAP API as a REST API. This means you can update your older back-end systems without needing to modify the code and take advantage of the greater level of integration of the REST APIs.

Use the following procedure to create a new APIM instance:

1. Open the Azure portal (https://portal.azure.com).
2. Click the Create A Resource button at the top of the Azure portal.
3. On the Create A Resource page, select Integration in the Categories column.
4. Select API Management in the Popular Azure Services column. If the API Management service doesn't appear in the Popular Azure Services column, you can use the Search The Marketplace text box to search for the API Management service.
5. On the API Management Service blade, type a name for your new APIM instance.
6. Select a subscription from the Subscription dropdown menu.
7. Select a resource group from the Resource Group dropdown menu. Alternatively, you can create a new one by clicking the Create New link below the dropdown menu.

8. Select a location from the Location dropdown menu.

9. In the Organization Name text box, type the name of your organization. This name appears on the developer's portal and email notifications.

10. In the Administrator Email text box, type the name of the email account that should receive all notifications from the APIM instance. By default, the value associated with this property is the email address of the logged-in user.

11. In the Pricing Tier dropdown menu, leave the Developer tier selected.

12. Click the Review + Create button at the bottom of the blade.

13. Click the Create button. The process of creating the APIM instance takes several minutes. When your new APIM instance is ready, you will receive a welcome email at the administrator email address that you configured in step 10.

> **NOTE   PRICING TIERS**
>
> The Developer pricing tier is appropriate for testing and development environments, but you should not use it for production because the Developer tier does not offer high-availability features and can be affected by disconnections during the updates of the node. You can review the full offer and the features available on each tier at *https://azure.microsoft.com/ en-us/pricing/details/api-management/.*

Create and document APIs

Once you have created your APIM instance, you can start adding APIs to your instance. In the following procedure, you will add two APIs. Although these APIs are fictitious, they provide a good example of two different ways to add an API to your APIM instance. To add the first API, we will use the OpenAPI definition of a fictitious API. The OpenAPI specification is a language for HTTP APIs that provides a standardized way to define an API so that others can use your API. You can consider OpenAPI as a way of documenting your API, so you should consider using this specification for any API that you may write from now on. For the second API, you will create a blank API definition and add only those methods that are appropriate for you.

1. Open the following URL in your favorite browser: *https://github.com/OAI/OpenAPI-Specification/blob/main/examples/v3.0/api-with-examples.json*

2. Download the api-with-examples.json file to your computer. You will need this file in a later step.

3. Open the Azure portal (*https://portal.azure.com*).

4. Type the name of your APIM instance in the Search text box at the top of the portal.

5. Select the name of your APIM instance in the results list.

6. Select APIs on the navigation menu on your APIM instance blade.

7. On the Add A New API blade, select OpenAPI in the Create From Definition section.

8. In the Create From OpenAPI Specification dialog box, shown in Figure 5-1, click the Select A File button, and select the JSON file with the OpenAPI specification that you downloaded in step 2.

9. Ensure that Azure automatically fills the Display Name and Name properties text boxes. This means that Azure was able to import the details of your API successfully.

10. Delete the content of the Display Name text box.

11. Type **library** in the Display Name text box.

12. Ensure that the Name text box has the value **library**.

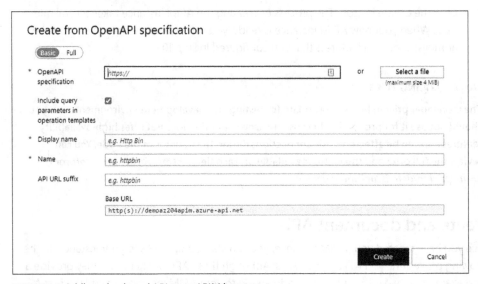

FIGURE 5-1 Adding a back-end API to an APIM instance

13. Type **library** in the API URL Suffix field. If you will connect more than one back-end API to the APIM instance, you will need to provide a suffix for each API. The APIM instance uses this suffix for differentiating between the different APIs that you connected to the instance.

14. Click the Create button at the bottom of the dialog box.

At this point, you have added your first back-end API to the APIM instance by using the OpenAPI specification of your back-end API. In the following steps, you will add another API without using any specification. Creating the endpoints using the Azure portal is useful if you need to connect only a few endpoints from your API or if you don't have the OpenAPI or SOAP specification of your API in any format:

1. Click APIs on the navigation menu in your APIM instance blade.

2. On the APIs blade, click Add API.

3. On the Add A New API page, select HTTP in the Define A New API section.

4. In the Create an HTTP API dialog box, type **Fake API** in the Display Name text box.

5. Leave the Name property with the default value.

6. Type **https://fakerestapi.azurewebsites.net** in the Web Service URL text box.

7. Type **fakeapi** in the API URL Suffix text box.

8. Click the Create button.

9. On the Design tab of the API blade with the newly added Fake API selected, select Add Operation.

10. In the Add Operation editor, shown in Figure 5-2, type **GetActivities** in the Display Name text box.

11. In the URL HTTP Method dropdown menu, ensure that the *GET* method is selected.

12. In the URL text box, type **/api/activities**.

13. Click the Save button at the bottom of the editor.

FIGURE 5-2 Adding an API operation to an API in an APIM instance

14. On the API blade, ensure that Fake API is selected.

15. Select the Test tab.

16. Select the GetActivities operation.

17. Click the Send button at the bottom of the GetActivities operation panel. Using this panel, you can test each of the operations that are defined in your API.

At this point, you have two back-end APIs connected to your APIM instance. As you can see in the previous example, you don't need to expose the entire back-end API. By adding the appropriate operations, you can publish only those parts of the back-end API that are useful for you. Once you have created the APIs in your APIM instance, you can grant access to these APIs to your developers by using the Developer portal. You can access the APIM Developer portal by using the URL *https://<your_APIM_name>.developer.azure-api.net/*.

> **NOTE** **AZURE API MANAGEMENT DEVELOPER PORTAL**
>
> The Azure API Management developer portal allows you to provide your customers and third parties that want to integrate with your API with a single point of contact for requesting access to your application and providing documentation about your API. You can read more about how to customize the developer experience by reviewing the following article at *https://docs. microsoft.com/en-us/azure/api-management/api-management-howto- developer-portal*.

Before you can use your API using the API Management service, you must associate a product to your API for publishing. Because you didn't associate your APIs with any product, your APIs won't be available to the external world. You can associate an API with more than one product. By default, Azure provides two products: Starter and Unlimited. These products are associated with the Echo API demo Azure automatically deploys when creating your API Management instance. Use the following procedure to create a product and associate it with your APIs:

1. Open the Azure portal (*https://portal.azure.com*).
2. Type the name of your APIM instance in the Search text box at the top-middle of the portal.
3. Select the name of your APIM instance in the results list.
4. Select Products on the navigation menu in your APIM instance blade.
5. Click the Add button at the top left of the Products blade.
6. Type a Name in the Display Name text box on the Add Product panel.
7. Leave the value in the ID text box as is.
8. Type a description in the Description text area.
9. Ensure that the Published value is checked. If you don't select this option now, you can publish later or publish the Product using its panel.
10. Click the button with a plus sign in the APIs section.
11. Select the Fake API option from the dropdown menu.
12. Repeat steps 10 and 11 for the Library API.
13. Click the Create button at the bottom of the Add Product panel.

By default, when you create a new product, only members of the Administrators built-in group can access the product. You can configure this by using the Access Control section in the product.

Configure authentication for APIs

Once you have imported your APIs, you must configure the authentication for accessing these APIs. When you configure the security options in the APIM instance, the back-end API delegates the security to the APIM instance. This means that even if your API has implemented its own authentication mechanism, it is never used when the API is accessed through the APIM instance.

This ability to hide the authentication of the back-end APIs is useful for unifying all the security using a consistent and unique authentication mechanism. You can manage the authentication options associated with a product or API by using subscriptions. A subscription manages the keys that a developer can use for accessing your API. If an HTTP request made to an API protected by a subscription does not provide a valid subscription key, the request is immediately rejected by the APIM gateway without reaching your API.

When you define a subscription, you can use three different scopes for applying it:

- **Product** The developer can access all the APIs configured in the product assigned to the subscription. Traditionally, the developer could request access to products by using the Developer portal. This is no longer a valid option. You need to provide access to the developer using the Azure portal and configure the appropriate APIM subscription.

- **All APIs** The developer can access all APIs in your APIM instance using the same subscription key.

- **API** The developer can access a single API in your APIM instance using a subscription key. There is no need for the API to be part of a product.

If you use the All APIs scope, you don't need to associate your API with a URL suffix. The subscription using this scope allows access directly to all the APIs configured in your API Management instance. You can use the following procedure for creating a subscription and associating it with a program:

1. Open the Azure portal (*https://portal.azure.com*).
2. Type the name of your APIM instance in the Search text box at the top of the portal.
3. Select the name of your APIM instance in the results list.
4. Select Subscriptions in the navigation menu in your APIM instance blade.
5. Click the Add Subscription button at the top left of the Subscriptions blade.
6. On the New Subscription panel shown in Figure 5-3, type a Name for the subscription. Beware that this name can only contain letters, numbers, and hyphens.

FIGURE 5-3 Creating a new API Management Subscription

7. In the Scope dropdown menu, select the Product value.

8. In the Product dropdown menu, select the name of the product that you created in the previous section.

9. Click the Create button at the bottom of the panel.

10. On the Subscription blade, click the ellipsis at the end of the row for your newly created subscription.

11. In the contextual menu, select Show/Hide keys. You can use either of these keys to access the APIs configured in the product associated with the subscription. You must use the Header Ocp-Apim-Subscription-Key for providing the subscription key in your HTTP requests.

When configuring a subscription, you can assign different users to the subscription by using the Users parameters in the New Subscription panel. This is a best practice method of providing different subscription keys to different groups of users.

NEED MORE REVIEW? **OTHER AUTHENTICATION METHODS**

Using subscription and subscription keys is not the only mechanism for protecting access to your APIs. API Management allows you to use OAuth 2.0, client certificates, and IP whitelisting. You can use the following articles to review how to use other authentication mechanisms for protecting your APIs:

- **IP whitelisting** *https://docs.microsoft.com/en-us/azure/api-management/ api-management-access-restriction-policies#RestrictCallerIPs*

- **OAuth 2.0 authentication using Azure AD** *https://docs.microsoft.com/en-us/azure/api-management/api-management-howto-protect-backend-with-aad*

- **Mutual authentication using client certificates** *https://docs.microsoft.com/en-us/azure/api-management/api-management-howto-mutual-certificates*

Implement policies for APIs

When you publish a back-end API using the API Management service, all the requests made to your APIM instance are forwarded to the correct back-end API, and the response is sent back to the requestor. None of these requests or responses are altered or modified by default, but there could be some situations for which you need to modify some requests and/or responses. An example of these modification needs is transforming the format of a response from XML to JSON. Another example could be throttling the number of incoming calls from a particular IP or user.

A policy is a mechanism that you can use to change the default behavior of the APIM gateway. Policies are XML documents that describe a sequence of inbound and outbound steps or statements. Each policy is made of four sections:

- **Inbound**   In this section, you can find any statement that applies to requests from the managed API clients.

- **Back End**   This section contains the steps that must be applied to the request that should be sent from the API gateway to the back-end API.

- **Outbound**   This section contains statements or modifications that you must apply to the response before it is sent to the requestor.

- **On-Error**   In case there is an error in any of the other sections, the engine stops processing the remaining steps on the faulty section and jumps to this section.

When configuring or defining a policy, you must keep in mind that you can apply it to different scope levels:

- **Global**   The policy applies to all APIs in your APIM instance. You can configure global policies by using the code editor on the All APIs policy editor in the APIs blade of your APIM instance.

- **Product**   The policy applies to all APIs associated with a product. You can configure product policies on the Policies blade of the product in your API instance.

- **API**   The policy applies to all operations configured in the API. You can configure API-scoped policies by using the code editor in the All Operations option on the Design Tab of the API in your APIM instance.

- **Operation**   The policy applies only to a specific operation in your API. You can configure operation-scoped policies by using the code editor in the specific operation.

Policies are a powerful and very flexible mechanism that allow you to do a lot of useful work, such as applying caching to the HTTP requests, performing monitoring on the request and responses, authenticating with your back-end API using different authentication mechanisms, or even interacting with external services, among others.

Use the following procedure to apply some transformations to the Library API that you configured in the "Create an APIM instance" section earlier in this chapter:

1. Open the Azure portal (*https://portal.azure.com*).

2. Type the name of your APIM instance in the Search text box at the top of the portal.

3. Select the name of your APIM instance in the results list.

4. Select APIs on the navigation menu in your APIM instance blade.

5. Select Library API in the APIs blade.

6. Select the List API Versions operation.

7. Select the Test tab.

8. Click the Send button at the bottom of the tab. This should send a request to the Library API and get results similar to those shown in Figure 5-4. In this procedure, you will transform the HTTP headers inside the red rectangles in Figure 5-4.

> **NOTE   TESTING DATA**
>
> Because we used a fictional OpenAPI definition, step 8 will give you an error. Nevertheless, all the steps in this procedure are valid and have been verified, so you can use them to connect your own API and create your own APIM policy.

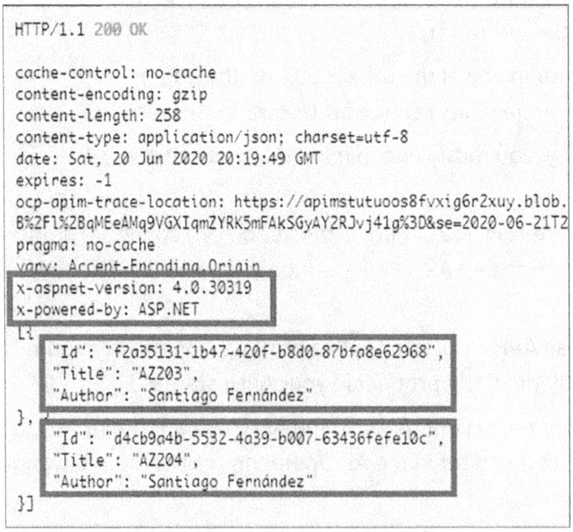

```
HTTP/1.1 200 OK

cache-control: no-cache
content-encoding: gzip
content-length: 258
content-type: application/json; charset=utf-8
date: Sat, 20 Jun 2020 20:19:49 GMT
expires: -1
ocp-apim-trace-location: https://apimstutuoos8fvxig6r2xuy.blob.
B%2F1%2BqMEeAMq9VGXIqmZYRK5mFAkSGyAY2RJvj41g%3D&se=2020-06-21T2
pragma: no-cache
vary: Accept-Encoding,Origin
x-aspnet-version: 4.0.30319
x-powered-by: ASP.NET
[{
    "Id": "f2a35131-1b47-420f-b8d0-87bfa8e62968",
    "Title": "AZ203",
    "Author": "Santiago Fernández"
},
{
    "Id": "d4cb9a4b-5532-4a39-b007-63436fefe10c",
    "Title": "AZ204",
    "Author": "Santiago Fernández"
}]
```

FIGURE 5-4 Testing an API operation

9. Select the Design tab.

10. Select All Operations in the list of available operations for this API.

11. Click the icon next to Policies in the Outbound Processing section.

12. In the Policy Editor, move your cursor inside the Outbound section, before the base tag, and add a new line by pressing the Enter key.

13. Click the Show Snippets button in the top right of the Policy Editor.

14. In the list of available policies on the right side of the Policy Editor, navigate to Transformation Policies.

15. Click the Set HTTP Header policy twice to insert the policies.

16. Modify the inserted policies with the following content:

```
<set-header name="X-Powered-By" exists-action="delete" />
<set-header name="X-AspNet-Version" exists-action="delete" />
```

17. Add a new line below the inserted policies.

18. Add the following code snippet:

```
<set-body>@{
    var response = context.Response.Body.As<string>();
    var arrayString = "{ \"Library\": " + response + "}";
    JObject books = JObject.Parse(arrayString);
    JArray modifiedBooks = new JArray();
    foreach (JObject book in books["Library"].ToObject<JArray>())
    {
        book.Add("URL", "https://az204books.azure-api.net/library/books/" +
book["Id"]);
        modifiedBooks.Add(book);
    }
        return (string)modifiedBooks.ToString(Newtonsoft.Json.Formatting.None);
    }</set-body>
```

19. Click the Save button at the bottom of the Policy Editor.

20. Repeat steps 6 to 8 to apply the transformation policies. You should notice that the headers X-Powered-By and X-AspNet-Version are missing. Also, you should see that all books have an additional property URL pointing to the URL of the book.

As you can see in the previous example, the policies in the API Management service are compelling. You can even use C# code to make elaborate modifications to your API's requests and responses. Although this example shows part of the power of using policies with the APIM service, you should not use this example for a production environment, since some critical verifications are missing from this example policy. Because we created this policy for All Operations in the Library API, any call made to an operation different from List API versions will fail.

Skill 5.2: Develop event-based solutions

One of the main principles of code development is to reuse code as much as possible. To make it possible to reuse the code, you must ensure that the code is as loosely coupled as possible, which reduces the dependencies with other parts of the code or other systems to a minimum.

With this principle in mind, to make loosely coupled systems communicate, you must use some kind of communication. Event-driven architectures allow communication between separate systems by sharing information through events.

In general, an event is a significant change in the system state that happens in the context of the system. An example of an event could be when a user adds an item to the shopping cart in an e-commerce application, or when an IoT device collects the information from its sensors.

Azure provides different services, such as Event Grid, notification hubs, or Event Hubs, to cover the different needs when implementing event-driven architectures.

In this section, we will review how to work with event-driven architectures. You should not get confused with message-driven architecture. In this type of architecture, the sender sends a message to a known receiver. Microsoft provides support for message-driven architectures through Azure Service Bus. In an event-driven architecture, the sender sends an event that multiple and unknown receivers can read.

> **This skill covers how to**
> - Implement solutions that use Azure Event Grid
> - Implement solutions that use Azure Event Hub

Implement solutions that use Azure Event Grid

Azure Event Grid allows you to create an application using serverless architecture by providing a confident platform for managing events. You can use Azure Event Grid for connecting to several types of data sources, such as Azure Blob Storage, Azure Subscription, Event Hubs, IoT

Hubs, and others; Azure Even Grid also allows you to use different event handlers to manage these events. You can also create your custom events for integrating your application with the Azure Event Grid. Before you can start using the Azure Event Grid in your solution, there are some basic concepts that we should review:

- **Event** This is a change of state in the source (for example, in an Azure Blob Storage or when an event happens when a new blob is added to the Azure Blob Storage).
- **Event source** This is the service or application when the event happens. There is an event source for every event type.
- **Event handler** This is the app or service that reacts to the event.
- **Topics** These are the endpoints where the event source can send the events. You can use topics for grouping several related events.
- **Event subscriptions** When a new event is added to a topic, one or more event handlers can process that event. The event subscription is an endpoint or built-in mechanism to distribute the events between the different event handlers. Also, you can use subscriptions to filter incoming events.

An important consideration that you must keep in mind is that an event does not contain the full information about the event itself. The event only contains information relevant to the event, such as the source of the event, a time when the event took place, and a unique identifier. For example, when a new blob is added to an Azure Blob Storage Account, the new blob event doesn't contain the blob. Instead, the event contains a reference to the blob in the Azure Blob Storage Account.

When working with events, you configure an event source to send events to a topic. Any system, or event handler, that needs to process those events subscribes to that topic. When new events arise, the event source pushes the event into the topic configured in the Azure Event Grids service. Any event handler subscribed to that topic reads the event and processes it according to its internal programming. There is no need for the event source to have event handlers subscribed to the topic; the event source pushes the event to the topic and forgets it.

The following steps show how to create a custom topic. Then you will create console applications using C# to send events to the topic and process those events.

1. Open the Azure portal (*https://portal.azure.com*).
2. In the Search Resources, Services, And Docs text box at the top of the Azure portal, type **event**.
3. Select Event Grid Topics in the results list.
4. On the Event Grid Topics blade, click the Create button at the top left of the blade.
5. On the Create Topic panel, select a subscription in the Subscription dropdown menu.
6. Select a resource group in the Resource Group dropdown menu. Alternatively, you can create a new resource group by clicking the Create New link below the dropdown menu.
7. In the Name text box, type a name for the Event Grid Topic.
8. Select a location in the Location dropdown menu.

9. Click the Review + Create button at the bottom of the panel.

10. Click the Create button.

When the Azure Resource Manager finishes creating your new Event Grid Topic, you can subscribe to the topic for processing the events. Also, you can send your custom events to this topic. Use the following steps to publish custom events to your newly created Event Grid Topic:

1. Open Visual Studio 2022.

2. In the Start window, select Create A New Project.

3. In the Create A New Project window, select the template Console App.

4. Click the Next button at the bottom right of the window.

5. Type a Project Name.

6. Select a location for your solution.

7. Click the Next button.

8. Click the Create button.

9. Select Tools > NuGet Package Manager > Manage NuGet Packages For Solution.

10. On the NuGet – Solution tab, select Browse.

11. In the Search text box, type **Azure.Messaging.EventGrid**.

12. Select Azure.Messaging.EventGrid in the results list.

13. On the right side of the NuGet – Solution tab, select the checkbox next to the name of your project.

14. Click the Install button.

15. In the Preview Changes window, click the OK button.

16. In the License Acceptance window, click the I Accept button.

17. Repeat steps 10 to 15 and install the Microsoft.Extensions.Configuration.Json NuGet Package.

18. In the Solution Explorer window, right-click your project's name.

19. On the contextual menu, select Add > New Item.

20. In the Add New Item window, click the Show All Templates button.

21. Type **json** on the Search text box at the upper right of the window.

22. Select the JSON File template.

23. Type **appsettings.json** in the Name text box.

24. Click the Add button at the bottom right of the window.

25. In the Solution Explorer window, select the appsettings.json file.

26. In the Properties window, set the Copy To Output Directory setting to Copy Always.

27. Open the appsettings.json file and replace the file's content with the content of Listing 5-1. You can get the access key from the Access Key blade in your Event Grid Topic.

LISTING 5-1 appsettings.json file

```
{
    "EventGridAccessKey": "<Your_EventGridTopic_Access_Key>",
    "EventGridTopicEndpoint": "https://<Your_EventGrid_Topic>.<region_name>-1.eventgrid.
azure.net/api/events"
}
```

28. In the Solution Explorer window, right-click your project's name.

29. In the contextual menu, select Add > New Item.

30. In the Add New Item window, select Class from the list of new items.

31. In the Name text box at the bottom of the window, type **NewItemCreatedEvent.cs.**

32. Click the Add button at the bottom right of the window.

33. Replace the content of the NewItemCreatedEvent.cs file with the content of Listing 5-2.

LISTING 5-2 NewItemCreatedEvent.cs

```
// C# .NET
using System.Text.Json.Serialization;
namespace <your_project_name>
{
    class NewItemCreatedEvent
    {
        [JsonPropertyName("name")]
        public string itemName;
    }
}
```

34. Open the Program.cs file.

35. Add the following using statements:

```
using Azure;
using Azure.Messaging.EventGrid;
using Microsoft.Extensions.Configuration;
```

36. Replace the content of the Main method with the content in Listing 5-3.

LISTING 5-3 Program.cs Main method

```
// C# .NET
IConfigurationBuilder builder = new ConfigurationBuilder().AddJsonFile("appsettings.json");
IConfigurationRoot configuration = builder.Build();

string topicEndpoint = configuration["EventGridTopicEndpoint"];
string apiKey = configuration["EventGridAccessKey"];

string topicHostname = new Uri(topicEndpoint).Host;
EventGridPublisherClient client = new EventGridPublisherClient(new Uri(topicEndpoint),
new AzureKeyCredential(apiKey));

List<EventGridEvent> events = new List<EventGridEvent>();
EventGridEvent newEvent = new EventGridEvent( subject: "Store A",
```

```
                                    eventType: "MyCompany.Items.NewItemCreatedEvent",
                                    dataVersion: "3.7",
                                    data: new NewItemCreatedEvent() { itemName =
                                                                "Item 1" });
events.Add(newEvent);

client.SendEvents(events);
Console.WriteLine("Published events to Event Grid topic");
Console.ReadLine();
```

At this point, your console application publishes events to the Event Grid topic that you created previously. Press F5 to run your console application and ensure that everything compiles and works correctly. You will not be able to see the published message yet.

Use the following steps to create a subscriber Azure Function that connects to the Event Grid Topic and processes these events:

1. Open Visual Studio 2022.

2. In the Start window, select Create A New Project.

3. In the Create A New Project window, select the template Azure Functions.

4. Click the Next button.

5. Type a Project Name.

6. Select a location for your project.

7. Click the Next button.

8. In the Azure Functions Additional Information window, click the Event Grid Trigger in the Function dropdown menu.

9. Leave the other options as is.

10. Click the Create button.

11. Create a new empty C# class called `NewItemCreatedEventData`.

12. Replace the content of the `NewItemCreatedEventData.cs` file with the content of Listing 5-4.

LISTING 5-4 NewItemCreatedEvent.cs

```
// C# .NET
using System.Text.Json.Serialization;

namespace <your_project_name>
{
    class NewItemCreatedEvent
    {
        [JsonPropertyName("name")]
        public string itemName;
    }
}
```

13. Replace the content of Function1.cs with the content in Listing 5-5.

LISTING 5-5 Function1.cs

```csharp
// C# .NET
using System;
using Microsoft.Azure.WebJobs;
using Microsoft.Azure.WebJobs.Extensions.EventGrid;
using Microsoft.Extensions.Logging;
using Azure.Messaging.EventGrid;
using Azure.Messaging.EventGrid.SystemEvents;

namespace <your_project's_name>
{
    public static class Function1
    {
        [FunctionName("EventGridTrigger")]
        public static void Run([EventGridTrigger]EventGridEvent eventGridEvent, ILogger log)
        {
            log.LogInformation("C# Event Grid trriger handling EventGrid Events.");

            log.LogInformation($"New event received: {eventGridEvent.Data}");

            if (eventGridEvent.TryGetSystemEventData(out var eventData))
            {
                switch (eventData)
                {
                    case SubscriptionValidationEventData subscriptionValidated:
                        Console.WriteLine(subscriptionValidated.ValidationCode);
                        break;
                    case StorageBlobCreatedEventData blobCreated:
                        Console.WriteLine(blobCreated.BlobType);
                        break;
                    // Handle any other system event type
                    default:
                        Console.WriteLine(eventGridEvent.EventType);
                        // We can get the raw Json for the event using data
                        Console.WriteLine(eventGridEvent.Data.ToString());
                        break;
                }
            }
            else
            {
                switch (eventGridEvent.EventType)
                {
                    case "MyCompany.Items.NewItemCreated":
                        NewItemCreatedEventData itemCreatedEventData = eventGridEvent.
Data.ToObjectFromJson<NewItemCreatedEventData>();
                        log.LogInformation($"New Item Custom Event,
Name {itemCreatedEventData.itemName}");
                        break;
                    // Handle any other custom event type
                    default:
                        Console.Write(eventGridEvent.EventType);
                        Console.WriteLine(eventGridEvent.Data.ToString());
```

```
                                     break;
                            }
                    }

                }
        }
}
```

14. Publish the Azure Function to your Azure subscription. Use the procedure at the follow-
    ing URL to publish an Azure Function to Azure: *https://docs.microsoft.com/en-us/azure/
    azure-functions/functions-develop-vs#publish-to-azure*.

15. Open your Event Grid Topic in the Azure portal.

16. On your Event Grid Topic Overview blade, click the Event Subscription button.

17. On the Create Event Subscription blade, shown in Figure 5-5, type a Name for the
    subscription.

18. In the Endpoint Type dropdown menu, select Azure Function.

FIGURE 5-5 Creating a subscription using an Azure Function endpoint

19. Click the Select An Endpoint link below the Azure Function endpoint type.

20. On the Select Azure Function panel, in the Function App dropdown menu, select the
    Azure Function that you published previously in this section.

21. Leave the Slot dropdown menu with the Production value.

22. Ensure that your Azure Function's name appears in the Function dropdown menu.

23. Click the Confirm Selection button.

24. Click the Create button.

At this point, you should be able to publish and process events using the Event Grid Topic that you created previously. Use the following steps to ensure that everything works correctly:

1. Open the publisher console application in Visual Studio 2022.

2. Run the console application to publish an event to the topic.

3. Open the Azure portal and navigate to your Azure Function.

4. On the Azure Functions blade, select the Monitor option in the Developer section.

5. You should be able to see a list of invocations when the function has been called because a new event arrived at the Event Grid Topic.

6. Click one of the successful invocations; you will get a result similar to Figure 5-6.

> *NOTE* **AZURE FUNCTION MONITORING**
> You must enable Application Insights integration to see the log messages generated from the Azure Function. Review the article about how to monitor Azure Functions using Application Insights at *https://docs.microsoft.com/en-us/azure/azure-functions/functions-monitoring*.

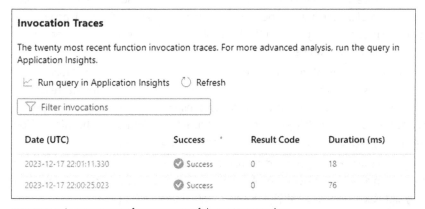

FIGURE 5-6 Log messages from a successful event processing

The Azure Function that we used in this example can manage not only custom events but also events from an Azure Storage Account. As an exercise, you can create a new subscription that listens only to Azure Storage Account events and uses the Azure Function that you published previously in this section to manage the events produced by the Azure Storage Account.

Another important consideration that you must deal with when you add a handler to an Azure Event Grid subscription is the handler validation. Depending on the type of handler you use, this validation process is performed automatically by the SDK, or you need to implement it manually. When you use an HTTP endpoint as an event handler, you need to deal with the subscription verification. This verification process consists of a verification code sent by the Event Grid service to the webhook endpoint. Your application must reply to the Event Grid service by using the same verification code. You can find a detailed example of how to perform this verification by reviewing the code available at *https://github.com/Azure-Samples/azure-event-grid-viewer*.

Implement solutions that use Azure Event Hub

Azure Event Grid is an excellent service for implementing event-driven solutions, but it is only one piece of a more complex pipeline. Although Event Grid is appropriate for working with event-driven, reactive programming, it is not the best solution when you need to ingest millions of events per second with low latency.

Azure Event Hub is a more suitable solution when you require a service that can receive and process millions of events per second and provide low-latency event processing. Azure Event Hub is the front door of a big data pipeline that processes millions of events. Once the Azure Event Hub receives the data, it can deliver the event to Azure Event Grid, store the information in an Azure Blob Storage Account, or store the data in an Azure Data Lake Storage.

When working with Event Hubs, you send events to the hub. The entity that sends events to the Event Hub is known as an event publisher. An event publisher can send events to the Event Hub by using any of these protocols: AMQP 1.0, Kafka 1.0 (or later), or HTTPS.

You can publish events to the Event Hub by sending a single event or grouping several events in a batch operation. Independently, if you publish a single event or a batch of them, you are limited to a maximum size of 1 MB of data per publication. When Azure Event Hub stores an event, it distributes the different events in different partitions based on the partition key provided as one of the data of the event. Using this pattern, Azure Event Hub ensures that all events sharing the same partition key are delivered in order to the same partition.

A partition stores the events as they arrive at the partition. This way, the newer events are added to the end of the partition. You cannot delete events from a partition. Instead, you must wait for the event to expire to be removed from the partition. As each partition is independent of other partitions in the Event Hub, the growth rates differ from partition to partition. You can define the number of partitions that your Event Hub contains during the creation of the Event Hub. You can create between 2 and 32 partitions, although you can extend the limit of 32 by contacting the Azure Event Hub team. Keep in mind that once you create the Event Hub and set the number of partitions, you cannot change this number later. When planning the number of partitions to assign to the Event Hub, consider the maximum number of parallels downstream that need to connect to the Event Hub.

You can connect event receiver applications to an Event Hub by using consumer groups. A consumer group is equivalent to a downstream in a stream-processing architecture. Using consumer groups, you can have different event receivers or consumers accessing different views (state, position, or offset) of the partitions in the Event Hub. Event consumers connect to the Event Hub by using the AMQP protocol that sends the event to the client as soon as new data is available.

The following procedure shows how to create an Azure Event Hub:

1. Open the Azure portal (*https://portal.azure.com*).

2. Expand the navigation menu by clicking the icon with three parallel lines at the top left of the Azure portal.

3. Select All Services on the navigation menu.

4. In the Filter Services text box, type **event**.

5. Select Event Hubs from the results list.

6. On the Event Hubs blade, click the Create button at the top left of the blade.

7. In the Create Namespace panel, ensure that the correct subscription is selected in the Subscription dropdown menu.

8. Select a resource group from the Resource Group dropdown menu. Alternatively, you can create a new resource group by clicking the Create New link below the dropdown menu.

9. Type a name for the Event Hub namespace.

10. Select a location in the Location dropdown menu.

11. Select the Basic tier in the Pricing Tier dropdown menu.

12. Leave the Throughput Units as 1.

13. Click the Review + Create button at the bottom of the panel.

14. Click the Create button.

15. Navigate to your newly created Event Hub namespace.

16. On the Overview blade in the Event Hub namespace blade, click the Event Hub button with the plus sign.

17. On the Create Event Hub panel, type a Name for the Event Hub. You will need this name in the next procedure.

18. Leave the Partition Count at 2. Remember that you cannot change this value once the Event Hub is created.

19. Click the Review + Create button.

20. Click the Create button.

21. Select Shared Access Policies in the navigation menu on the left side of the Event Hub namespace.

22. Select the `RootManageSharedAccessKey` policy.

23. Copy the Connection String-Primary Key value. You need this value for a later step in the next procedure.

Once you have created your Event Hub's namespace and your hub, you can start sending and consuming events from the hub. Use the following procedure to create two console applications, one for sending events and another for receiving events:

1. Open Visual Studio 2022.

2. On the Welcome screen, select Create A New Project.

3. Select the Console App template.

4. Click the Next button.

5. Type a Project Name.

6. Select a location for the project.

7. Click the Next button.

8. In the Additional Information window, leave the Framework dropdown menu with the default value.

9. Click the Create button.

10. Install the Azure.Messaging.EventHubs NuGet package.

11. Replace the content of the Program.cs file with the content of Listing 5-6. You received the Event Hub Namespace connection string in the last step of the previous procedure.

LISTING 5-6 Function1.cs

```
// C# .NET
using Azure.Messaging.EventHubs;
using Azure.Messaging.EventHubs.Producer;
using System.Text;

EventHubProducerClient eventHubClient;
const string EventHubConnectionString = "<Your_event_hub_namespace_connection_string>";
const string EventHubName = "<your_event_hub_name>";
const int numMessagesToSend = 100;

eventHubClient = new EventHubProducerClient(
        EventHubConnectionString,
        EventHubName
    );

using EventDataBatch eventBatch = await eventHubClient.CreateBatchAsync();

for (var i = 0; i < numMessagesToSend; i++)
{
    try
    {
        var message = $"Message {i}";
```

```
        try
        {
            eventBatch.TryAdd(new EventData(Encoding.UTF8.GetBytes(message)));
        }
        catch (EventHubsException ex)
        {
            Console.WriteLine($"Error while adding the message '{message}' to the batch:
{ex.Message}");
        }
    }
    catch (Exception exception)
    {
        Console.WriteLine($"{DateTime.Now} > Exception: {exception.Message}");
    }

}

try
{
    await eventHubClient.SendAsync(eventBatch);
    Console.WriteLine($"{numMessagesToSend} messages sent.");
}
catch (EventHubsException ex)
{
    Console.WriteLine($"Error while sending the batch of messages: {ex.Message}");
}
finally
{
    await eventHubClient.DisposeAsync();
}

Console.WriteLine("Press ENTER to exit.");
Console.ReadLine();
```

At this point, you can press F5 and run the console application. This application console
sends 100 messages to the Event Hub that you configured in the EventHubName constant. In
the next procedure, you will create another application console for implementing an Event
Processor Host. The Event Processor Host is an agent that helps you receive events from the
Event Hub. The Event Processor automatically manages the persistent checkpoints and parallel
event reception. The Event Processor Host requires an Azure Storage Account to process the
persistent checkpoints.

> **NOTE** **EXAMPLE REQUIREMENTS**
>
> You must create an Azure Blob Storage container to run this example. You can review how to
> create a blob container and how to get the access key by reading the following articles:
>
> - **Create a container** *https://docs.microsoft.com/en-us/azure/storage/blobs/
>   storage-quickstart-blobs-portal#create-a-container*
>
> - **Get access keys** *https://docs.microsoft.com/en-us/azure/storage/common/
>   storage-account-manage#access-keys*

Follow these steps to create the console application that implements the Event Processor Host:

1. Open Visual Studio 2022.
2. On the Welcome screen, Select Create A New Project.
3. Select the Console App template.
4. Click the Next button.
5. Type a Project Name.
6. Select a location for the project.
7. Click the Next button.
8. In the Additional Information window, leave the Framework dropdown menu with the default value.
9. Click the Create button.
10. Install the following NuGet packages:
    - Azure.Messaging.EventHubs
    - Azure.Messaging.EventHubs.Processor
11. Replace the content of the Program.cs file with the content of Listing 5-7.

LISTING 5-7 Program.cs

```csharp
// C# .NET
using Azure.Messaging.EventHubs.Consumer;
using Azure.Messaging.EventHubs.Processor;
using Azure.Messaging.EventHubs;
using Azure.Storage.Blobs;
using System.Text;

const string eventHubConnectionString =  "<your_event_hub_namespace_connection_string>";
const string eventHubName = "<your_event_hub_name>";
const string storageContainerName = "<your_container_name>";
const string storageAccountName = "<your_storage_account_name>";
const string storageAccountKey = "<your_storage_account_access_key>";
string storageConnectionString = string.
Format($"DefaultEndpointsProtocol=https;AccountName={storageAccountName};" +
AccountKey={storageAccountKey}");


BlobContainerClient blobContainerClient = new BlobContainerClient
(storageConnectionString, storageContainerName);

var eventHubConsumerClient = new EventProcessorClient(blobContainerClient,
EventHubConsumerClient.DefaultConsumerGroupName, eventHubConnectionString,
eventHubName);

// Register the processor handlers.
eventHubConsumerClient.ProcessEventAsync += ProcessEventHandler;
eventHubConsumerClient.ProcessErrorAsync += ProcessErrorHandler;
```

```
// Start the processing.

await eventHubConsumerClient.StartProcessingAsync();

// Wait for 10 seconds for the events to be processed.
await Task.Delay(TimeSpan.FromSeconds(10));

// Stop the processing.
await eventHubConsumerClient.StopProcessingAsync();

async Task ProcessEventHandler(ProcessEventArgs eventArgs)
{
    // Write the body of the event to the console window.
    Console.WriteLine("\tReceived event: {0}", Encoding.UTF8.GetString
(eventArgs.Data.Body.ToArray()));
    // Update checkpoint in the blob storage so that the app receives only new events
the next time it's run.
    await eventArgs.UpdateCheckpointAsync(eventArgs.CancellationToken);
}

Task ProcessErrorHandler(ProcessErrorEventArgs eventArgs)
{
    // Write details about the error to the console window.
    Console.WriteLine($"\tPartition '{ eventArgs.PartitionId}': an unhandled exception
was encountered. This was not expected to happen.");
    Console.WriteLine(eventArgs.Exception.Message);
    return Task.CompletedTask;
}
```

Now, you can press F5 and run your console application. The console application registers itself as an Event Processor and starts waiting for events not processed in the Event Hub.
Because the default expiration time for the events in the Event Hub is one hour, you should
receive all the messages sent by your publishing console application in the previous example.
If you run your event publisher console application without stopping the event processor console application, you should be able to see the messages in the event processor console almost
in real-time as they are sent to the Event Hub by the event publishing console. This simple
example also shows how the Event Hub distributes the events across the different partitions.

> **NOTE SECURITY ON PRODUCTION ENVIRONMENTS.**
>
> As you might notice, the examples in this section use connection strings for connecting to the
> different services. In a real-world scenario, you should take advantage of the Managed
> Identities and Microsoft Entra ID authentication and use passwordless authentication. You can
> review the following Microsoft Article to learn how to use passwordless authentication
> with Azure Event Hub: *https://learn.microsoft.com/en-us/azure/event-hubs/*
> *event-hubs-dotnet-standard-getstarted-send?tabs=passwordless%2Croles-azure-portal.*

Skill 5.3: Develop message-based solutions

In the previous skill, we reviewed how to use event-driven services in which a publisher pushes a lightweight notification or event to the events management system and then forgets about how the event is handled or whether it is even processed.

In this section, we will review how to develop message-based solutions using Azure services. In general terms, a message is raw data produced by a service with the goal of being stored or processed elsewhere. This means that the publisher of the messages has an expectation of some other system or subscriber processing the message. Because of this expectation, the subscriber must notify the publisher about the status of the message.

This skill covers how to
- Implement solutions that use Azure Service Bus
- Implement solutions that use Azure Queue Storage queues

Implement solutions that use Azure Service Bus

Azure Service Bus is an enterprise-level integration message broker that allows different applications to communicate with each other in a reliable way. A message is raw data that an application sends asynchronously to the broker to be processed by another application connected to the broker. The message can contain JSON, XML, or text information.

Here are some concepts that you should review before starting to work with the Azure Service Bus:

- **Namespace** A container for all the components of the messaging. A single namespace can contain multiple queues and topics. You can use namespaces as application containers, associating a single solution to a single namespace. The different components of your solution connect to the topics and queues in the namespace.

- **Queue** A queue is the container of messages. The queue stores the message until the receiving application retrieves and processes the message. The message queue works as a FIFO (First-In, First-Out) stack. As a new message arrives at the queue, the Service Bus service assigns a timestamp to the message. Once the message is processed, the message is held in redundant storage. Queues are appropriate for point-to-point communication scenarios in which a single application needs to communicate with another single application.

- **Topic** You use topics for sending and receiving messages. The difference between queues and topics is that topics can have several applications receiving messages used in publish/subscribe scenarios. A topic can have multiple subscriptions in which each subscription in a topic receives a copy of the message sent to the topic.

Use the following procedure to create an Azure Service Bus namespace. Then, you can create a topic in the namespace. We will use that topic to create two console applications to send and receive the messages from the topic:

1. Open the Azure portal (*https://portal.azure.com*).
2. Click the Create A Resource button at the top of the portal.
3. Type **bus** in the Search Services And Marketplace text box.
4. Select the Service Bus option in the Create dropdown menu in the Service Bus rectangle in the results table.
5. On the Create Namespace panel, ensure that the correct subscription is selected in the Subscription dropdown menu.
6. Select a resource group in the Resource Group dropdown menu. Alternatively, you can create a new resource group by clicking the Create New link below the dropdown menu.
7. Type a name for the Service Bus in the Namespace Name text box.
8. Select a location in the Location dropdown menu.
9. Select the Standard tier in the Pricing Tier dropdown menu. You cannot create topics in the Basic pricing tier; you must use at least the Standard tier.

10. Click the Review + Create button at the bottom of the panel.

11. Click the Create button.

12. Go to the resource once the Azure Resource Manager finishes the deployment of your new Service Bus Namespace.

13. On the Overview blade in the Service Bus Namespace, click the Topic button.

14. On the Create Topic panel, shown in Figure 5-7, type a Name for the topic.

FIGURE 5-7 Creating a new topic

15. Leave the Max Topic Size and Message Time To Live parameters as they are.

16. Select Enable Duplicate Detection. This option ensures that the topic doesn't store duplicated messages during the configured detection window.

17. Click the Create button.

18. Select Topics in the Entities section on the navigation menu on the left side of the Service Bus Namespace.

19. Select your topic.

20. On the Overview blade on the Service Bus Topic, click the Subscription button.

21. On the Create Subscription panel, shown in Figure 5-8, type a name for the subscription.

22. Type **10** in the Max Delivery Count text box. This is the number of retries for delivering a message before moving the message to the Dead Letter Queue.

23. Leave the other properties as they are.

24. Click the Create button at the bottom of the panel.

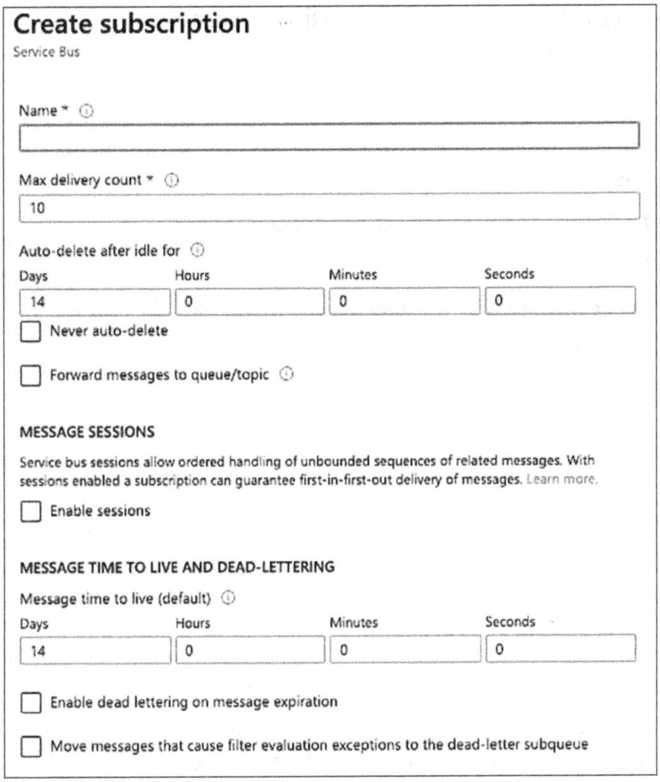

FIGURE 5-8 Creating a new subscription

Now, you will create two console applications. One console application will publish messages to the Service Bus Topic; the other console application will subscribe to the Service Bus Topic, process the message, and update the processed message. Use the following procedure to create the console application that publishes messages to the Service Bus Topic:

1. Open the Azure portal (*https://portal.azure.com*).

2. In the Search Resources, Services, And Docs text box at the top of the portal, type the name of your Service Bus Namespace.

3. Select your Service Bus Namespace from the results list.

4. On the Service Bus Namespace blade, select the Access Control (IAM) option on the navigation menu.

5. Select the Add Role Assignment option in the Add dropdown menu at the top left of the Access Control (IAM) blade.

6. Select the Azure Service Bus Data Receiver role.

7. Click the Next button.

8. Click the Select Members button.

9. In the Select Members panel, in the Select textbox, type the username you use in your Visual Studio to connect to your Azure Subscription.

10. Select your username from the results list.

11. Click the Select button.

12. Click the Review + Assign button twice.

13. Repeat steps 5 through 12 and assign the *Azure Service Bus Data Sender* role.

14. Open Visual Studio 2022.

15. On the Welcome screen, select Create A New Project.

16. Select the Console App template.

17. Click the Next button.

18. Type a Project Name.

19. Select a location for the project.

20. Click the Next button.

21. In the Additional Information window, leave the Framework dropdown menu with the default value.

22. Click the Create button.

23. Install the Azure.Messaging.ServiceBus and Azure.Identity NuGet packages.

24. Replace the content of the Program.cs file with the content of Listing 5-8. Remember that you copied the connection string needed for this code in step 20 of the previous example.

LISTING 5-8 Program.cs

```
// C# .NET
using Azure.Identity;
using Azure.Messaging.ServiceBus;

const string serviceBusNamespace = "<your_service_bus_namespace>";
const string topicName = "<your_topic_name>";
const int numberOfMessagesToSend = 100;

ServiceBusClientOptions clientOptions = new ServiceBusClientOptions { TransportType =
ServiceBusTransportType.AmqpWebSockets };
ServiceBusClient client = new ServiceBusClient(
    $"{serviceBusNamespace}.servicebus.windows.net",
    new DefaultAzureCredential(),
    clientOptions);

ServiceBusSender sender = client.CreateSender(topicName);

// Create a batch of messages
using ServiceBusMessageBatch messageBatch = await sender.CreateMessageBatchAsync();
for (int i = 1; i <= numberOfMessagesToSend; i++)
{
    // Try adding a message to the batch
    if (!messageBatch.TryAddMessage(new ServiceBusMessage($"Message {i}")))
```

```
        {
            // If it is too large for the batch
            throw new Exception($"The message {i} is too large to fit in the batch.");
        }
}


try
{
    // Use the producer client to send the batch of messages to the Service Bus topic
    await sender.SendMessagesAsync(messageBatch);
}
catch (Exception ex)
{
    Console.WriteLine($"{DateTime.Now} :: Exception: {ex.Message}");
}
finally
{
    await sender.DisposeAsync();
    await client.DisposeAsync();
}
```

You can now press F5 and publish messages to the topic. Once you publish the messages, you should be able to see an increase in the Message Count column on the Overview blade of your Service Bus Topic. The next steps show how to create the second console application that subscribes to the topic and processes the messages in the topic:

1. Open Visual Studio 2022.

2. On the Welcome screen, select Create A New Project.

3. Select the Console App template.

4. Click the Next button.

5. Type a Project Name.

6. Select a location for the project.

7. Click the Next button.

8. In the Additional Information window, leave the Framework dropdown menu with the default value.

9. Click the Create button.

10. Install the Azure.Messaging.ServiceBus and Azure.Identity NuGet packages.

11. Replace the content of the Program.cs file with the content of Listing 5-9.

LISTING 5-9 Program.cs

```
// C# .NET
using Azure.Identity;
using Azure.Messaging.ServiceBus;

const string serviceBusNamespace = "<your_servicebus_namespace>";
const string topicName = "<your_servicebus_topic>";
const string subscriptionName = "<your_topic_subscription>";
```

```
ServiceBusClientOptions clientOptions = new ServiceBusClientOptions
{ TransportType = ServiceBusTransportType.AmqpWebSockets };
ServiceBusClient client = new ServiceBusClient(
    $"{serviceBusNamespace}.servicebus.windows.net",
    new DefaultAzureCredential(),
    clientOptions);

ServiceBusProcessor processor = client.CreateProcessor(topicName, subscriptionName,
new ServiceBusProcessorOptions());

try
{
    processor.ProcessMessageAsync += MessageHandler;
    processor.ProcessErrorAsync += ErrorHandler;

    await processor.StartProcessingAsync();

    Console.WriteLine("Waiting a minute for processing the messages");
    await Task.Delay(TimeSpan.FromMinutes(1));

    // Stop processing
    Console.WriteLine("\nStopping the processor...");
    await processor.StopProcessingAsync();
    Console.WriteLine("Stopped receiving messages");
}
catch (Exception ex)
{
    Console.WriteLine($"An exception ocurred while receiving messages: {ex.ToString()}");
    throw;
}
finally
{
    // Cleaning connections
    await processor.DisposeAsync();
    await client.DisposeAsync();
}

static async Task MessageHandler(ProcessMessageEventArgs args)
{
    string body = args.Message.Body.ToString();
    Console.WriteLine($"Received: {body}");
    // Complete the message. Message is deleted from the queue.
    await args.CompleteMessageAsync(args.Message);
}

static Task ErrorHandler(ProcessErrorEventArgs args)
{
    Console.WriteLine($"Error processing message: {args.Exception.ToString()}");
    return Task.CompletedTask;
}
```

You can now press F5 and run the console application. As the console application processes the messages in the topic, you can see that the count of the messages in the subscription is decreasing. In this example, you assigned the Azure Service Bus Data Sender and Azure Service Bus Data Receiver roles to the same user. In a real-world scenario, you should create a service principal for each sender and receiver application and grant the corresponding role. For example, if you deploy the console application into an Azure Container Instance, or an Azure Kubernetes Services pod, you should enable the Managed Identities on that service and grant the appropriate role to the Managed Identity.

NEED MORE REVIEW? **SERVICE BUS ADVANCED FEATURES**

You can learn more about Service Bus features in the following articles:

- **Queues, Topics, and Subscriptions** *https://docs.microsoft.com/en-us/azure/service-bus-messaging/service-bus-queues-topics-subscriptions*

- **Service Bus Performance Improvements** *https://docs.microsoft.com/en-us/azure/service-bus-messaging/service-bus-performance-improvements*

- **Topic Filters and Actions** *https://docs.microsoft.com/en-us/azure/service-bus-messaging/topic-filters*

Implement solutions that use Azure Queue Storage

Azure Queue Storage is the first service that Microsoft released for managing message queues. Although Azure Service Bus and Azure Queue Storage share some features, such as providing message queue services, Azure Queue Storage is more appropriate when your application needs to store more than 80 GB of messages in a queue. Another important feature of the Azure Queue Storage service you need to consider is that although the queues in the service work as a FIFO (First-In, First-Out) stack, the order of the message is not guaranteed.

NOTE **AZURE QUEUE STORAGE VS. AZURE SERVICE BUS**

You can review a complete list of differences between these two queuing services at *https://docs.microsoft.com/en-us/azure/service-bus-messaging/service-bus-azure-and-service-bus- queues-compared-contrasted*.

The maximum size of a single message that you can send to an Azure Queue is 64 KB, although the total size of the queue can grow to over 80 GB. You can only access an Azure Queue by using the REST API or by using the .NET Azure Storage SDK.

Here are the steps for creating an Azure Queue Storage Account and a queue for sending and receiving messages:

1. Open the Azure portal (*https://portal.azure.com*).

2. Select Create A Resource at the top of the portal.

3. Select Storage in the Categories column.

4. Click the Create link Storage Account option in the Popular Azure Services column.

5. On the Create Storage Account blade, select a subscription in the Subscription dropdown menu.

6. Select a resource group in the Resource Group dropdown menu.

7. Type a Storage Account Name.

8. Select a location in the Location dropdown menu.

9. Select Locally-Redundant Storage in the Replication dropdown menu.

10. Leave the other properties as is.

11. Click the Review button.

12. Click the Create button.

13. Click the Go To Resource button once the deployment finishes.

14. Select Access Control (IAM) on the navigation menu in the Azure Storage account blade.

15. Select the Add Role Assignment option in the Add dropdown menu at the top left of the Access Control (IAM) blade.

16. Select the Storage Queue Data Contributor role.

17. Click the Next button.

18. Click the Select members button.

19. In the Select Members panel, in the Select text box, type the username you use in your Visual Studio to connect to your Azure Subscription.

20. Select your username from the results list.

21. Click the Select button.

22. Click the Review + Assign button twice.

At this point, you can create queues in your Azure Storage account by using the Azure portal. You can also add messages to the queue using the Azure portal. This approach is useful for development or testing purposes, but it is not suitable for applications.

Use the following steps to create a console application that creates a new queue in your Azure Storage Account. The application also sends and reads messages from the queue:

1. Open Visual Studio 2022.

2. On the Welcome screen, select Create A New Project.

3. Select the Console App template.

4. Click the Next button.

5. Type a Project Name.

6. Select a location for the project.

7. Click the Next button.

8. In the Additional Information window, leave the Framework dropdown menu with the default value.

9. Click the Create button.

10. Install the following NuGet packages:

- Azure.Storage.Common
- Azure.Storage.Queue
- Azure.Identity

11. Replace the content of the Program.cs file with the content of Listing 5-10.

LISTING 5-10 Program.cs

```
// C# .NET
using Azure.Storage.Queues.Models;
using Azure.Storage.Queues;
using Azure.Identity;

const string storageAccountName = "<your_storage_account_name>";
const string queueName = "az204queue";
const int maxNumOfMessages = 10;

QueueClient queueClient = new QueueClient(
    new Uri($"https://{storageAccountName}.queue.core.windows.net/{queueName}"),
    new DefaultAzureCredential());

//Create the queue
queueClient.CreateIfNotExists();

//Sending messages to the queue.
for (int i = 0; i < maxNumOfMessages; i++)
{
    await queueClient.SendMessageAsync($"Message {i} {DateTime.Now}");
}

//Getting the length of the queue
QueueProperties queueProperties = queueClient.GetProperties();
int? cachedMessageCount = queueProperties.ApproximateMessagesCount;

//Reading messages from the queue without removing the message
Console.WriteLine("Reading message from the queue without removing them from the queue");
PeekedMessage[] peekedMessages = queueClient.PeekMessages((int)cachedMessageCount);

foreach (PeekedMessage peekedMessage in peekedMessages)
{
    Console.WriteLine($"Message read from the queue: {peekedMessage.MessageText}");

    //Getting the length of the queue
    queueProperties = queueClient.GetProperties();
    int? queueLength = queueProperties.ApproximateMessagesCount;
    Console.WriteLine($"Current length of the queue {queueLength}");
}

//Reading message and removing it from the queue
Console.WriteLine("Reading message from the queue removing");
QueueMessage[] messages = queueClient.ReceiveMessages((int)
                                    cachedMessageCount);
```

```
foreach (QueueMessage message in messages)
{
    Console.WriteLine($"Message read from the queue: {message.MessageText}");
    //You need to process the message in less than 30 seconds.
    queueClient.DeleteMessage(message.MessageId, message.PopReceipt);

    //Getting the length of the queue
    queueProperties = queueClient.GetProperties();
    int? queueLength = queueProperties.ApproximateMessagesCount;
    Console.WriteLine($"Current length of the queue {queueLength}");
}
```

Press F5 to execute the console application that sends and reads messages from the queue. You can see how the messages are added to the queue by using the Azure portal and navigating to your Azure Storage account > Queues > az204queue. You should see a queue similar to the one shown in Figure 5-9.

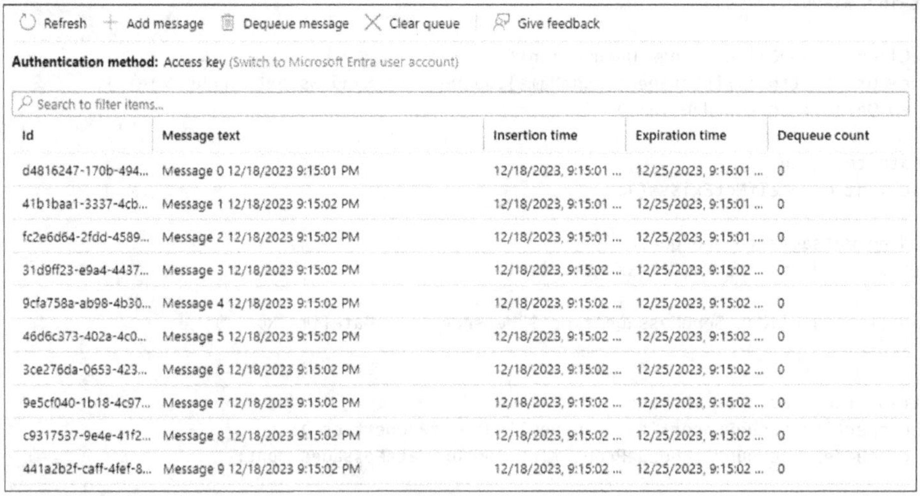

Refresh
Add message
Dequeue message
Clear queue
Give feedback
Authentication method: Access key (Switch to Microsoft Entra user account)
Search to filter items...

Id	Message text	Insertion time	Expiration time	Dequeue count
d4816247-170b-494...	Message 0 12/18/2023 9:15:01 PM	12/18/2023, 9:15:01 ...	12/25/2023, 9:15:01 ...	0
41b1baa1-3337-4cb...	Message 1 12/18/2023 9:15:02 PM	12/18/2023, 9:15:01 ...	12/25/2023, 9:15:01 ...	0
fc2e6d64-2fdd-4589...	Message 2 12/18/2023 9:15:02 PM	12/18/2023, 9:15:01 ...	12/25/2023, 9:15:01 ...	0
31d9ff23-e9a4-4437...	Message 3 12/18/2023 9:15:02 PM	12/18/2023, 9:15:02 ...	12/25/2023, 9:15:02 ...	0
9cfa758a-ab98-4b30...	Message 4 12/18/2023 9:15:02 PM	12/18/2023, 9:15:02 ...	12/25/2023, 9:15:02 ...	0
46d6c373-402a-4c0...	Message 5 12/18/2023 9:15:02 PM	12/18/2023, 9:15:02 ...	12/25/2023, 9:15:02 ...	0
3ce276da-0653-423...	Message 6 12/18/2023 9:15:02 PM	12/18/2023, 9:15:02 ...	12/25/2023, 9:15:02 ...	0
9e5cf040-1b18-4c97...	Message 7 12/18/2023 9:15:02 PM	12/18/2023, 9:15:02 ...	12/25/2023, 9:15:02 ...	0
c9317537-9e4e-41f2...	Message 8 12/18/2023 9:15:02 PM	12/18/2023, 9:15:02 ...	12/25/2023, 9:15:02 ...	0
441a2b2f-caff-4fef-8...	Message 9 12/18/2023 9:15:02 PM	12/18/2023, 9:15:02 ...	12/25/2023, 9:15:02 ...	0

FIGURE 5-9 View queue messages

NEED MORE REVIEW? **PUBLISH-SUBSCRIBE PATTERN**

Although the Azure Queue Storage service doesn't provide the ability to create subscriptions to the queues, you can easily implement the publish-subscribe pattern for communicating applications using Azure Queue Storage. You can learn how to implement this pattern by reviewing the article at *https://docs.microsoft.com/en-us/learn/modules/communicate-between-apps-with-azure-queue-storage/*.

Chapter summary

- The API Management service allows you to publish your back-end REST or SOAP APIs using a common and secure front end.
- You need to create subscriptions in the APIM service for authenticating the access to the API.
- You need to create a product for publishing a back-end API.
- You can publish only some operations of your back-end APIs.
- APIM Policies allow you to modify the behavior of the APIM gateway.
- An event is a change in the state of an entity.
- In an event-driven architecture, the publisher doesn't have the expectation that the event is processed or stored by a subscriber.
- Azure Event Grid is a service for implementing event-driven architectures.
- An Event Grid Topic is an endpoint where a publisher service can send events.
- Subscribers are services that read events from an Event Grid Topic.
- You can configure several types of services as event sources or event subscribers in Azure Event Grid.
- You can create custom events to send to the Event Grid.
- The Azure Notification Hub service unifies push notifications on mobile platforms.
- You can connect the push notification services from different manufacturers to the Azure Notification Hub.
- The Azure Event Hub is the entry point for Big Data event pipelines.
- The Azure Event Hub specializes in ingesting millions of events per second with low latency.
- You can use Azure Event Hub as an event source for the Event Grid service.
- You can use AMQP, Kafka, and HTTPS for connecting to Azure Event Hub.
- In a message-driven architecture, the publisher application has the expectation that the message is processed or stored by the subscriber.
- The subscriber must change the state once the message is processed.
- A message is raw data sent by a publisher that needs to be processed by a subscriber.
- Azure Service Bus and Azure Queue message are message broker services.

Thought experiment

In this thought experiment, demonstrate your skills and knowledge of the topics covered in this chapter. You can find answers to this thought experiment in the next section.

Your organization has several Line-Of-Business (LOB) applications deployed on Azure and on-premises environments. The information managed by some of these LOB applications overlaps between applications. All your LOB applications allow you to use SOAP or REST API for connecting to the applications.

Your organization needs to implement some business processes that require sharing information between the LOB applications. Answer the following questions about connecting Azure services and third-party applications:

1. Your company needs to share some information managed by one of the LOB applications with a partner. The LOB application uses a SOAP API for accessing the data. You need to ensure that the partner is authenticated before accessing the information. Your partner needs to get the information from your application in JSON format, so you also need to ensure that the information provided by your application is published using a REST API. Which service should you use?

2. One of the LOB applications of your company is becoming obsolete. Your company has decided to develop a new web application for replacing the legacy LOB application. You are designing the architecture for the new web application. You need to implement a decoupled architecture that needs to process millions of events per second. Which service should you use?

Thought experiment answers

This section contains the solution to the thought experiment. Each answer explains why the answer choice is correct.

1. You should use the API Management service. This service allows you to share your backed APIs with partners and external developers securely. Using the APIM policies, you can also convert the XML message provided by the SOAP API to JSON documents needed for REST APIs. You can use Azure AD, mutual certificate authentication, or API keys for authenticating access to the API.

2. You should use Azure Event Hub. This service is specially designed to ingest millions of events per second. Once the service has ingested the events, you forward the event to other services such as Azure Storage, Azure Data Lake, or Azure Event Grid. The critical point for choosing Azure Event Hub instead of Event Grid is the number of events that need to be ingested. Another clue for choosing Event Hub instead of Azure Queue Storage or Azure Service Bus is that you need to process events instead of messages. Azure Queue or Azure Service Bus are services aimed for use in message-driven architectures.

CHAPTER 6

AZ-204 developing solutions for Microsoft Azure exam updates

The purpose of this chapter

For all other chapters, the content should remain unchanged throughout this edition of the book. Instead, this chapter will change over time, with an updated PDF posted online so you can see the latest version of the chapter, even after you purchase this book.

Why do we need a chapter that updates over time? For three reasons:

1. To add more technical content to the book before it is time to replace the current book edition with the next edition. This chapter will include additional technology content and possibly additional PDFs containing more content.

2. To communicate details about the next version of the exam, to tell you about our publishing plans for that edition, and to help you understand what that means to you.

3. To provide an accurate mapping of the current exam objectives to existing chapter content. While exam objectives evolve and are updated, and products are renamed, much of the content in this book will remain accurate and relevant. In addition to covering any content gaps that appear through additions to the objectives, this chapter will provide explanatory notes on how the new objectives map to the current text.

After the initial publication of this book, Microsoft Press will provide supplemental updates as digital downloads for minor exam updates. If an exam has major changes or accumulates enough minor changes, we will then announce a new edition. We will do our best to provide any updates to you free of charge before we release a new edition. However, if the updates are significant enough in between editions, we may release the updates as a low-priced standalone eBook.

If we do produce a free updated version of this chapter, you can access it on the book's product page. Simply visit *MicrosoftPressStore.com/ERAZ2043e/downloads* to view and download the updated material.

About possible exam updates

Microsoft reviews exam content periodically to ensure that it aligns with the technology and job role associated with the exam. This includes, but is not limited to, incorporating functionality and features related to technology changes, changing skills needed for success within a job role, and revisions to product names. Microsoft updates the exam details page to notify candidates when changes occur. If you have registered this book and an update occurs to this chapter, you will be notified by Microsoft Press of the availability of this updated chapter.

Impact on you and your study plan

Microsoft's information helps you plan, but it also means that the exam might change before you pass the current exam. That impacts you, affecting how we deliver this book to you. This chapter enables us to communicate in detail about those changes as they occur. But you should watch other spaces as well.

For other information sources to watch, bookmark and check these sites for news. In particular:

Microsoft Learn: Check the main source for up-to-date information: *microsoft.com/ learn*. Be sure to sign up for automatic notifications on that page.

Microsoft Press: Find information about products, offers, discounts, and free downloads: *microsoftpressstore.com*. Be sure to register your purchased products.

As changes arise, we will update this chapter with more detail about exam and book content. At that point, we will publish an updated version of this chapter, listing our content plans. That detail will likely include the following:

- Content removed, so if you plan to take the new exam version, you can ignore that content when studying.
- New content planned per new exam topics, so you know what's coming.

The remainder of the chapter shows the new content that may change over time.

News and commentary about the exam objective updates

The current official Microsoft Study Guide for the AZ-204 Developing Solutions for Microsoft Azure exam is located at *https://learn.microsoft.com/en-us/certifications/resources/study-guides/az-204*. This page has the most recent version of the exam objective domain.

This statement was last updated in October 2023, before the publication of *Exam Ref AZ-204 Developing Solutions for Microsoft Azure*. The content of this book has been updated to reflect the change of the Microsoft cloud identity solution from Azure AD to Microsoft Entra ID. We also cover the evolution of the libraries and tools to work with the identity platform that now receives the name of Microsoft Identity Platform.

This version of this chapter has no news to share about the next exam release.

The most recent version of this Chapter, the AZ-204 Developing Solutions for Microsoft Azure exam version number was released on October 18, 2023.

Updated technical content

The current version of this chapter has no additional technical content.

Objective mapping

This *Exam Ref* is structured by the author based on the topics and technologies covered on the exam and is not structured based on the specific order of topics in the exam objectives. Table 6-1 maps the current version of the exam objectives to chapter content, allowing you to locate where a specific exam objective item has coverage without having to consult the index.

TABLE 6-1 Exam objectives mapped to chapters

Exam Objective	Chapter
Develop an Azure Infrastructure as a Service solution	
Implement containerized solutions	1
▪ Create and manage container images for solutions	
▪ Publish an image to the Azure Container Registry	
▪ Run containers by using an Azure Container Instance	
▪ Create solutions by using Azure Container Apps	
Implement Azure App Service web apps	1
▪ Create an Azure App Service web app	
▪ Enable diagnostics logging	
▪ Deploy code to a web app	
▪ Configure web app settings including Secure Sockets Layer, API settings, and connection strings	
▪ Implement autoscaling rules, including scheduled autoscaling and scaling by operational or system metrics	
▪ Configure deployment slots	
Implement Azure Functions	1
▪ Create and configure an Azure Function App	
▪ Implement input and output bindings for a function	
▪ Implement function triggers by using data operations, timers, and webhooks	
Develop for Azure storage	
Develop solutions that use Cosmos DB storage	2
▪ Perform operations on containers and items by using the SDK	
▪ Set the appropriate consistency level for operations	
▪ Implement change feed notifications	

Exam Objective	Chapter
Develop for Azure storage	
Develop solutions that use Blob Storage	2
■ Set and retrieve properties and metadata	
■ Interact with data using the appropriate SDK	
■ Implement storage policies and data life cycle managementImplement static site hosting	
Implement Azure security	
Implement user authentication and authorization	3
■ Authenticate and authorize users by using the Microsoft Identity platform	
■ Authenticate and authorize users and apps by using Microsoft Entra ID	
■ Create and implement shared access signatures	
■ Implement solutions that interact with Microsoft Graph	
Implement secure cloud solutions	3
■ Secure app configuration data by using App Configuration or Azure Key Vault	
■ Develop code that uses keys, secrets, and certificates stored in Azure Key Vault	
■ Implement Managed Identities for Azure resources	
Monitor, troubleshoot, and optimize Azure solutions	
Implement caching for solutions	4
■ Configure cache and expiration policies for Azure Cache for Redis	
■ Implement secure and optimized application cache patterns including data sizing, connections, encryption, and expiration	
■ Implement Azure Content Delivery Network endpoints and profiles	
Troubleshoot solutions by using Application Insights	4
■ Configure an app or service to use Application Insights	
■ Monitor and analyze metrics, logs, and traces	
■ Implement Application Insights Web Tests and Alerts	
Connect to and consume Azure services and third-party services	
Implement API Management	5
■ Create an APIM instance	
■ Create and document APIs	
■ Configure authentication for APIs	
■ Implement policies for APIs	
Develop event-based solutions	5
■ Implement solutions that use Azure Event Grid	
■ Implement solutions that use Azure Event Hub	
Develop message-based solutions	5
■ Implement solutions that use Azure Service Bus	
■ Implement solutions that use Azure Queue Storage	

Index

A

C

D

E

F

T

U

V

W-X-Y-Z